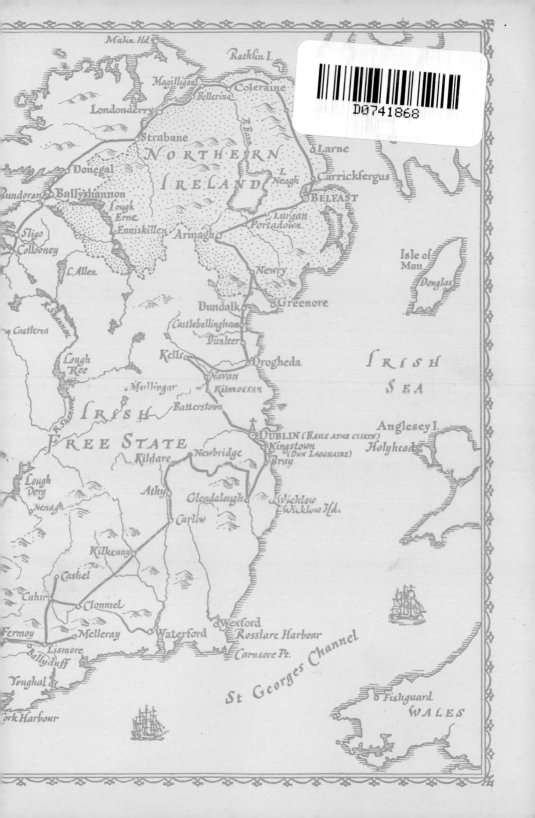

IN SEARCH OF IRELAND

Photo. W. J. Henley, Wembley

TWO CONNEMARA GIRLS

IN SEARCH OF IRELAND

BY

H. V. MORTON

WITH ILLUSTRATIONS AND A MAP

The people are thus inclined, religious, frank, amorous,
sufferable of infinite paines, verie glorious, manie
sorcerers, excellent horsemen, delighted with wars,
great alms-givers, parting in hospitalite.
—HOLINSHED'S CHRONICLES

DODD, MEAD AND COMPANY
NEW YORK   1936

Published February 1931
Second Printing August 1931
Third Printing October 1931
Fourth Printing March 1932
Fifth Printing October 1933
Sixth Printing November 1934
Seventh Printing September 1935
Eighth Printing October 1936

PRINTED IN THE UNITED STATES OF AMERICA
BY THE VAIL-BALLOU PRESS, INC., BINGHAMTON, N. Y.

TO
THE RAKING OF THE FIRE
AND THE NEW FLAME
IN THE MORNING

INTRODUCTION

Ireland will always be "the old country" to a large proportion of Americans. I hope that those citizens of the United States in whose veins run that vivid and deathless dash of Irish will recognize in these pages something true and something new.

Books about Ireland written by Englishmen have for centuries formed a peculiar and annoying class of literature. Unable to understand the Irish, baffled by their point of view, out of sympathy with their religion and blind to their racial grievances, writers, especially of the 18th and early 19th centuries, dealt with Ireland in supercilious but tolerant amusement. It was a comic country, a mad country, an incomprehensible country.

This "ruling class" view of Ireland was blown sky-high with the Dublin Four Courts in the Rebellion of Easter Week 1916. The Treaty of 1922 which established the Irish Free State, or Saorstát Eireann, on the same constitutional basis in the British Empire as the Dominion of Canada, New Zealand, the Commonwealth of Australia and the Union of South Africa has made it necessary for Englishmen to revise their attitude to Ireland. Here at our doors is a separate political entity, a new nation. We must give to it the sympathy and the respect that we extend to foreign races.

This book is the first of its kind to appear since the formation of the Irish Free State. I hope it may, no matter how faintly, blaze a trail for other Englishmen who will go to Ireland not to laugh but to understand. The building up of this nation by men still young all of whom took up arms to gain recognition for their country is a magnificent and stimulating sight. No man can visit Ireland without wishing God-speed to this youngest and yet oldest of European states.

I find it difficult to express my gratitude to those Irishmen and Irishwomen who opened their homes to me with a warmth and a hospitality which is characteristic of their race. The memory of their generosity, their humour, their attractive melancholy and their swift sympathy will remain with me always as something that is—just Ireland.

London.
January 1931.

BIBLIOGRAPHY

THE visitor to Ireland should read some of the following books. Many are out of print, but second-hand bookshops can generally procure them.

Irish Nationality, by Alice Stopford Green (Home University Library).

The History of the Irish State to 1014, by Alice Stopford Green (Macmillan).

The Making of Ireland and its Undoing, by Alice Stopford Green (Macmillan).

A Short History of Ireland, by P. W. Joyce (Longmans Green & Co.).

Ireland and the Making of Britain, by Benedict Fitzpatrick (Funk & Wagnalls Co.).

Ireland, by Stephen Gwynn (Ernest Benn).

Ireland, by Stephen Gwynn (The Kitbag Travel Books; Harrap).

The Fair Hills of Ireland, by Stephen Gwynn (Maunsel & Co.).

The Famous Cities of Ireland, by Stephen Gwynn (Maunsel & Co.).

A Holiday in Connemara, by Stephen Gwynn (Methuen).

Irish Books and Irish People, by Stephen Gwynn (T. Fisher Unwin).

The Archaeology of Ireland, by R. A. S. Macalister (Methuen).

Ireland a Nation, by Robert Lynd (Mills & Boon).

Rambles in Ireland, by Robert Lynd (Mills & Boon).

The Riddle of the Irish, by J. Chartres Molony (Methuen).

Tramping Through Ireland, by John Gibbons (Methuen).

The Road Round Ireland, by Padraic Colum (Macmillan).

The Leaders of Public Opinion in Ireland, by William E. H. Lecky (Longmans).

The Victory of Sinn Fein, by P. S. O'Hegarty (Dublin: The Talbot Press).

Michael Collins and the Making of a New Ireland, by Piaras Beaslai (Harrap).

With Michael Collins Through the Fight for Irish Independence, by Batt O'Connor (Peter Davies).

With the Dublin Brigade, by Charles Dalton (Peter Davies).

The Book of Kells (The Studio).

Hail and Farewell, by George Moore (Heinemann).

Some Experiences of an Irish R. M., by E. Œ. Somerville and Martin Ross (Longmans & Co.).

The Romance of Irish History, by John G. Rowe (The Talbot Press, Dublin).

The poems and plays of W. B. Yeats, J. M. Synge, Francis Ledwidge, Douglas Hyde, P. H. Pearse, Thomas MacDonagh, A. E., Moira O'Neill.

Ireland awaits inclusion in Dr. Muirhead's "Blue Guides" series. The best existing guide is out of print and out of date: *Ireland,* by C. S. Ward, 2 vols. (Dulau & Co.). Murray's excellent "Handbook" is also out of date. Messrs. Ward, Lock & Co. publish seven volumes in their guide-book series which cover the country.

CONTENTS

CONTENTS

LIST OF ILLUSTRATIONS

CHAPTER I

I go in search of Ireland, arrive in Dublin, meet a poet, am
warmly received, listen to Irish conversation, visit Dáil
Eireann, and enter a house which hid Michael Collins

1

THE roses on the saloon tables trembled slightly and shed
an occasional petal into the salad. That, and a furtive
creak of mahogany, was the only indication that we were
at sea. If we glanced through the portholes we saw that the
Holyhead boat moved towards Ireland over calm, green
waters. It was June.

There were three American families on board, on their
way, I suppose, to visit in a Daimler car the village which
their ancestors left on foot. There were Englishmen with
rods and golf clubs, our usual missionaries of leisure,
hearty, pink Englishmen, washed and polished; and there
were Englishwomen of the country kind in tweed costumes
who always remind me of a phrase employed exclusively
by publishers—"these companionable volumes."

Two priests walked the deck. They were as foreign as
Frenchmen on a Channel boat. Their faces, beneath unfriendly, religious hats, were those of farmers, and I
thought as I watched them, how swiftly they would be "up
to" all the tricks of a peasant parish. As they tramped the
deck in sombre conversation, their thick boots seemed separated only by sanctity from boots that follow a plough.
Two nuns sat close together as though for mutual protection, wearing that expression, common to all nuns who
travel, of having strayed innocently and with folded hands

1

out of some past age. And we were all, for our various reasons, going to Ireland, some of us, no doubt, like myself, for the first time.

I felt rather like the fool of the party because I was bound on perhaps the most stupid and thankless task which a man can set for himself: I was going to add another book to that mountain of books about Ireland. Other people were going merely to fish, to play golf, to look at the old home or to rebuke the sinner. But I was on much more difficult and dangerous ground, and well I knew it.

In order to refrain from brooding and also to satisfy a natural curiosity, I explored the steerage which was, I discovered, more interesting than the upper regions of this ship. Here were hearty young Irishmen drinking too much at a bar. They were excited. They were full of good humour. One of them told me that he was a barman in the Edgware Road. Most of his friends were either chauffeurs, barmen or young men who fulfil the mysterious domestic duties covered by the title of house-parlourman. They were going home on holiday.

There were also many young maids with vivid eyes, highly-strung girls, voluble and un-English. They were servants, also on holiday, or going home to spend a week with mother before they satisfied the Irish urge to move on to some distant land. The men stood together at the bar and the girls sat together apart. Now and then one of the men would carry over a small glass of port and make some gallant remark which would send the girls into peals of laughter:

"Get along with ye, Mick," cried a big, dark-eyed wench. "I'll be telling your mother about your goings-on in Hyde Park, I will now. . . ."

And everybody roared with laughter. It was all very friendly.

This little bit of Ireland on its way home fascinated me.
They all knew each other. It was Bridie This and Kate
That and Pat This and Mick the Other, so that you might
have thought they all worked together in the same district.
I found that it was not so. They were dotted about all over
London but they managed to meet on their nights-out
either in Hyde Park, which seemed to hold no terror for
them, or at Irish clubs and Irish dances. They were a clannish community which perhaps the strangeness and the
immensity of London helped to hold together. And I
thought what a lot of plotting had gone on in kitchens,
garages and bars all over London to bring this group of
young friends together on the same homeward boat.

"Come on, Mick, now, give us 'Danny Boy,' " shouted
one of the men.

"I will not," said my friend of the Edgware Road.

More drinks came round. Everybody was rather glass-
eyed. Somebody began to hum a tune and, after a lot of
fussing about, the young barman finished his stout and
sang in a rather girlish tenor that song which is, to my
mind, one of the great songs of the world:

Oh Danny Boy, the pipes, the pipes are calling
From glen to glen, and down the mountain side,
The summer's gone and all the roses falling,
It's you, it's you, must go and I must bide. . . .
But come ye back when summer's in the meadow,
Or when the valley's hushed and white with snow,
It's I'll be here in sunshine or in shadow,
Oh, Danny Boy, I love you so, I love you so.

This song, that goes to the exquisite "Londonderry
Air," stilled all the gaiety in the bar. In the brief silence
that followed we were aware of the propellers threshing
the water and of the banging about of sailors and all the

noises of a ship. Then, as if to force away a mood of melancholy, more drinks were called for, everybody began to shout and laugh, and I slipped away.

On deck again, I leaned over the rail and looked towards Ireland. What was it going to be like? I was eager and excited.

What little did I know about Ireland? As a schoolboy I had been a sentimental Home Ruler when I encountered the literature of the Gaelic League, although I was never quite sure what Kathleen was crying about. That did not, of course, matter in the face of the prose of Æ. and the verse of Yeats. What youth would not run instinctively to a beautiful, tearful woman?

The Irishmen I had met during the War had resembled the Englishmen unless they were drunk, when they became either intensely violent and smashed camp furniture or incredibly pathetic, which was harder to bear. In such moments they lost an English accent and lapsed into a faint brogue, using words which I suppose they had learnt in childhood from gamekeepers and grooms. When you put them to bed you were never quite sure whether they would try to hit you or kiss you. Sometimes they would try to hit you first and kiss you afterwards.

But even they did not know why Kathleen was crying. It was very puzzling. There were things about their own country which these Irishmen did not understand.

Many of these good fellows, and they were a hearty, generous slap-dash type, had their creameries and their country houses burnt out in the Rebellion of 1916, which was the first inkling I received—for few Englishmen read Irish history—that Irishmen were of two kinds: the Irishmen of English descent, generally Protestants and officers, and the Irishmen of Irish descent, generally Catholics

and sometimes sergeants. Although the Protestant officers
would have been infuriated had you called them English
—and, in fact, had been known in the splendour of their
cups to cry "to hell with England"—the Catholic sergeants considered them to be a kind of English, which
was very confusing to anyone brought up in the easy
English tradition that bygones should be bygones.

Then came that time, the Rebellion of 1916, when Ireland's army (few Englishmen know that she gave 250,000
men to the Services) was hissed through the streets of
France with the cry of "Shinners" and "Traitors," a
pretty cruel moment for them.

I was aware that the time has come when England must
look at Ireland in a new light. She is no longer an English
county that has somehow gone bad. She has fought for, and
won, Dominion status. The commissioned officers have been
flung out and the sergeants are in command. The Irish
"Question"—a political term, which, it seemed, wilfully
disguised a racial struggle—has ended in an Irish nation.

I was going not to the land of clowns and "bulls,"
which amused the ruling class of two centuries, but to a
small country that has stood its guns through a consistent War of Independence that dragged its weary, blood-
stained way through nine centuries—the longest struggle
in the history of the world.

Before me on the sky-line was the Irish Free State.

2

I met a pleasant young man on deck who told me that
his object in life was to sell legal stationery to solicitors
in the Free State: a profession which I gathered left him
no spare time. In the course of his extensive wanderings
by motor-car he had come to know the country well. When

I told him that I was paying a first visit he wrote out for me introductions to solicitors all over Ireland. These I was never able to use, because I lost them.

"You'll like Ireland," said the young man. "You can't help it. It's got a way with it. But don't argue. They'll try to make you argue. It's a national vice. If you become pro-Irish they'll become pro-English, and you won't know where you are! And don't believe them when they tell you that they wish the English were back—except when you hear it on the Curragh; and even then take it with a grain of salt."

"How deeply do they hate the English?"

"Have you ever read an Irish history of Ireland? You know then that the history of Ireland is very simple: it is just her resistance to England. Why? Because we are different races. The real Irishman is as different from us as a Spaniard or an Italian. We tried for centuries to make him into a kind of Englishman; and we failed. But they don't hate English people. I think they like us better than they like most foreigners; but they detest our politicians."

A rim of land grew clearer, and slowly the Wicklow Hills shouldered their way out of the sea. My first impression of them was that they were foreign hills. They were not like any hills in England or Scotland, and it was difficult to say why. The light was, perhaps, different over them; even the clouds seemed to be Irish clouds.

Dunleary—or Dun Laoghaire—which used to be called Kingstown, was an interesting contrast to these foreign hills. Here was an old-fashioned English port with an old-fashioned English railway station. It was rather like going back half a century into the reign of Queen Victoria. Mr. Philip Guedalla has described it well in one of his essays:

"The comfortable air of 1888 lay close about it," he says. "There was about that station an almost sacramental atmosphere of long tradition, of all the jokes that *Punch* had ever printed about railway stations. Surely that porter in the peaked cap that was just too small for him was the very porter who had once pronounced unforgettably that cats was dogs and birds was dogs, but tortoises . . . These dogs, too, in the corner over there—must they not just this moment have eaten their labels? And some cheerful passenger in that adorable little train, which magic beyond our understanding had recalled from the dead past, would surely inform a nervous fellow-traveller that her Bill *could* make her go when he had a drop in him."

The Customs Officer handed me a list and asked if I had anything to declare. There was something apologetic about him. He asked me to open a bag. He went through it with an air which suggested that to do so was a deplorable breach of good manners. The man next to me had among his bags a leather silk-hat box.

"And what might that be?" asked the Customs official, pointing to the box.

"A silk hat. I'm going to a funeral," replied the passenger.

"Och—God help ye!" replied the official, and at once marked every piece of this man's luggage with chalk.

That was my first impression of Ireland; and one that I was to recall time and again.

3

Dublin in the early morning, with the sun shining, is a city the colour of claret. The red-brick Georgian mansions, with fine doors, fanlights, and little iron balconies at the first-floor windows, stand back in well-bred reticence against wide roads, quiet and dignified, as if the family has just left by stage-coach. Dublin shares with Edinburgh the air of having been a great capital.

This city is as completely a creation of the eighteenth century as Bath. It is a superb, indolent aristocrat among cities, with an easy manner and a fine air of unstudied elegance. The Liffey, crossed by eight bridges, some of them good-looking, cuts the city into a north and south division, and there is pervading Dublin that subtle something as vivid and distinctive as the feel of ships and docks, due to the nearness of great mountains. Just behind Dublin the long, smooth Wicklow Hills lie piled, clear-cut against the sky, brown-green in colour, and from them, on clear days I am told, a man can see across the Irish Sea to the mountains of Wales.

One of the first things that charmed me, as it must charm all visitors, is the Irish voice. The Irish do not like the "Dublin accent," but it is not so much a matter of accent as of intonation. I found myself listening to people in the street. The cadence of the Irish voice is catching. The habit of giving a little upward kick to the end of a sentence is a charming habit; in women it is adorable.

Why has Dublin been called "dear dirty Dublin"? This surely is an ancient libel. The roads outside Dublin are apparently dirty on the evidence of the omnibus wheels, to which are attached small hanging brooms of stiff bristles. These brooms tickle the tires when the wheels are in motion and brush off the mud. But the city itself is as clean as a Dutch dresser.

In the streets stand among the taxicabs many of the oldest horse-cabs on earth, objects of remarkable antiquity which surely, by some virtue of the Irish temperament, continue to function, and there is also that strange but famous vehicle, known to the English as a "jaunting car," but called in Ireland an "outside-car." I imagine that the outside-car is to Dublin what the few remaining hansom cabs are to London—a sentimental refuge for Americans. When you hire one of them and sit sideways to the world, Dublin smiles indulgently at you from the pavement. I went round behind a spanking bay pony while the jarvey pointed out the sights with his whip.

In O'Connell Street he indicated a line of shattered buildings, and remarked that they had been destroyed during the "crossness."

"You mean," I said, "the fighting."

"Och, sure," he replied, "it was the crossness, I said."

I thought this description quite the kindest and most generous I had ever heard!

Sentries, smart in green uniforms and brown leggings, marched before the Government building, which flies the tricolour of the Free State. A hefty young man, armed with a revolver, stood on the steps. In a barrack square we saw a company of young soldiers at bayonet drill, practising a lunge and parry, which looked to me something new in warfare.

The crowds in the Dublin streets are vastly different from English crowds. You do not see the haggard money look which is becoming characteristic of all large English cities. There is more laughter. There is no painful rushing about. There is a cheerful ease about Dublin, a casual good temper, which makes it difficult to realize the dark times through which this city has passed. There are certain apparent superficialities which, however, possess a deep significance. The English red has vanished from the streets; the pillar-boxes are green. So are the envelopes in which telegrams are delivered. So are the mail vans. And the names of the streets are written in Gaelic, which not one in a thousand Dubliners can read! Still this proves a change in ownership and a striving to be Irish.

When we came to the end of the journey the jarvey said, when I asked how much he wanted:

"I'll leave it to yourself."

A Frenchman would have taken my enormous bribe with a surly doubtfulness, but he was quite frankly overpaid, and showed it with Irish candour. "God bless ye," he said. "And now what about a bit of a drive tomorrow?"

In the hotels of Dublin at tea-time enter men in riding-breeches and girls in habits with mud on their boots and wind in the cheeks. In the season they hunt with the Meath of Kildare Hounds and get back to Dublin in time for tea. This nearness to the country and to that abiding passion of the Irish, a horse, is another of Dublin's Georgianisms. A Dublin man can shoot grouse on the hills within six miles of the General Post Office. He can grass trout within the same distance. He can take a day from business, ride to hounds, and be home in time to look through the evening post.

This gives Dublin a balanced sanity. She is an ancient capital with the health of a county town. She is Georgian not only in her architecture but in her attitude to life.

4

In London, and in other large capitals, social life is formal and meetings are premeditated. This is not so in Dublin. There are, of course, a fair proportion of stately dinners, but more important, and more socially interesting, are the unorganized parties that just happen night after night. It must be impossible to be alone in Dublin.

The Irish have a genius for improvisation and—they hate
to be alone! A man may meet a friend casually in a tramcar in Dublin at noon and find himself saying good-bye
to this man at 3 a.m., having visited together during the
night several houses where they have been sincerely welcomed as an interesting conversational turn, much as one
might welcome a couple of strolling players.

They care nothing for appearances in Dublin. An
Englishman who arrives at a function in morning-clothes
when everyone else has dressed feels unhappy; but this
does not matter in Dublin. Neither does money. Talk matters. Wit matters. Laughter matters. And the man who
has something interesting to say has more platforms than
he can occupy.

The hospitality of Dublin is almost embarrassing to an
English visitor. If a stranger knows one person he soon
knows hundreds. They open their houses to him and let
him find his way about. There can be no other capital in
the world more generous in its welcome and more devastat-
ing in its disapproval. For through Irish life and conversation there runs a bitter spitefulness that at first
puzzles you until you understand that it is a national gift.
A Catholic bishop once told Padraic Colum that spite
and envy are the Catholic vices—the other side of the Catholic virtue of equality—just as harsh individualism and
snobbery are the Protestant vices. There may be something in this, in spite of the fact that these vices seem to
me shared in equal parts by Catholics and Protestants!
But it is a fact that the Irish have a genius for satire.
When they get together they love to tell stories that reveal those whom they admire, or those who are important
and prominent, in a rather cruelly amusing and belittling
light. It is rather confusing at first.

What is George Moore's *Hail and Farewell* and James

Joyce's *Ulysses* but this Irish gift for satire that always borders on the malicious?

A stranger lost in the confusing maze of Irish conversation feels at first that nothing is sacred to these people until, finding himself outside in the small hours in company with a man who has been sparkling all evening, he discovers that the former brilliance of his companion has been thrown off as an actor throws off a cloak after a play. The amusing Touchstone of the evening becomes a sombre Hamlet. As he walks through the empty street he contradicts everything he has previously said in a voice that comes out from him drenched in an abysmal melancholy.

You then realize that talk in Ireland is a game with no rules.

*   *   *

In the cold light of morning you wonder why it sounded so brilliant!

5

When the Poet, who says he is an atheist, grew weary of defending the Church from the attacks of a devout Catholic, we left the cabaret, and, walking some distance through the quiet streets, entered a low door and fell down a flight of dark steps into the wings of the Abbey Theatre. We were welcomed as an unrehearsed effect and conducted to the green-room, which, unlike all other green-rooms, is really green. The Poet took off his coat and immediately started an argument on the superiority of the Saxon to the Celt, which looked like being the best hare started that evening until the call-boy put his head round the door and killed it stone dead.

"What'll we do now?" asked the Poet unhappily, as he

prowled round the picture gallery. "Isn't James Stephens like a leprechaun? Let's go to Michael's. You'll like Mrs. Mike. . . ."

It is a habit in Dublin to go out in search of mental refreshment on a kind of house-to-house canvass of friends. (The expense of having friends in Dublin must be fearful!)

The Poet knocked at a door, and before it opened he had time to curse the Celtic twilight, the Gaelic League, the Government, the Opposition, and the Holy Roman Empire. He was in good form.

"Good evening to you, lady of the house," recited the Poet, making a low bow as the door opened. "It's meself that's come to you at the close of day with the turf in me hair and the bog myrtle in me ears, and me eating nothing since the sun went down. . . ."

"Don't be an ass, Pat," said the lady of the house. "Come in!"

"Have you any bacon and eggs?" asked the Poet anxiously.

"In the kitchen," said his hostess.

His arrival there was signalled by a loud crash. A door was opened and I went into a room blue with tobacco smoke. It was not built to hold so many people. Dark Irishmen and fair Irishmen, elderly Irishmen, and young Irishmen lounged about in chairs. A number of girls sat on the floor. Everyone was talking at the same moment, but a young man with red hair was winning.

"What we want in Ireland," he shouted at the top of his voice, "is a king. . . ."

"To hell with him!" came the instinctive cry.

"I suggest," went on the young man, "that we have George Bernard Shaw as king, with W. B. Yeats as heir apparent. . . ."

"That's a good idea!" someone said, "and if we want a court jester, what about Tim Healy?"

"Look here!" cut in someone. "We can't have a king without a national anthem. The 'Soldiers' Song' is as dull as the 'Red Flag.' We must have an Irish National Anthem!"

"I know one," shouted the red-haired youth, springing to his feet. "It was written by my old friend Gerald Kelly." He then sang to the tune of "Paddy McGinty's Goat":

God save the Free State, Tim Healy, and the King,
The Harp and the Shamrock and the old Claddagh Ring,
The round tower of Clonmacnoise, the pistol and the bomb,
But when we get the Republic, boys, we'll make the old
    land hum.

There was a roar of laughter. He sang it solemnly again.

"That," he cried, "is the ideal National Anthem because it has a kind word to say for everybody. It is unbiassed. It is more than impartial, it is—"

We were interrupted by the Poet, deeply injured, who said that he could not find a frying-pan.

Irish conversation is always subject to these crazy upheavals. The most solemn discussion is always in danger of becoming wrecked on a joke. When this happens wit is carried to fantastic lengths, and it takes time for things to settle down again.

The rapidity of thought is also remarkable. An Irishman appears to jump from topic to topic. What really happens is that his thought is so much swifter than speech that he leaps over an obvious idea in the assumption that his listener has jumped with him.

"The curse of Ireland," said a young man, "is that the country is no place for youth. In the lower stations of life we are brought up side by side with the ghost of an emigrant ship. A bit higher up we know that if we want to get a living wage we must go to England for it—"

"I hate England," murmured a gentle-looking young girl.

(Someone whispered to me that she had carried bombs in an attache-case at the age of eighteen.)

"I don't hate England," said another girl, "but I do hate Lloyd George."

"I don't hate anybody," began a young man.

"Then you're a disgrace to Ireland!"

"But what I do hate," he continued, "is our respect for seniority. It is a relic of tribalism. It's patriarchal. Why can't we give youth a chance? If a man of twenty and a man of forty applied for the same work, and were both successful, the young man would get three pounds a week and the older man six pounds a week just because he was older. If every Irishman were forced to earn his living in London for two years—"

"God forbid!" came the gloomy voice of the Poet from the corner, where he was eating bacon and eggs. "The beauty of Ireland is the fact that we are untouched by the Reformation and the Industrial Revolution. We have the chance now to make a magnificent experiment. We can create the unmaterialistic State."

"Codology!" shouted a voice.

"It's not," said the Poet. "We can never do big business, and why should we try? Has it made other countries happy? It's not our line. What we should do is to become efficient in the things we can do. We might, for instance, make farming a business instead of a sentimental disease. . . ."

Someone asked him to define the word "Progress," and in ten seconds the room was in pandemonium.

The charm of Irish conversation is that it is undisciplined. It is a riot of good things. Unfortunately, you cannot hear much because of the conversation! Irish thought and expression are simultaneous, and an Irishman is continually surprising himself by his brilliance. That perhaps is why he laughs at his own jokes.

"Of course, the greatest joke about Ireland," said a sad, thoughtful man, who had not contributed much to the mental riot, "are the English statesmen who have died saying: 'Thank God I was born to solve the Irish problem! I gave them all they wanted!' "

Someone discovered that it was 2 a.m. The Poet began to feel hungry again and wanted to move on. So we said good-morning and went away.

6

The Poet came on the following day to say that he would show me the most interesting sight in Dublin:

"We are," he explained, "going to see Dáil Eireann which, as you may know, is the Parliament of the Free State."

The Dáil meets in a large eighteenth-century house, formerly the residence of the Dukes of Leinster. In front of it is a statue of Queen Victoria, which, while not complimentary, is not so bad as the one that sits so heavily on Manchester.

"That," explained the Poet, pointing to the statue, "is known with justice as 'Ireland's Revenge.' "

The entrance to the Dáil is like that to any big London club. Members enter smoking pipes and cigarettes, collect their letters from a porter's box on the right, and go on through Grosvenor Square galleries and up wide ducal stairways to the "House."

The Free State Parliament meets in the old lecture theatre of the Royal Dublin Society, which was founded in 1731 for the purpose of promoting useful arts and sciences. The gallery has recently been altered and fitted with protective railings to prevent the accidental fall of spectators or other objects on the deputies' heads, but the floor of the theatre has been fitted with shining mahogany seats, which rise in tiers in a horseshoe round the Speaker's chair. The House is dignified. Beneath the gallery are old prints of Dublin in Hogarth frames.

One's first impression is that immense pains have been taken to introduce as much green into the landscape as possible. Members hold green question papers. When they turn them in unison it is as if a breeze has blown through a forest! The files are green. The note-books are bound in green. Now and then messengers tiptoe down through the seats to deliver emerald green telegrams. At the top of the steps and at the doors stand the most competent-looking chuckers-out seen in public since the heyday of the old music hall. I would give a man of average physique two seconds to maintain a real row in the Dáil!

An electric bell rang outside in the corridors, members drifted in casually and took their seats. Mr. Cosgrave slipped into his place on the Government benches and Dáil Eireann opened as quickly as a directors' meeting when the chairman has to catch a train.

When Mr. Guedalla looked down on the Dáil he wondered what Mr. Gladstone would have thought of "the last of all his dreams." And Padraic Colum was inspired by the penetrating thought as he watched Mr. Cosgrave that "the former Irish leaders, even when they were intellectuals like John Dillon, or country gentlemen like

John Redmond, all had the air of being chieftains. President Cosgrave looks the magistrate rather than the chieftain, and that contrast lets us know that the Irish nationalism is no longer a revolt, a rally, a forlorn hope; it is now an established thing, a directive force: Ireland a Nation has become Ireland a National State."

As I watched this rather frail-looking man with light-coloured hair that stands up like a cockatoo's crest and light-coloured moustache and pale eyes, I thought that I had never seen any man who looked less like a rebel. It was difficult to believe not only that this man had suffered in prison for his convictions but that he also possessed the greater courage necessary to steer the government of the Free State through its first years. (I could not forget Griffith, Michael Collins, and O'Higgins.) As his even voice, calm and unassuming, went on with the business as though he were controlling a city council I realized that he was the outstanding personality of the Dáil. One looked at Mr. de Valera with curiosity but at Mr. Cosgrave with respect. He has contributed something new to the conduct of Irish affairs: dignity, calmness, a sense of balance, authority, and prestige.

The green question paper of the Dáil is puzzling to a stranger. It is, in slight, innocuous patches, bilingual, but not sufficiently so to baffle a foreigner. Questions to Ministers are addressed first in Irish and then, in case no one can understand them, in English. Irishmen have two names, one in English and one more difficult to pronounce, in Irish.

Most members prefer to be known in the Dáil by their Gaelic names, so that one comes across in the question paper heroic-sounding names, which suggest the battles of giants.

I looked down on the Dáil, thinking that Ireland is

never what you expect it to be. I expected eloquence. I
expected that some politician would rise up and make me
burn with indignation about something. But no; Dáil
Eireann was even harder to listen to than the British
House of Commons! Where was the Irish wit? Where the
Irish pugnacity? Where the sly Irish humour? Where the
quick cut and thrust encountered in conversation round
the Irish fireside? Where were those amazingly clever
things that slip out of an Irishman's mouth before he
knows what he has said? They were not in the Dáil! I was
surprised that a nation of good talkers could put up such
a mumbling show in Parliament.

Then it occurred to me that, of course, they were all
very much in earnest. There was nothing playful about
them as there is now and then about Westminster. They
had fought to get there not only with votes but also with
guns. Their Parliament was steeped in the blood of their
companions and schoolfellows.

Their voices went on level, solemn, and unemotional,
and as I followed the Poet downstairs I thought that this
was a good omen for Ireland.

7

The feelings of an unprejudiced Englishman after a
first contact with Irish life have been perfectly described
by Mr. H. W. Nevinson in a preface to one of his fine
books. He says that after meeting Irish friends and discussing England with them he feels as though he has been
exquisitely operated on for a disease he never had. He
was infected by their hatred for the English.

This is so true. The stranger must always be on his
guard in case he becomes a too violent Sinn Feiner. There
is something extravagant in the air of Ireland which, com-

bined with the engaging and convincing manners of its people, goes right to the heart and sometimes to the head. Many of the greatest Irish nationalists have been English or Anglo-Irish. It is a good plan for a visiting Englishman to say to himself every night before he goes to bed: "My first duty is to England. I will be true to her in the face of this awful temptation!"

The Irish are, of course, sometimes unfair, which, I think, proceeds from the fact that they possess no sense of historical perspective. Even educated Irishmen will talk about Cromwell's campaign as though it was the work of the present British Government. A wrong has never died in Ireland. Every injustice inflicted on Ireland since the time of Strongbow is as real as last year's Budget. No allowance is made for the greater brutality of past centuries, and if you venture to argue about it they bring out the Black and Tans to prove that the "Saxon" (this is an amusing term) was always a brute.

It sometimes happens that a man is forced to hear the confession of a friend's wife. You may know the man only as a good fellow, sincere, upright, and honest. And the woman tells you that she is suing for divorce on grounds of cruelty. It is difficult to believe it. How is it possible that this fine fellow has knocked this woman about and intimidated her? You listen in horror to her story of mental and physical suffering.

The incompatibility of temperament between England and Ireland affects you in exactly the same way; and you look at the Free State Flag and say:

"Well—thank heaven, she got her divorce!"

When the stranger locks himself up with an armful of books on Irish history he learns with surprise, if he is English, and also with pain, that if Ireland's struggle had been staged elsewhere in Europe, and had the ruling race been French, Italian or Turkish, no greater sympathy, no deeper indignation and no more eager support would have been forthcoming than that of England. Byrons in great numbers would have gone out in support of her national ideals.

He discovers, too, having previously taken his opinions of the Irish from the comic pictures in *Punch* or, perhaps, from eighteenth-century fiction, that a resistance to England which he believed sprang from an innate pugilism heated by immature whisky has had its roots for centuries in one of the deepest of human passions, a sense of nationality. How, he asks himself, can the Irish be called traitors if they never professed to be loyalists? The germ of nationalism never died, even in those times when England and Ireland seemed to be blending into one nation.

It is curious that those qualities of grim perseverance and dogged determination which are supposed to be purely English characteristics should have been shown to a far greater degree by Ireland. Her struggle has been one of the most consistent events in history. When banishment and emigration drove her people overseas they broadened the base of rebellion and returned to the attack.

The history of Ireland is the struggle of the Gael. The old stock was dispossessed but never suppressed. It found an outlet for its resistance even if it had to enlist in foreign armies and intrigue, sometimes hopelessly, in foreign countries. And always behind the hedge in Ireland was there a Mac with a pitch-fork who felt himself to be the real ruler of the land and the scion of kings.

Now for the first time since the Battle of Kinsale the men who control Ireland are the old stock, the O's and the Mac's. Ireland has ceased to be a "Question" and has become a Nation.

Every man, no matter of what nationality, must be glad that this generation has seen the end of the fight and the victory of the Gael.

8

I was swapping war stories with an ex-officer of the Munsters. He was a violent Gael. He believed that it would some day be Ireland's mission to re-Christianize the world; but we had been entertaining one another for some time and we may have been slightly irresponsible. He told me a story about a sergeant in France. We will call him Sergeant Murphy.

One day Murphy's leave came through and he departed for a village in the south of Ireland, somewhere in Kerry I believe it was. When he returned to France my friend said to him:

"Well, sergeant, and did you have a good leave? How's the old country looking and what did you do with yourself?"

"Well, sor," replied Sergeant Murphy, "I took off me uniform and drilled the Sinn Feiners. . . ."

This is not really, I feel, a funny story; but it is a true one.

9

Dublin is the only European capital that has known real war. Berlin and those capitals which have experienced sudden political crises have seen barricades and police charges, but no capital except Dublin came to regard armed hostilities as a matter of course.

You cannot go out to dinner in Dublin without hearing some reminiscence, generally humorous, of the Rebellion or the Civil War, or some story, generally tragic, of the hated Black and Tans.

I went to call on a young Irishman who had played a part in the fight for independence. He lives in a small villa in one of the suburbs of Dublin. It is a house with a small front garden and a general air of rectitude quite English. His study was upstairs.

"Michael Collins hid here when he was on the run," he explained.

The houses in Dublin in which Michael Collins sought refuge are as numerous as the English beds in which Queen Elizabeth slept. I wondered as I looked around the ordinary little room whether I was not seeing something which future generations would wish modern Irishmen to preserve.

I shall always regret that I missed Michael Collins by five minutes when he was in London, moving about rather furtively and shyly and refusing to become a social sight, as so many hosteses in Mayfair wished him to be. To produce "Mick" Collins at a dinner-party was the dream of many a foolish woman's life just before the signing of the Treaty.

This ex-postal clerk was one of those remarkable characters which nations, in moments of good-fortune, throw up, frequently in the least likely direction. Although Irishmen do not talk much of him today I believe that future ages may perhaps think of him as the Bonnie Prince Charlie of Ireland. Like Prince Charles Edward he was young, handsome, fearless, and a fugitive. Romance will in the generosity of time claim him. But, unlike Charles Edward, he was successful and he died, as Charles should have died in Culloden Moor, before times of peace could ruin a reputation gained in war. The only fortunate warriors are those who are lucky enough to perish in the moment of victory.

I have talked to many English soldiers and to many journalists who acted as special correspondents during the "Trouble"—most of whom, by the way, had sympathy with Sinn Fein—and I have never heard anything but admiration for the military skill and the personal courage of Michael Collins. I have read an enormous book about him in two volumes by Piaras Beaslaí, but it does not give me a picture of the man so vivid as that which comes through now and then in less pretentious and more portable reminiscences of the time. Batt O'Connor, for instance, who has written a sincere book called *With Michael Collins Through the Fight for Irish Independence*, describes the superb coolness of Michael Collins in the face of danger; and danger in those days meant a firing squad:

"On one occasion when the Sinn Fein headquarters at No. 6 Harcourt Street were raided Michael Collins was in an upstairs room. He had an office in the building. He succeeded in bluffing the first policeman who came into the room, and passing out leisurely, as if he were an unimportant assistant clerk, he ran lightly up to the floor above and escaped through the skylight.

"His papers fell into the hands of the raiders, and No. 6 being now useless he gave me instructions to buy a house which was for sale further up the street—No. 76.

"As I was in the building trade it was easy for me to buy houses without arousing suspicion. We had to move cautiously not only with an eye upon the enemy, but upon the people with whom we did business. With the propertied class Sinn Fein naturally was not popular. The owner of a house in Stephen's Green had refused to sell when he discovered that it would be used as one of our offices.

"So we learned to keep our own counsel, and when I was commissioned to buy a house for the offices of one of our Departments—and I did nearly all this part of the business—I took care to buy it for 'a client,' or some 'friend of mine' who wanted a 'nice residence in Dublin' or 'good business offices,' and the house was purchased in his or her supposed name.

"When we had completed the purchase of No. 76 I went to Michael Collins.

" 'Michael,' said I, 'they raided No. 6, and it is within the bounds of possibility that they will spot and raid No. 76. How about my putting in a hiding-place for your papers?'

"He was pleased with the idea, and I found a recess suitable for my purpose in a fitted-in wardrobe in one of the rooms. It was a simple job to partition off a portion of the wardrobe, and, having made it accessible by a secret spring, to repaper the whole while the general papering and painting was being done.

"I also arranged a means of escape for him through the skylight, leaving a light ladder in readiness which he could pull up after him. Two or three doors off there was an hotel, and we took the proprietors into our confidence. They agreed that their skylight should be used in the event of a raid on No. 76. These gentlemen were not of our way of thinking, and it was against their religious principles to take part in any kind of violence, but they were of chivalrous nature, men who would be naturally on the side of the oppressed, and they showed true friendship towards us on this and many other occasions. We also arranged with the boots of the hotel that the skylight should never be bolted.

"All these precautions bore good fruit when, before long, No. 76 also fell to the enemy. Michael used the skylights, and dropped into the hotel after nearly breaking his ribs on the rail of the stairs. The skylight happened to be situated immediately over the well of the stairs, so that he had to swing his body backwards and forwards before dropping, and only escaped falling through the well by landing on the rail. He passed out of the hotel as one of the visitors, and, mingling among the crowd in the street, he watched the raid as it proceeded."

The author's house in Brendan Road should have a significance for the future Ireland, because it was here that the Dáil Loan of £25,071 in gold was hidden from July 1920 until September 1922:

"Money was needed for the new Administration," writes Mr. O'Connor, "and for carrying out the plans of reconstruction agreed to by Dáil Eireann, and, as Minister of Finance, Michael Collins raised the Dáil Loan of 1919–1920. He asked for £250,000, but, in fact, £400,000 was subscribed, and of this £25,000 was in gold.

" 'Bring it to me in gold, Batt,' he said, when I went to him with the subscriptions I had collected.

"I obeyed. I got shopkeepers and business men whom I knew to hoard every sovereign and half sovereign which came into their hands, and I exchanged notes for the gold from time to time.

"When the Loan closed in July 1920, the gold was entrusted to me, but to be put into a safe hiding-place. The Loan, of course, had been declared illegal, and anyone found and convicted of subscribing to it or collecting for it was imprisoned. But while this did not interfere with its success (quite the contrary) it meant that if any of the money had been discovered it would have been confiscated.

"Doctor Fogarty, Bishop of Killaloe, a splendid patriotic Irishman, and one of our truest friends, was one of the many trustees, and I think Lord Monteagle was another. The main fund in notes was banked in their names; and the gold—packed in four boxes each weighing about two cwt., and a baby's coffin—was placed in my keeping.

"I worked all night alone burying the boxes beneath the concrete floor of my house in Brendan Road. Lying on my side, I had to work myself forward beneath the floor. Backwards and forwards I moved wriggling like a worm, upon my hip and elbow, bringing one box at a time, pushing it in front of me in the confined two foot space between the cement floor of the house and the wooden floor of the room in which I worked.

"I was gasping for want of air and pouring with sweat, so that early in my work I had stripped myself nearly to the skin. It took me seven hours to complete the job. One of my difficulties was having so little room to raise my arm to any height before bringing down my hammer to break through the concrete foundation. But I persevered, and having dug the necessary cavities and buried the boxes, I made good the concrete again. I did the work with great care and neatness, and I got my reward, because, though the house was raided several times, the appearance of the floor never aroused suspicions. The hiding-place was known only to my wife and myself. Michael never asked me where I had hidden the gold. He knew it was in the safest place I could think of, and that was all he cared about.

"It remained undisturbed until September 1922, when, shortly after his death, I was requested by the Accountant-General of Dáil Eireann, George McGrath, to produce the boxes so that the gold could be deposited in the vaults of the Bank of Ireland.

"This was done in the presence of the Accountant-General. Fourteen bank-clerks counted the money after the Bank had closed to the public at three o'clock. Each box had a tag on the inside, showing the amount it contained, and in each case the figure mentioned on the tag was right to a half sovereign.

"The gold coin amounted to £24,957, and some bags containing gold bars and foreign coins were valued at £114. A receipt was given by the Bank to the Accountant-General for this total—£25,071.

"That was very soon after Michael was killed, and while we were still stricken with desolation at his loss. That day in the Bank, looking at those labels which he had touched with his own hands, I felt that we were back again in the first days of our mourning. I saw him, in my imagination, three years before, in some secluded place, proudly counting and labelling the gold which was to support us in the struggle on which he entered with such hope."

No Englishman can read the story of the Irish Revolution fought by a handful of young men against organized and fantastic odds—marred as it was on both sides by madness and murder—without the feeling that it would have been a duty and a privilege to have acted in this way for England.

10

The only Gaelic word which seems to be universally known in Ireland is "Slainte," which is a good beginning. Men say it when they lift their glasses.

What luck will attend the young men who are building the Irish State in their attempt to revive the Gaelic no stranger can possibly say. The names of all the Dublin streets are written up in Gaelic in the type which Queen Elizabeth sent over. The Government advertisements are printed in English and Gaelic. A distinguished Gaelic scholar told me that this custom has developed a "Government Gaelic" which to a student of the pure Gaelic reads more or less as though an English proclamation were written in the language of an omnibus conductor from Bethnal Green.

But the revival of the Gaelic is at the very root of the Irish Revolution. Its opponents say that it can never be commonly employed by a modern State. Its supporters believe in it almost with fanaticism as the one means of building up a national spirit. There are others who admire it as a literary language and would like to see it take its place in schools with Greek and Latin.

Professor R. A. S. Macalister has this interesting comment to make in *The Archaeology of Ireland*:

"Notwithstanding her heritage of one of the noblest literatures of all time, the English of current speech is rapidly degenerating into a conglomerate of lazy abbreviations such as 'bike,' 'flu,' 'soccer,' 'pram,' 'veg,' 'marj,' and so forth, studded in a repulsive magma of exotic gibberish imported and naturalized by the 'picture-drome' as it features 'stars' in 'gripping thrills' and 'intriguing stunts.' The literary standard still remains for the time being, but sooner or later it must collapse under these assaults upon its integrity. Those abominable words 'bus' and 'cab' have completely established themselves in literary English; 'bike,' 'flu,' and 'pram' have almost succeeded in doing so; before very long the only language of the ordinary Englishman will be this noisome jargon which is growing up to maturity before our eyes, and Shakespeare will be as incomprehensible as Cynewulf to the man in the street. Opponents of the Gaelic revival, read, mark, and learn! In that day it will be good for us to have, as a second string to our bow, a language which, with all its flexibility, does not lend itself to such barbarous mishandling. It will stabilize us even in our use of English."

But will it ever be possible for a woman to go shopping in Gaelic? What is the Gaelic for suspenders?

CHAPTER II

I see the book of Kells, stand at the tomb of Strongbow, watch the making of Dublin's "Black Wine," am invited to breakfast at the Zoo, discover a church full of mummies, and eventually escape from Dublin

1

THE stranger passing through the gates of Trinity College beneath the gaze of Burke and Goldsmith finds himself on a wide expanse of cobble-stones planted by some ancient humorist to torture the bunions of learned men. Most cities possess a sanctuary which offers, or appears to offer, an escape from everyday things, and, like the Temple in London and Cheetham's Hospital in Manchester, such places become more impressive when they lie in the very heart of the city. This is so with Trinity College. You pass through its gates into a rather thoughtful world.

Trinity College is the only monument to the Elizabethan age in Dublin.

"Its foundation is the first real landmark in the Dublin that we know—the metropolis of Ireland; and it expresses the positive or constructive side of Elizabethan rule," writes Mr. Stephen Gwynn in *The Famous Cities of Ireland*. "English statesmen had now fully determined to make Ireland into a Protestant nation, and men of English race in Ireland saw that such a nation needed the machinery of instruction both to educate Protestants and also to convert the Catholics. At the entreaty of several distin-

31

guished clerics, among whom were Adam Loftus, the Archbishop, and Henry Ussher, the Archdeacon of Dublin, a
charter was obtained from Elizabeth for the foundation of
a University. Its site was placed on the lands of the Augus-
tinian monastery of All Hallows. In the confiscation under
Henry VIII the Mayor and Corporation had become possessed of its buildings, and they now granted both to the
new institution. But funds were slow of coming in, and
the best proof that the settlers felt a real need for knowledge is the manner in which provision was made. When the
Spanish forces in Kinsale and the Irish army under Hugh
O'Neill and Red Hugh O'Donnell were defeated in 1601
by Mountjoy and Carew, the victorious soldiers offered
their booty as an endowment to the new college. They had
conquered with the sword the forces of Popery; the conquest had to be extended with the arm of science.

"From the beginning of the seventeenth century on-
wards the University has been there, not cloistered and
apart like those of Oxford and Cambridge, on whose model
it was planned, but making part of the metropolitan life:
closely in touch with the governing powers of Ireland,
sharing officially their point of view, repressing, indeed,
so far as in it lay, any turbulent tendencies among its
students, but, when all is said, providing there a kind of
vat in which the life of Ireland's Protestant youth worked
out its fermentation."

Trinity has always been criticized as a stronghold of
the Protestant intruder, and I am told that during the
1916 Rebellion letters were intercepted which referred to
it as "the foreign college."

Mr. J. Chartres Molony has some interesting criticisms
of Trinity in a recent book which has not received the
attention it deserves—*The Riddle of the Irish:*

"It is rather the misfortune of Ireland than the fault of Trinity that few men enter, or in my day did enter, the College without some definite practical end in view. Some sought to turn scholarship, or, at least, academic success, to immediately profitable account; others joined at once the 'professional schools' (law, medicine, engineering, divinity) with the set purpose of obtaining a qualification that would win for them a livelihood. A capital benefit that the English universities confer on England takes form in the many men who pass through a University, and then mingle in the life of England, turning to no direct practical use that which they had learned, but bringing with them the University atmosphere of broadmindedness, of tolerance of opposing opinions and aspirations. Ireland may not have so numerous a class as England of men who can afford to spend three or four years simply in the acquiring of a culture that offers no direct pecuniary recompense, but small though the actual number of such men in Ireland may be, it would be to the inestimable benefit of the country that these should for a time rub shoulders with their fellow-Irishmen under the conditions of University life. Half of the distracted disunitedness of Ireland has arisen from the fact that the natural leaders of the Irish people, the gentlemen of Ireland, did not lead, were not capable of leading. They were separated from the mass of the people, and separated one from another. They had no common standard of values; and each man ordinarily had an infinitely and absurdly exaggerated idea of his individual importance, and of the importance of his own social class. The squires or squireens of my own county I now look back on with a half-whimsical pity. I do not recall them as bad men, but as men crassly unenlightened, as men utterly unable to grasp the significance of that which was happening about them, to understand its meaning. Each man isolated in his country 'place' expected the world to stand still, and felt aggrieved when the world refused to do anything of the sort."

Every visitor to Dublin should go to Trinity to see one of the most precious books in existence—the famous Book of Kells. This book is taken from its case every evening and locked in a safe in the vaults; every morning it is carried reverently to its glass-case again, and one leaf is turned each day.

What is the value of the Book of Kells? Many men have wondered. Professors have been known to speculate in the sanctity of the family circle how much it would mean a year if Trinity sold the beastly book and devoted the proceeds to the staff! (This, of course, is an Irish joke!)

The value of the Book of Kells is the sum which one millionaire, bidding against another millionaire, would pay at Sotheby's for it. This depends, in its turn, on the depth of hatred and rivalry between them. Both of them might think they had won, for instance, if the price was £500,000! And the Book of Kells is not insured! There can be no other book of its character in the world which is not insured. The college authorities, and no doubt wisely, feel that money could not produce another such book, so that the best insurance is to spend a fraction of the premium that would be necessary on extra fire-hoses and watchmen.

I was permitted by the courtesy of the librarian to examine the book. He even allowed me to turn one of its thick vellum pages.

What is the Book of Kells?

When the barbarian was exploring the ruins of Roman cities in England and the imported gods howled for blood along the sea-coast of Norfolk, Irish monks decided to set sail for England and bear into that distressful country the light of Christian learning.

London at this time was a haunted Roman ruin on a

hill, with the brambles over London Wall and the camp fires of the East Angles shining in the marsh beyond the city, which they were afraid to enter; Paris was a desolation, and the sun was setting over Rome. But Armagh, the religious capital of Ireland, was the centre of European culture. During the three darkest centuries of English history Ireland was saving Greek and Latin culture for Europe. It was from Ireland—by way of Iona and Lindisfarne, that sandy little island off the Northumbrian coast—that Christianity came to the north of England.

At the beginning of this time an unknown Irish monk was writing the Gospels in an abbey at Kells in Meath, founded by St. Columba. He was one of the world's greatest artists. In Italy of the Renaissance he might have been another Michael Angelo.

He enriched his book with a thousand phantasies and a thousand beauties of intricate design. He poured into this book all the power of his imagination. Men looking at it today wonder not only at the fertility of his brain but also at the keenness of his eyes. How is it possible that a man, unless he employed a type of magnifying glass unknown in his day, could pen such microscopic designs, so perfect that sections of them no larger than a postage stamp when photographed and enlarged show no flaw in the intricate interlocking of lines and spirals?

This great relic of Irish art was placed in a costly gold shrine. Later in history a thief stole it from the sacristy of the Abbey of Kells. It was found two months afterwards hidden in the earth. The thief had taken it for the shrine; and so the book, flung carelessly away, was recovered, and remains the most perfect expression of Christian art which has survived from the Golden Age of Ireland.

The technical excellence of the Book of Kells and of

other Irish manuscripts must interest and puzzle everyone who sees them:

"The ink used," writes Professor Macalister in *The
Archaeology of Ireland*, "was a decoction of galls which in
most cases has retained its intense blackness until the
present day. Sometimes an inferior ink was supplied in
the monastic *scriptoria*, and this has faded to a brownish
colour. Complaints of bad ink and bad pens are sometimes
scribbled on the margins of manuscripts. A sixteenth-
century student engaged in copying extracts from the
great manuscript called *The Speckled Book* was especially troubled. On page 17 of the manuscript he wrote,
O Mary help the ink!—justifiable, for it is of a very poor
faint brown colour. Later at page 141 we find *O Mary,
are you better now?* At page 197 he lost all patience, and
broke out in these words, *My God, do you still serve us
for ink? I am Cormac son of Cosnomach, testing it at Dun
Doighre* (Duniry, Galway), *and I'm afraid that we'll get
great annoyance out of this ink. Anno Domini* 1575. Incidentally we may remark that there is much of human
nature in these and similar marginalia, although many
of them are extremely tantalizing. What was the trouble
in the monastery which induced one student to write a
heartfelt *Thank God I was not in last night?* And why
did another student write *Brian is a naughty boy?* There
is a manuscript of miscellany of legal and other matters,
now in the British Museum Library, which was written by a
jurist named Domhnall o Duibhdabhoireann—a name that
would be Anglicized 'Donal O'Davoren'—in the sixteenth
century. It contains a marginal note which shows that
one of the most fruitful sources of trouble for literary men
is no new thing: *My curse, and God's curse in addition to
it, be on the women who have disarranged all my ink, and*

my colours, and my books. And God's curse be on anyone who reads this and who doesn't curse them. My God, this is a bad job! Donal seems to have possessed what in modern jargon is known as a temperament. He had some justification, however, for his womenkind took unpardonable liberties with his papers. Soon after he had thus relieved his feelings one of them, prying inquisitively, discovered the note and wrote in the book a couple of pages later: *I'm not the woman, Donal!"*

Near the Book of Kells they show you the "Harp of Ireland," supposed to be the famous harp that sounded "once through Tara's halls," but no one believes this. It is, however, the national emblem of the Free State.

"The story is," the guide will tell you, "that after Brian Boru was killed at the battle of Clontarf this harp was given to the Pope Alexander II. It remained in the Vatican for nearly 500 years, and was given, in 1521, to Henry VIII in recognition of his defence of the Seven Sacraments. Twenty years later Henry VIII gave the harp to the Earl of Clanicarde, and it was handed down until it came into the possession of a Limerick antiquary. . . . I myself remember when there were strings on the harp, but they've gone now. . . ."

It is a pretty story, but the archaeologists say that the harp is not older than the fourteenth century.

It is in the Book of Kells that Ireland's remote past lives gloriously in subtle line and perfect colour. When a man turns the pages of that great book he turns back the centuries to a world of Irish saints, of Irish poems, of Irish legends, of Irish boats sailing over the sea taking the light of the Christian Church into the dark places of the world.

2

The Book of Kells and the "gold room" in Dublin's remarkable museum must astonish those who do not know the position occupied by this country from A. D. 600 to about A. D. 800.

I wonder what new light on Irish culture lies hidden in museum manuscripts. It will be the task of Irish scholars to unlock this treasure-house within the next few years. If there is an Englishman who believes that early Ireland was as savage as Anglo-Saxon England, let him go to the "Gold Room"—one of the most interesting rooms in Dublin—and examine the beaten gold torcs, the shining lunulae, the jewelled shrines, the metal croziers, the exquisite cups and vases, all stamped with a vigorous art and a stern convention as different from anything known to us as the art of Egypt differs from that of Greece.

I think that one of the most exqusite things in Dublin is the Tara brooch. It was found on the beach near Bettystown, near Drogheda, in 1850. There is no connexion between this brooch and Tara. The name was given to it by the jeweller into whose possession it came. It is a bronze pin shaped like a Roman fibula. It is decorated with panels in fine gold filigree work, enamel, amber, and glass. It is as characteristic as the Book of Kells. It is decorated at the back and the front with every form of Celtic ornamentation: spirals, interlacing, human heads, and zoomorphic decorations.

3

The verger of Christ Church Cathedral—which is one of Dublin's three cathedrals—loves to take a stranger down into the ghostly crypt, which is said to have been built by the Danes in the time when Sigtrygg Silkbeard was King of Dublin. In this cold spot, where the electric light serves only to increase the gloom of the arches which spring from a forest of stunted pillars, are the roots of Dublin.

When this crypt was built there were men alive who remembered the Homeric battle of Clontarf, and how the great battle-ax of Prince Murragh, the eldest son of Brian Boru, rose and fell dripping red in the fight as he headed his Dalcassians against 1,000 picked Norsemen clad in chain armour. Perhaps the very men whose hands placed these stones one upon the other had seen the fight that swayed round the tent of Brian when it became known that Brodar the sea king had rushed in and killed the aged monarch as he knelt in prayer, giving God thanks for victory.

But the verger, accustomed to dealing with English and American visitors, leads you to a bricked-up doorway, and tells you that in the old days a secret passage ran from Christ Church under the earth. It was sealed up in the eighteenth century when a British officer who had attended the funeral of a general was locked by accident in the crypt, to be discovered weeks afterwards dead. (He goes into gruesome details of the discovery.) Then he takes you to a glass-case, and striking a match, holds the flickering flame above the mummified forms of a cat and a rat. Both creatures died in life-like positions: the cat springing after the rat and the rat in full flight from the cat. He tells you that the cat followed the rat into an organ pipe which became their tomb. . . .

All the time your mind strays from these country-fair stories to the grim arcades, trying to visualize the history out of which they spring. Christ Church was built twenty-four years after the battle of Clontarf. Between that time

and the building of the crypt the Kingdom of Ireland re-
lapsed again into petty States, and history is a mist that
blows aside for a moment now and then, to show us the long
boats of the Danes beached on the east coast of Ireland,
battles, defeats, victories, and, at length, a little Danish
settlement on Dublin Bay.

The verger takes you up into the church, and you see
a fine Norman transept, and, not far away, in the nave
lies the body of a stone Crusader in full armour. This is
the tomb of Strongbow. With him Ireland's troubles began. He held Dublin for Henry II, and founded the Irish
problem.

Some memory of Strongbow's ruthlessness lingers on at
least in the mind of the verger of Christ Church. He tells
you how Strongbow broke his way in through Dublin
wall, slaughtering and pillaging. Then he points to a
small stone effigy that lies beside the Norman. It is that of
a young boy, but it is cut off at the waist.

"And do ye not know who that is?" asks the verger,
leading up dramatically to the information. "That's the
son of Strongbow. He was only a lad, and his father said
he had shown fear in the battle, so he killed him and cut
his body in two as a warning to all cowards. That's the
kind of man, a cruel, hard man, he was entirely. . . .
Now come this way and I'll show ye the heart of St.
Laurence O'Toole."

He points to a heart-shaped metal case, the size of a
cushion, chained and padlocked to the wall. In this case
is the heart of the famous Laurence O'Toole, Archbishop
of Dublin, who died in Normandy in 1180.

But of all the mysteries, grotesque and historic, locked
away in Christ Church, I think the verger's special pride
is the statue of an orphan, down whose cheek runs a stone
tear. He lights a match and holds it near the statue.

"Do you see it?" he asks.

It is, I suppose, a greater marvel to his visitors than the grim and terrible memories called up by the church that was founded by Sigtrygg Silkbeard. . . .

In St. Patrick's Cathedral, near by, you come with something of a shock to the graves of Swift and Stella, together at last in death. You have to search for that famous epitaph hard and bitter as its author, which no one but Swift could have written. It was removed from his tomb many years ago, and is now to be seen over the door of the robing room:

> *Here lies the Body of*
> *Jonathan Swift,*
> *for thirty years dean*
> *of this cathedral,*
> *where suvage indignation can*
> *no longer gnaw his heart.*
> *Go, traveller, and*
> *imitate, if you can, one who*
> *played a man's part in defence*
> *of Liberty.*

Those words have gone round the world. And how poor and commonplace in comparison are those not far away which commemorate Stella.

There are many things to be seen in St. Patrick's—the flags of the disbanded Irish regiments, the stalls of the Knights of St. Patrick, and a number of fine memorials—but always one returns to the two stones in the nave which cover the bodies of the two most mysterious lovers in English literature.

4

There is in Ireland a science unknown to us in England called codology. Nearly every true Irishman is either a graduate or a professor. The American for codology is "bunk," or perhaps "blah"; the English is "leg-pulling." There is nothing your true Irishman likes better than putting over a tall story on an Englishman.

When I received an invitation to breakfast at the Dublin Zoo I thought that I could detect the hand of the chief codologist, but it took me only a few minutes to discover that a summons to a Zoo breakfast in Dublin is not only a compliment, but also a solemn and historic social event. In the cold morning, with a wind blowing from the Wicklow Hills, I took one of Dublin's most decayed taxicabs and drove to Phoenix Park. I was met at the Zoo gates and conducted to a room decorated with dead animals in which a table was set for breakfast.

A dozen grave professional men were standing about eating porridge in little bowls. It is a tradition with the zoologists of Dublin that porridge is never consumed from a sitting position. My hosts were the Council of the Royal Zoological Society of Ireland, and they have breakfasted at the Zoo once a week for over ninety years. When breakfast is over they hold a council meeting:

"How did it begin?" I asked.

"With the liver brigade who used to ride every morning in Phoenix Park," said Dr. Farrer, the superintendent.

"In those days the council's method of inspecting the gardens was not satisfactory, so it was established in 1837 that members should take breakfast here once a week, and at the end of the year the three worst attenders should be struck off the council. So you see these breakfasts keep us up to the mark."

When breakfast was over an elephant's foot was handed to me for inspection. It is the most tragic relic preserved in the council-room, and bears the inscription:

SITA,
who killed her keeper
and was shot,
June 11, 1903

After the toast and marmalade the council prepared for business. I bade them good-bye and retired.

How many people know that Dublin is famous for the export of lion cubs? I do not refer to the young playwrights and poets who dawn so pleasantly on Mayfair from time to time, but to the young of the undomesticated lion. The factory is in Phoenix Park and is known as the Zoo.

As I was walking round the gardens I met Mr. Christopher Flood, who has been in charge of the only lion stud in the world for over forty years. Stories of Mr. Flood and of his power over wild beasts, so marvellous and so authentic that they could have come only out of Ireland, were in circulation in France during the War, when every soldier who had passed through a Dublin hospital added to them and even, now and then, if an Irishman, improved on them.

"And what's the secret of breeding lions?" echoed Mr. Flood. "Sure, and what's better in all this world than the air of Dublin?"

"But you don't suggest that young lions are brought up like nations on hot air?"

"We also make stout in Dublin," said Mr. Flood playfully.

We were surrounded by what all distinguished naturalist, big game hunters, members and directors of zoological societies and other expert persons agree are the finest lions in captivity in any country on earth. People who frequent zoos are familiar with the debauched-looking, string-hocked monarchs of the jungle who sit in dreadful apathy with tear-ducts at the corner of their eyes and moth in the tail, too depressed even to be stimulated by the sight of a nice pink baby. There is no more dreadful sight.

There is nothing like this about the lions of Dublin. Their muscles ripple under their honey-coloured skins, and their eyes are as clear as two amber rings in lake water. There is a fearful vitality about them. They are real lions.

Some of them would give anything to devour Mr. Flood; others like to lie on their backs and have their beards tickled as he goes by.

We went into the maternity ward. Two fat cubs were playing together. They are the latest addition to a family which, spread now throughout the zoological gardens of the world, numbers hundreds. Lion cubs are born in most zoos, but they are rarely reared. If they are not eaten by their parent they die off before they are six months old. The remarkable thing about Mr. Flood is that he has bred hundreds of lion cubs and never lost one.

He will tell you that the secret is understanding lions, which does not carry you far. How do you understand a lion? No two lions are alike, he will tell you. Each one is a personality with moods and feelings like a human being. Their tastes and appetites are different. Their food has to be watched as a matron watches, or is supposed to watch, the food in a nursing home.

"I suppose the secret," says Mr. Flood, "is that I live for them. I couldn't do anything else. Ever since I was a bit of a boy I wanted to look after lions. I've done it, and I'm happy."

"Are the stories about your power over wild animals true?"

"In parts. It's a question of voice. There's something in my voice, in the tone of it, you understand, which they obey. I never shout at them. I've never taken a stick to an animal in my life. I just speak to them. They know. They have to obey me. I developed this power over them unconsciously. You notice that every animal in this place is watching me, and only me. It's the same when the lion house is packed with people. If I come in quietly and stand at the back they know. They don't see anybody else. . . ."

This is true, as any Dublin man can prove today by going into the lion house with Mr. Flood and trying to attract the eyes of a lion.

Dublin's export of lions began nearly half a century ago. The record price for a grown lion was £250. You can buy a cub for £50.

When the Germans bombarded Antwerp at the beginning of the war the shells dropped into the zoo. Those animals who were not killed were mercifully slaughtered. The Antwerp Zoo, believing optimistically that the war would end in a few months, at once wrote to Dublin and ordered a new supply of lion cubs. A litter was reserved for them and delivered five years later as full-grown animals.

There are Dublin lions in Adelaide and Toronto. There are Dublin lions travelling round the world in fairs and menageries.

The most famous lioness was Nigeria, a magnificent creature presented by King Edward. She had twenty-six cubs during her long and productive life, every one of which lived. The Dublin Zoo contains several of Nigeria's great-grandchildren. She was a youthful-looking old lady, and Mr. Flood will tell you that she looked younger than her grandchildren almost until she died.

The Dublin Zoo was opened in 1831. Its early history is a mystery because there is no printed record. Members of the Royal Zoological Society of London will be interested to know that Major Vigors, who took part in forming the London Zoo, helped to establish it, and that Mr. Decimus Burton, architect to the Zoological Society of London, designed it. Its first animals were presented by William IV from the royal menagerie in Windsor Park. From the Tower of London he sent a wolf, a leopard, and a hyena.

Zoo breakfasts are a strange and entertaining feature of Dublin life, and it is so right in this land of paradox that the capital of Ireland should be famed for breeding the symbol of England!

5

Stout is a drink which in some mysterious way has become wedded to the oyster. It is the robust and slightly heavier brother of beer. Most men like it, and thin women drink it as a duty. We are constantly told that "it is good for us."

This dark and satisfying fluid is occasionally mixed by those of exotic taste with port or sherry, producing a drink which is famed as a "corpse reviver."

Dublin is the home of stout. Guinness's brewery is the world's largest brewery, and it is, speaking industrially, Dublin. It is the greatest employer of labour in the Irish capital, and the only firm with a world-wide reputation. A jet black river of Guinness trickles into every corner of the thirsty world, taking with it the name of Dublin.

When I went there to learn the mysteries of stout I entered a walled city devoted to drink. There are railway lines in it, and a canal on which sail barges with cargoes from all the barley fields of Ireland.

Now and then these barges, which are a distinctive

feature of the landscape, draw from loungers on the banks
the ironic shout:

"Will ye bring us back a parrot?"

The recipe for stout is simple: it is hops (Kentish and
Californian mixed), pale malt, and a certain quantity of
roast malt or barley. Roast malt looks exactly like coffee,
which explains the Ethiopian colour of the "wine of
Ireland."

Now, the first ordeal endured by potential Guinness is
that of the brew-house, in which it is, after mixing, drawn
off as a thin, sweet, coffee-like liquid known as "wort."
The "wort" is next boiled with hops and pumped through
long pipes into the fermenting house.

Yeast is added to assist fermentation, and as you look
through a door you see this khaki-coloured scum moving
in a slow, repulsive manner, opening and closing a bubbly
eye here and there with a kind of obscene intelligence.

The brewery joke is to take a visitor to these vats, and
wait for that inevitable moment when he puts his head over
them to see better. Then, with the speed of an electric
shock, something far superior to the world's worst smell
leaps out and hits him in the face. It is not a smell: it is a
gas. If a man were held in this gas for five seconds he could
not breathe, and if for ten he would be dead.

We opened a door and entered a long shed in which
three hundred men and boys were working in a pungent
smell of burning oak chips. This is to me the most interesting section of the brewery. These men are coopers, the
survivors of a dying industry which, during the Middle
Ages, was one of the most powerful of trade guilds. Today
the Dublin cooperage is the last great one in existence.

Cooperage is an hereditary and closely-guarded trade.
Boys, every one the son of a cooper, are apprenticed to a
master cooper and are paid not by the brewery, but by

their instructors. There is a mediæval discipline in the fact that if a master cooper finds his pupil slacking he docks the boy's money.

Every portion of the cask's interior is charred over a fire of oak shavings in order to remove certain qualities in the wood which might injure the stout.

Outside the cooperage you see twenty-five men putting their noses to the bung-holes of empty barrels. They smell them so systematically that one's first thought that they may be bent on pleasure is obviously unworthy. These men belong to one of the least-known of the queer professions —that of smeller of empty stout barrels.

Their delicate noses, accustomed to all the smells of cooperage, tell them at once when a cask is sweet and clean enough to be refilled and sent out once more to cheer the world.

Every visitor to the brewery ends up in the tasting-room, where the choicest vintage is ready for him. A wise man drinks only one tankard of that mysterious beverage known as "foreign extra." This is a stout of liqueur-like potency which has matured often for five or seven years. It is designed for foreign consumption, and is said that it reconciles exiles all over the world to the sadness of their fate. The kick of a full-grown mule is in each bottle.

"Och!" said my guide, "they call it the drink of heaven!"

I am sure that is not a good name for it.

The joke in this room is to give the visitor two bottles of "foreign extra" and then watch him walk to the gate.

6

The most gruesome sight I have encountered in any city is to be seen beneath the Church of St. Michan, in Dublin.

St. Michan is said to have been a Danish bishop who founded a church in the year A. D. 1095, above vaults built on the site of an ancient oak forest. The church was rebuilt on town-hall lines during the eighteenth century. The only objects of interest contained in it are a Stool of Repentance, a pulpit which at one time could be swung round to face any section of the congregation, and a good-looking organ, sprouting gilded cherubs, on which Handel, so they say, practised his "Messiah" before the first performance in Dublin.

Visitors go to St. Michan's to look at the bodies in the vaults beneath. These are preserved by some peculiarity of the atmosphere as perfectly as Egyptian mummies. Morbid persons, and those who like to feel their flesh creeping, will find it worth while to visit Dublin to see this awful place, because it is unique in Ireland; and there is certainly nothing like it in England. I seem to remember once seeing rows of mummified monks in the crypt of a church at Bonn, on the Rhine, but, unless my memory is at fault, they were skeletons compared with the mummies of St. Michan's.

The sexton takes you outside through the churchyard and approaches heavy iron doors on the ground level against the wall of the church. These he unlocks, and you look down a steep flight of stone steps into the darkness of the charnelhouse. You notice as you descend that the air is not the chilled, clammy air of a crypt: it is almost warm, and of a surprising freshness.

"This," says the sexton, as he goes down before you, "is the best air in Dublin."

A number of high-vaulted cells lead off from each side of a central passage running east and west beneath the church. They are fitted with iron gates. The sexton takes an electric lamp, opens a gate, and, leading the way into one of the vaults, flashes his torch over the most ghastly sight you can imagine.

Coffins lie stacked one on top of another almost to the roof. You are in the vault of a noble family. Lords and ladies, generals and statesmen, known and unknown, lie round you in human strata. The last coffin placed in position rest on others, which in their turn rest on that of the great-great-grandfather. The lower coffins are of a shape and colour long out-dated. Some, which bear coats of arms, are covered in red velvet, which has not decayed much or faded in colour; others are bound in black leather, and are studded with big brass nails which have not tarnished.

When you look more closely you notice that the weight of the dead pressing on the dead has caused the coffins to collapse into one another, exposing here a hand, there an arm, a leg, or a head. The idea of dead men pushing their ancestors from their coffins is worthy of Edgar Allan Poe. But what does startle and horrify is that these men and women, many of whom have been dead for 500 years and more, have not gone back to the dust; they are like mummies, their flesh is the texture of tough leather, and, stranger still, their joint bones work.

"Look!" said the sexton, moving a knee, anxious that I should miss nothing.

In a corner I saw the body of a man lying with one leg crossed over the other, the traditional death posture of a Crusader. This indicated that he had been to the Holy Land. You can see this position sculptured in stone on the tombs in the Temple Church, London, and in thousands of other Norman memorials up and down England, but I never thought it possible to see the Crusader himself.

"You can shake hands with him!" said the sexton. I

bent down and examined the nails of a man who has been dead for nearly 800 years.

In the same vault is the body of a woman, said to be a nun, whose feet and right hand have been amputated. The story is that she was tortured and mutilated hundreds of years ago.

We went into many other vaults, notably that of a family which has died out. This place was a nightmare. Intimate fragments of this family were lying about the floor in a thin brown dust of decayed coffins.

The only living creatures in these vaults are spiders. In certain places they have spun thin grey shrouds from roof to floor. In one vault they have made a merciful curtain over the door.

"What do they live on?"

"Themselves," says the sexton. "Men who study spiders come here from all over the place, and I have been told that spiders are cannibals. . . ."

The generally accepted theory, which explains the remarkable preservative quality of the vault, is that the air is chemically impregnated by the remains of the oak forest which stood there in ancient times. So long as the vaults are kept perfectly dry decay ceases. Let only a little moisture enter, then bodies and coffins crumble into fine dust. When the two brothers, John and Henry Sheares, who were beheaded in the eighteenth century, were re-coffined in 1853—they used to stand upright in a vault with their heads beside their feet—the people of Dublin brought wreaths and flowers to the vault. The moisture in these flowers wrecked everything in the vault within a year.

I was glad to reach the cold air and the daylight.

"Do you show these vaults to women?" I asked.

"I always warn ladies," he said, "or I'd be having them fainting on me. . . . I'll not forget the first time I came here fourteen years ago, and me not knowing a thing about it at all. I took a candle—there was no electric light then—and went down to have a look. I got the biggest fright of my life. . . .

"Yes, they do tell a ghost story about it. It's about a thief who went down one dark night to take a ring from a lady's finger, and, as he was working away, the lady sat up in her coffin and stepped out over the side and walked away. Yes, she did! And they say she lived for years after. But that's all blarney, sir. . . ."

St. Michan's is Dublin's chamber of horrors!

7

It occurred to me at about three o'clock one morning that I must tear myself away from the terrible friendliness of Dublin and see Ireland. I knew that I could not face all my sudden friends and say:

"I am going away at once!"

They would have replied:

"But what's the hurry? Come on now and we'll go and see So-and-So!"

And I would have been flattered, swayed, and conquered. So I made secret arrangements for a motor-car, wrote a lot of apologies, and early one morning escaped from Dublin like a criminal.

CHAPTER III

The road runs over the hills to Glendalough and its churches. I
hear the legend of St. Kevin and go on to the Curragh where I
see horses and stud farms. I go to an Irish race meeting and
win some money

1

IT was a warm summer morning and the dew still on the
grass when I took the road over the hills.

No such wilderness as the Dublin hills lies at the door
of any great city. The Peak District, at the back door of
Sheffield, is tame compared with the miles of melancholy
peat bog which never have given, and never will give, food
or shelter to man.

You could be lost in the hills within an hour of Dublin;
you could wander for days without meeting a soul; you
could, if injured, lie there and die in the bog because your
chance of finding help would be indeed remote.

The great hills, more savage even than Dartmoor, lie
fold on fold, some long and of gentle outline, others sharp
and conical; and in their hollows you come unexpectedly
to deep lakes, such as Lough Dan, lying like a patch of
fallen sky. Little brown streams trickle through the peat.
The whole landscape is a study in various browns; brown
peat like dark chocolate; black brown water; light brown
grass; dark brown pyramids of cut peat stacked at intervals along the brown road.

But in the evening the hills turn blue. White mists rise
in the hollows and lie there like thin veils hung from hill to
hill. The sun sets. And there is no sound but the wind

53

blowing through the tough grass and the thin trickle of water running to the valleys.

A man might be among the dead mountains of the moon.

So I have come into Wicklow, where the fields are sharply green, where a wild beauty hides in the glens, where sudden surprising vistas open up as the road rises and falls; and here I smell for the first time the incense of Ireland, the smoke of turf fires, and here for the first time I see the face of the Irish countryside.

It is not an easy, comfortable countryside like that of England. It has not the same settled confidence. It has a strange and foreign look. I feel at times that I am in France. No half-timbered cottages stand rooted in the soil wearing thatches like old hats; no cosy inns call themselves "The Nag's Head" or "The Fox and Hounds."

There are instead small one-story houses of stone, whitewashed so that they hurt the eyes as they shine in the sun. Some are so small that a child might think them the houses of fairies. Often a full-sized Irish face looks out from a window no bigger than a table-napkin. All these houses standing against the road have little green doors designed for contemplation. It is possible to make half doors of them on which a thoughtful man may lean and smoke his pipe and watch the world go past, just as if he were leaning on the rail of a ship.

When these doors are open I can see into the half dusk of a small room in which a small red flame burns before a little shrine.

In a field near-by a farmer stands among his herds, a pipe in his mouth, a stick in his hand, and an eye on the main road; his wife sets out towards the next town leading a small donkey in a small cart. And down the country roads of Ireland walk some of the best-looking country girls in the world. Some are small and red-faced, with dark eyes; others are fair and freckled about the nose, with blue eyes. They possess great dignity of bearing.

I saw a hatless girl carrying a basket on one arm and on the other a baby wrapped in the fold of a black shawl. There was nothing of the peasant in her appearance. She had a fine face and thoroughbred ankles.

A man cannot go far along an Irish road without meeting a horseman. Often a priest talks to a young farmer who leans slightly from the saddle and pats his horse while he replies to "his riv'rence," and the horse is not the English farmer's nag; there is blood in him.

I miss flowers in cottage gardens. I go through village after village thinking that if I were an Irishman I would start a society for the planting of them in little gardens all over the land. But most of all I miss that triumph of the English landscape—the village Inn.

There is, it is true, in every town a drink saloon called after the name of past or present owner, "Casey's" or "Dempsey's," dull and ugly buildings so strange and uncouth in a country noted for its sociability and its good manners. Outside at thirsty moments of the day gather numerous gigs, traps, jaunting cars and sometimes a shaggy little donkey and cart.

But over it all—the white houses, the green fields with their stone walls, the long road winding, the slow herds coming along in the knee-deep dust, the sweet smell of turf burning, the little carts with coloured shafts, the soft Irish voices, the quick Irish smiles—over it all, and in it as if imprisoned in the stone and brick of this country, as if buried beneath the grass and hidden in the trees, is something that is half magic and half music.

There is something in a minor key that a man never

quite hears. Perhaps no stranger ever hears it. But I think
the Irish do. It is something drawn up out of the earth of
Ireland, out of the water in the streams and the grass and
flowers in the fields, something of the sky and of the
earth—a something that is mysterious and like a fall of
dew over the land.

What it is I shall probably never know. It is what people mean when they say that Ireland "gets you" or that
Ireland is "fascinating."

It is something subtle and deeply rooted and very old,
something that may be the blessing or the curse of Ireland. If you could translate it into sound I imagine it
would be rather like the twittering of a fiddle.

I am sure that this minor note which just escapes the
ear is important. If a man could hear it he would know
all there is to know about Ireland.

At night I took out the books I carry with me and
looked through the few books of Irish verse in the hope of
finding something that might help me to explain a feeling
which is so vague and difficult to put into words that I
fear few people without a dash of Celtic blood in them will
be able to understand a word of it. And I found in the
few Irish poems I had with me an interesting insistence
on the sounds of Ireland. Synge in particular describes a
landscape ever and again in terms of sound. Take the
tramp's speech in "The Shadow of the Glen":

"Come along with me, now, lady of the house, and it's
not my blather you'll be hearing only, but you'll be hearing the herons crying out over the black lakes, and you'll
be hearing the grouse and the owls with them, and the
larks and the big thrushes when the days are warm; and
it's not from the like of them you'll be hearing a talk of
getting old like Peggy Cavanagh and losing the hair off
you, and the light of your eyes, but it's fine songs you'll

be hearing when the sun goes up, and there'll be no old
fellow wheezing, the like of a sick sheep, close to your ear."

And Nora Burke's speech in the same play:

"When you do be sitting and looking out from a door
the like of that door and seeing nothing but the mists
rolling down the bog and hearing nothing but the wind
crying out in the bits of broken trees left from the great
storm, and the streams roaring with the rain."

And again in "The Well of the Saints":

"I'm smelling the furze a while back sprouting on the
hill, and if you'd hold your tongue you'd hear the lambs
of Grianan, though it's near drowned their crying is with
the full river making noises in the glen."

Take the poems of Francis Ledwidge:

And when the war is over I shall take
My lute a-down to it and sing again
Songs of the whispering things amongst the brake.

It is these "whispering things" that are never far away
from you in Ireland. But you cannot hear what they are
saying.

2

I have stood on the windy sands of Lindisfarne, where
St. Cuthbert made his cell, and on that hill in Somerset
where, so they say, St. Joseph of Arimathea planted the
Holy Thorn, but no place has given me a clearer picture
of early Christianity than the strange little ruin city of
Glendalough, in Co. Wicklow.

I do not think Ireland can have anything more lovely to show than this heavenly little valley, with its two small lakes lying cupped in a hollow of the hills. So high are the hills and so deep the lakes that even on a sunny day the waters are still and black.

A tall, round tower rises above the trees at the lakeside, one of those towers peculiar to Ireland, and built nearly 1,000 years ago as a belfry and a refuge from the Danes. The doors are high up in these towers, so that refugees could pull up the ladder after them and feel secure from attack.

Round the tower, lost in trees, covered in green moss and tangled in brambles, or perched high on ledges of the cliffs, are the ruins of a religious community which was established centuries before England was a Christian country.

The bells rang for Mass in Glendalough when there was no sound in England but the meeting of the sword on sword and the cries of the Vikings beaching their ships.

They tell you at Glendalough that the ruins are those of the Seven Churches, but this, as Professor Macalister points out in *The Archaeology of Ireland*, is a number never found grouped together:

"A notable peculiarity of Irish ecclesiastical establishments," he writes, "is the multiplication of small church buildings. At Glendalough, Ucht Hama, Clonmacnois, Kilmacduach, Inis Cealtra, and elsewhere, there are to be found within one and the same enclosure a number of independent churches, most of them of small size. There may be any number of these; at some places there are two or three, at others as many as thirteen. One number which, as it happens, *never* found is *seven;* notwithstanding this such groups frequently bear the popular name 'The Seven Churches,' with the ridiculous assumption that the Seven

Photo. Irish Tourist Association, Dublin

GLENDALOUGH

Churches of the Apocalypse are thereby represented in symbol. Such a symbolism would be quite pointless in any case; and even if there were any conceivable reason why the church builders should affect it, the non-existence of any actual group of seven churches, and the fact that the component elements of the groups are sometimes not churches at all but domestic buildings and that they were obviously at different times, would be enough to show that it never entered their heads to do so.

"To understand the real meaning of these groups of buildings we have only to think of a mediæval cathedral or large collegiate church, with its complication of chantry chapels, each containing an altar. Now, imagine the unity of such a building to be dissolved, so that each of these chapels becomes a separate church: we shall then find ourselves with a group of churches as is presented by the Irish monastic sites. Each church is essentially a chantry chapel, founded by some benefactor of the establishment."

I sat on a bridge over a brown, troutful stream, watching two boys approach leading a donkey laden with wood in panniers. They promised to send the boatman to me, so that I could go over the lake and climb to St. Kevin's Bed.

St. Kevin was the founder of Glendalough. He came to it about the year 520—was there one Christian in England at that date?—to lead a hermit's life.

There is an ancient tradition, the source of a thousand songs and poems, that he was driven into solitude by the passion of a beautiful girl named Kathleen, who favoured him with rentless ardour. The old chronicle states that "the holy youth rejected all these allurements."

One day finding the young monk alone in the fields, she approached him and clasped him in her arms. "But the soldier of Christ, arming himself with the sacred sign and full of the Holy Ghost, made strong resistance against her, and rushed out of her arms into the wood, and finding nettles, took secretly a bunch of them and struck her with them many time in the face, hands, and feet. And when she was blistered with the nettles, the pleasure of her love became extinct."

So says legend. Another version, exploited by the poet Moore, is that St. Kevin, in order to rid himself of his fair admirer, pushed her into the lake!

The historic fact remains that the young hermit retired to Glendalough, where he lived at first in a hollow tree and later in a small cave which he discovered high up in the sheer face of the cliff.

Disciples came from near and far. Gradually there grew up round the lake a little sanctuary of holy men. St. Kevin lived to see his disciples go from Glendalough to found schools and monasteries in other parts of Ireland. This little ruined city—an Irish Thebaid—was a school of Irish saints.

"Good evening, sir."

I looked up, and saw the boatman standing before me wearing one of those deathless bowlars seen only in Ireland. They are, I think, handed down the centuries from father to son.

"And it's the saint's bed ye'll be seeing this evening?" he asked.

"Wait now while I get the boat out. . . . Step aisy, now!"

As we went over the still, dark water and he told me the story of St. Kevin and his struggle with the ardent Kathleen I asked him if it was true that the saint pushed her into the lake.

"Begor," he said, "and what kind of a saint would he be to treat a young lady like that? The truth of it is that he bothered her with nettles, and she was cured of her love and became a nun. Now, sir, look back there!"

He pursed up his mouth and looked solemn, as his type does before "putting over" a bit of blarney: "On that stone Kathleen appears every night at ten. I've seen her with me own eyes, that I have, and the loveliest creature that ever stepped she is."

"How deep is the lake?"

"It's that deep, sir, that my sister went bathing there a while back and sank. . . ." He paused solemnly, and added, "We heard not a word from her until we got a letter from Manchester asking us to post her some dry clothes. That's how deep it is, sir."

I knew that the man was acting up to a tradition established by centuries of tourists. He was expected to talk like this and to tell tall stories; and I could not help admiring him because he did it so well.

St. Kevin's Bed—the cell in which the saint lived before the "Seven Churches" were built—is high up in the cliff. It is a perilous climb, but thousands do it every year. Once in the cave you can sit down and contemplate the waters and wonder how on earth you are going to get down again.

The boatman then recites in a curious, high-pitched chant Moore's poem on the pushing of Kathleen into the lake. The first verse is:

> *By the lake whose gloomy shore*
> *Skylark never warbles o'er,*
> *Where the cliff hangs high and steep,*
> *Young St. Kevin stole to sleep.*

"Here at last," he calmly said,
"Woman ne'er shall find my bed."
Ah! the good saint little knew
What the wily sex can do. . . .

"And that's thrue, sir, for if a lady sets her heart on a man, be he saint or sinner, he's got to watch himself, that he has. . . . Now take three wishes and they'll come thrue!"

I went west over the Wicklow hills into Kildare. I saw a bill in a shop window which advertised races on the Curragh and I decided to go to the meeting. On the way I stopped in a small country town for a drink and a sandwich. I met a man who seemed to like me. He swore that he would go down on his knees and hobble the length of the main street if he could see the British army come marching back to the Curragh. I told him flatly that I did not believe him. He swore again that he was speaking the truth. I have an idea that people who say things like this to a visitor from England do so out of a natural politeness, although on the Curragh the withdrawal of the army must have made a sad hole in the income of the local people:

"Surely you are proud of your country's independence?" I asked him.

"It's from bad to worse we go every time, captain," he replied.

I was surprised to find myself addressed as captain, a rank and a tribute to one's youth, nowadays only given occasionally by those furtive newsvendors in Piccadilly who know something for the three-thirty. But it rather illuminated the strange being: he thought that he was talking to an English officer. He spat with disgust:

"It's from bad to worse we go," he repeated. "Shure, it's an awful misfortunate country; and that's the fact of it."

I was vaguely annoyed with him. I was sorry if he really felt like this, and I was ashamed to think if he were trying to please me that he should consider me such a simple fool as to believe him. I gave him up as a bad job and went on towards Kildare, thinking that when the bar opened again he would probably be discovered denouncing the iniquity of England to a more sympathetic audience than I had proved to be.

Kildare had reached the end of its market day. A few desolate cows were being led home down the hilly street.

I went to sleep that night below a mildewed engraving showing Lord Roberts, in fatherly mood, sitting with a little long-haired girl on his knees:

"Can't you see I'm busy?" his lordship was saying to an urgent A.D.C. who stood at the door anxious to intrude with the South African War.

What a truly mildewed voice from the past!

8

It is seven o'clock in the morning. The air is like iced wine. The sun is bright over the Curragh, which is the Salisbury Plain of Ireland. Clouds are vast above it, and far off on the sky the Dublin Mountains lie in a blue mist, fold on fold.

My horse throws up his head and fidgets to fling himself through the morning over the green grass; and I hold him in, loving his impatience and the shining life in him which is something pure and classic from the beginning of the world. I pat his neck and whisper to him, denying him cruelly, telling him to be patient.

"Let me go," he seems to say. "Let me match the beauty of my strength with the beauty of the world!"

"Go, go—*now!*" I press my knees lightly to him; and, with a kind of elemental ecstasy, he springs forward into the sunlight; and—I forget everything but the rush of the wind, the rhythm of his hoof-beats on the turf, and the heady joy of riding a horse in the early morning!

The whole bright world rushes towards us. I see a gleam of snow-white rails above the grass: the deserted Curragh Racecourse. But the plain is awake. It is dotted with race-horses at exercise or gallops. This place is a nursery of racehorses, the finest in the world. As I pass them trotting, walking, galloping, I wish that I had an Irishman with me to say to me in a reverent whisper:

"There goes so and so who sired many a winner!"

To the men of the Curragh these horses are the local heroes. The spirit of the Curragh is a lightly-stepping thoroughbred—fetlocks in brown bandages—the very incarnation of nervous energy, speed, and breeding.

I come into the little town of Kildare. It is shuttered and asleep in the early morning, save for a drover and his kine. There is a sudden great clatter of horses, and round the corner, riding one and leading one, comes a squadron of Free State cavalry at early morning exercise. The years drop from me, and I follow them longingly with my eyes—fancy following an early morning parade longingly!—as they go at a heavy jog-trot down the hill towards the miles of open country.

As I follow slowly I hear behind me the sound of hoofs, but very different from the hearty clatter of a cavalry squadron. It is a delicate, nervous, lady-like sound, and, turning, I see a string of racehorses. There are sixteen of them. Beauties!

A stable-boy walks at the head of each holding a white band attached to the head collar. Each horse wears knee-caps and fetlock bandages. Following the long file comes a dogcart containing a man who looks at the horses with the expression of a mother. He is the manager of a stud farm watching the stately procession of a year's hard work and devotion.

These horses are yearlings. They are as nervous as kittens. The very sound of their shoes on the road startles them. To pass from sunlight into a tree shadow causes them to sidestep and fling up their lovely narrow heads.

"They are going to the yearling sales at Newmarket," says the man in the dogcart. "And a better batch of yearlings has never left the Curragh. Poor little devils! They don't know what's up this morning! This is the first time they've been on the roads. See that filly, the fourth from the end, she's worth ten thousand pounds if she's worth a penny! I reckon there's seventy thousand pounds worth of horseflesh in front of us this morning. . . .

"Yes; it's an anxious job taking yearlings to England. We have a special train, then the boat to Holyhead, and a special train to Newmarket. But yearlings don't understand travel. An experienced old racehorse will lean against the box in the train and rest himself, and he'll let himself go with the rise and fall of a ship; but, bless you, yearlings are just little children! They knock themselves about in the train and panic on the boat. It takes pounds off their weight. Come along and watch them look at their first railway engine!"

The nervous line halted some distance from the railway bridge, every ear pricked to heaven, every nerve on edge. A sudden start at the head of the line would pass right down to the last horse.

The manager and I walked to the station, where a special train of horse-boxes stood in a siding, driven by a discreet locomotive that had shut off steam.

"That's right," said the stud manager. "These drivers are used to horses."

"When you shunt," said the manager to the engine driver, "don't let the buffers bang. . . ."

"Sure I won't," said the driver, with a grin. "I'll come back as swate and gentle as a drame!"

The manager waved his hand, and the £70,000 worth of speed and aristocracy advanced delicately and doubtfully over the bridge.

The sides of the horse-boxes were let down with a bang that shook the yearling to the heart. They stood with pricked ears looking over the wall at the engine and the train, wondering, interested, startled. Straw was flung over the gangways, and the first yearling was led, slowly and with every kind of endearment known to stables, towards the train. The rest watched him.

He walked quietly towards the box, then suddenly shied away from it. His groom coaxed him and brought him head on to it. He shook his head and whinnied. There was an answering whinny from the other horses on the road.

"Hup-hup-hup; hey, boy, there's the pretty lad, there's the big feller; come boy, come—hup-hup-hup . . ." coaxed the groom.

The lovely thing put out one leg and touched the gang-plank delicately, then shivered with doubt and fear.

"Hup-hup-hup, hey, there's the pretty boy, there's the great big feller . . ."

He tested the plank with both feet, and, finding it firm under the straw, entered the box with a great thud of hooves. His groom entered with him, and the sides of the box were bolted on them.

"The stable-boys go all the way with them?"

"They never let go the head-ropes from the Curragh to Newmarket," said the manager. "They're the lads who've looked after them since they were foaled. Yes; it's like seeing your children leave home."

One by one the sixteen yearlings were placed in their padded boxes as the engine driver shunted his train "as swately and softly as a drame." There was no trouble. No horse was cut. Only the £10,000 filly exercised certain feminine prerogatives, and kicked up a fuss; but she was soothed and persuaded.

"Well, I've never seen yearlings boxed with less trouble," said the manager. "Of course, they'll sweat pounds off themselves. When I get to Newmarket I'll give them a bran mash and let them rest for a while. . . . Now, boys," he said, walking the length of the train, "don't let go the head ropes for a second . . ."

"We won't!" came back in muffled tones from the darkness of the boxes, and down the train sounded from every box the love-making of stables, the sound of sleek bodies being patted and Irish voices saying, "There's a lovely lad, there's a darlin' bhoy; shure he's a grand big feller . . ."

"And now," said the manager, "that's over! I've bred them since they were foaled, looking as much like a race-horse as a rat, and now I'm proud of them, and they're fit for any stable in the land. Is there a Derby winner in that little lot I wonder!

"It's a wonderful thing to see thoroughbred yearlings go off like this, some of them to become famous all over the world . . . wonderful."

A whistle blew. The shuttered line of horse-boxes moved. There was a protest of whinnies. The untried, unchristened potential heroes of the turf moved off from Ireland on their first adventure, sure of nothing but their pedigrees.

4

"Ye can talk about Newmarket," said the ancient man who was propping up Kildare market hall, "if it's grand horses ye're wanting it's to Ireland ye must come for thim. What horses have won the big races in England this year? Irish ivery wan o' thim! Faith, the Curragh's just mate and dhrink to thim! Divil a spot in the world to put such bone on a horse. . . ."

"It is so," agreed the friends of this old man, who at the magic sound of the word "horses" gathered from afar like old ravens.

I asked the way to the National Stud and then tore myself violently from the crowd for every casual street-corner conversation in Ireland has the dangerous charm of eternal friendship. Ireland is full of old men at street corners, who appear to have been in conference since the days of Brian Boru.

The stud farms of the Curragh look like a compromise between hunting stables and sanatoria. The National Stud, which breeds, sells, and trains racehorses, is not, as many people possibly imagine, the property of the Free State; it belongs to the British Government. It is run from Whitehall, and its profits—it makes a good profit—go to the Treasury. These 2,000 acres were, until 1916, the private stud of Colonel Hall Walker, now Lord Wavertree, who in that year gave them to the Government with sires, brood mares, yearlings, foals, and horses in training.

A small red house guards the entrance of the stud, and in it lives the manager, Mr. P. C. Purcell, a cheerful, ruddy, middle-aged man with a faint but puzzling English accent. I closed my eyes, listened, and then I got it—Birmingham!

Mr. Purcell is known wherever racehorses own men. His life has been spent in making racehorses. He knows as much about horses as mothers of enormous families know about children, which is, of course, everything.

Were I Mrs. Purcell, however, I would live in fear that Mr. Purcell might, at any moment, turn into a centaur and go cantering off into the woods.

The National Stud can stable 150 horses. Its pastures could, I imagine, sustain a number of cavalry divisions. Mr. Purcell took me to a wide square around which are the stables. The place was as swept and garnished as a flagship, and in fact, a stray straw lying about gave one the same twinge of horror that a match gives one on a quarter-deck.

"Now, here are the beauties!" said Mr. Purcell, opening stable doors.

Inside were the twenty-six yearlings he has brought to perfection during the past twelve months. Many of them were sired by the National Stud stallions Diligence and Silvern.

"And don't they look like it?" cried Mr. Purcell, as black and brown yearlings pricked their ears at us.

I noticed that he had a different manner for each yearling: with some he was affectionate, with some jocular, with some cold and distant, with some he even pretended to be harsh.

"Bless you, every one's a personality to me! Haven't I bred them since they were that high. Most of them are off to England this week to be sold at Newmarket. . . ."

"You'll never come back, old boy," he said, patting a brown child of Diligence, "never. Perhaps the next I shall hear of you will be from New Zealand or India. . . ."

"It's good-bye tomorrow old lady," he said to a black filly. "You're a beauty, you are, you're a racehorse, you are, you're a lovely little girl—ah! would you, you little vixen! You're too cheeky by half! Bite me, would you?" . . .

And he snapped his fingers and looked threatening; but in his eyes were a year's love and devotion. Mr. Purcell would not admit, of course, that he feels any tenderness once a year when his beautiful, swift children go out into the world; but his manner with them, his personal knowledge of them and their sires, above all his interest in their future careers and his prophetic sense of their capabilities, remind me of a great head-master.

It seemed to me as we continued our walk, discussing this yearling and its sire and its sire's sire, that the National Stud is a public school on four legs. It is a kind of eugenic Eton of the turf. Here, foals of historic strain come in annual procession, go through the same process of education and depart into a world of achievement.

And Mr. Purcell seemed to me a fortunate schoolmaster —his scholars are scientifically bred.

"Here's the maternity ward!"

We inspected a side of the square in which mares with foals are stabled. Nothing looks less like a racehorse than a fluffy foal. It is not possible to imagine these infants flashing round Newmarket or Epsom with a jockey crouched over their withers. Every time we opened a stable door the mare would look round at us, the foal would run to the shelter of her shadow and stand prettily to receive the reassuring touch of her nose on his little body.

"See them in a year's time," said Mr. Purcell. "That one is sired by Diligence!"

The strangest little fawn-like creature looked up at us

from the straw. I wondered whether it would ever win the Derby!

And for the first time in my life I felt the attraction of a racing stable. I realized that were I a millionaire I would breed racehorses, not only in order to keep in touch with the fascinating and absolutely distinct race of men who live for horses—they exude a sort of earthy humanity and a prehistoric cunning—but because few things can be more absorbing than this constant mixing of blood, this transmutation of breed into speed.

I was shown Silvern and Diligence, vast and rather threatening, in their padded stalls. They blew out their nostrils at us and stood, studies in collected energy, ready, it seemed to me, to kick down the doors and leap over us into the stable yard.

How truly I had compared the National Stud to a public school!

There is a circular building, open to the sky in the centre, in which young racehorses are taught the secrets of their profession. It is deep in straw. The whole building has a protective air. Has it not guarded the first stumbles of classic heroes? But right round the building, in a bright metallic circle, are nailed the shoes of all National Stud horses which have won honours on the turf.

But no schoolmaster ever exhibited the scholarship shields with half the pride that Mr. Purcell walked round the riding school, noting the names of winners and the stake money gained each year since 1917. Last year National Stud horses won £12,607 in stakes. In 1922 they won £34,750. The bare stake money won in this school since 1917 amounts to £130,946.

"Why is the Curragh so famous for horse breeding?"

"It's a limestone plain, and the Curragh pasture is the best bone-making country in the world."

"Is it uniformly good, or does it lie in patches?"

"If you want to make a stud farm here you must prospect for it and choose the best ground, but, having found it, you'll raise up real horses on it."

Adjoining, and connected with, the National Stud is one of the unknown jewels of Ireland. This is the garden of Lord Wavertree's old house. The house is unoccupied, but the garden had been cared for largely through the devotion of an old gardener, Mr. Taylor, who loves every inch of it.

It is an astonishing little paradise to discover on the edge of the Curragh. A stream sings through it, ancient trees cast their shade, and great banks of flowers bloom and die with none to admire them, for this garden is unknown, and no one visits it.

Mr. Taylor took me through his paradise to a wicket gate, which opens on the most marvellous Japanese garden I have ever seen. It was laid out years ago by a Japanese landscape artist—and he was a genius. He had forty-five assistants, and the garden was four years in the making.

It is, of course, symbolic. It is a novel in stone and flowers. It tells the story of a man's life, from his birth to his death. You start with him in a dark tunnel, which represents the mystery of birth; you follow his straggling steps through youth to manhood; you mount to a parting of two paths, which symbolizes the perplexities of early life; you wind round rocks and cross streams and climb a hill, which represents ambition; you follow him through a love-affair of flowers to his marriage, where two stones welded together side by side cross a stream.

Married life is not easy. The steps which mount a hill are far apart and difficult to climb. You come to a quarrel and two paths go on: the man one way, the woman another. But round the hill they join again—the quarrel is made up. So it goes on, twisting and turning, crossing streams, every year full of poetic symbols.

This Japanese garden in Ireland which belongs to England, is a sheer joy from beginning to end.

5

An old man wearing a hat like black batter pudding stands with his back to a canvas tent as he makes faint twitterings on a fiddle. No one seems to notice him. No one gives him money. Above the hubbub of the race meeting — and specially when they cry, "They're off!" and a silence falls on the crowd in which I can hear the larks in the sky—his fiddle goes on and on, wheezing like nestlings in a thatch. He plays the same jig over and again, never moving his bow more than an inch either way across the strings. He has wicked pale blue eyes, pink crab-apple cheeks, and the absurd little cupid's bow of a mouth which so many Irishmen of his type possess. He is inconceivably decayed. He is queerly detached. He plays rapidly, his eyes all the time fixed on the grass a yard before him as though he is playing a jig for some invisible dancing dwarf.

I give him half a crown.

What is half a crown? Nothing! Thirty pence. But as it lies in his grimy palm with the sun on it that half-crown gathers compound interest at a surprising and abnormal rate as he looks at it and then at me. He holds it up near his eyes and I realize that he is almost blind. Then life comes into his pale eyes, and still he stands with the bright coin in his hand and the sun on it. He looks at me as though I had given him a purse of gold:

"Glory be to God!" he cries, "and the blessing of the holy saints on ye!"

Before I can reply to this overwhelming return for half a crown he pushes his way into the crowd towards a tent where they sell drink.

High gold clouds are wheeling above the Curragh. The white racecourse rails sweep round into the green distance. There is a feeling of space, air, birds in the sky, and over the broad roads come traps and jaunting-cars in puffs of dust; over the green turf of the plain come in long, easy canters men and women on horseback and small children in corduroy breeches astride fat ponies. A little encampment of tents has grown up against the white rails. There is a smell of wood smoke and turf. There is a smell of crushed grass. There are shabby tinkers' carts festooned with pots and pans. There are booths shining with yellow lemonade and vivid cakes. There are long, crowded canvas bars where men toss down porter or Irish whisky. There are stalls stacked with pigs' feet, ready to eat and looking as horrible as the Cockney's jellied eels. There are small circular gaming tables on which people can lose any money they may win on horses. There are bookies shouting. There are thousands of men and women talking; and the bright light gives a sparkle to it all, flings up the colours so that it might be some fine, shining canvas which contains the essential essence of all race meetings.

Race meetings in Ireland seem to attract every eccentric character in the neighbourhood. Ireland is a country of vivid personalities, as England was in the eighteenth and nineteenth centuries before life was influenced by standardization. The only remaining characters in England now are the old farmer and labourers in remote places. They will soon pass away and leave the stage to sons who look alike and think alike, who use the same advertised razors and shaving-soap, who buy the same cars, take in the same newspapers, and manipulate the same wireless sets. The individuality of an Irish crowd is stimulating. It is full of vitality. It is full of originality. There is a Hogarthian robustness about it.

An old woman whose matted grey hair escapes from a shawl begs in a gracious voice as soft as light falling through stained glass in a church; and when you give her a coin she pours a benediction over you that, like the gratitude of most Irish beggars, really warms the cockles of your heart. She goes into a booth and taps the drink-wet counter with a coin.

"A glass of whisky if ye plaze. . . ."

The barman regards her with grave disapproval:

"Have I not tould ye, Bridget O'Brien, that if ye drink any more this day it's the police that'll come to ye and lock ye up as they locked ye up at Punchestown? . . ."

"The polis!" she cries suddenly, abandoning her Madonna-pose and baring her teeth as she leans furiously over the counter, "the polis!"

The word police seemed to let loose some fury in her.

"Bring them to me," she cries with extravagant rage. "There's not a polisman in the land who'll be laying his dirty hands on me this day. Bring them to me! . . ."

She stands there like some champion offering ordeal by battle.

"Now get along out o' this, will ye?" says the barman soothingly, "for it's no whisky I've got for ye."

"To hell wid the polis!" she cries, becoming a raving virago. "To hell wid them all, I say; and me an O'Brien!"

She shakes her head and glooms. Her wrath falls from her. She has descended into some abysmal pit of sorrow where apparently she communes with the soul of all O'Briens. She looks up with tears in her eyes: an injured aristocrat.

"Och, it's not hard ye'd be on a poor ould woman. Come now, just one glass and it's not troubling ye' I'll be all the day."

She gazes at the barman as if she had seen him for the first time and discovered something incredible about him.

"And can a handsome, civil young man like yerself turn an ould woman away wid hard words and she asking no more than she can pay for. . . . Arrah, come on wid ye now and——"

The barman, at the end of all his patience, makes as though he would come round and turn her out. She instantly flares up again.

"To hell wid ye!" she screams, banging her hand on the bar, which is only a trestle table with oilcloth over it, so that it rebounds under her rage. "Bad luck on ye and may the divil take ye. . . . The polis! It is the polis ye'd bring to me? Is it insulting me ye'd be?"

At this moment a young Civic Guard appears in the opening of the tent. He says nothing. He just stands there. The old woman stabs the barman between the eyes with a glance. It is the glance of a tragedy queen. There is in it anger, dignity, pride, a colossal sense of injury, and a magnificent exaggeration which crops up so often in Irish affairs. She moves over the grass of the tent into the sunlight. The Civic Guard winks at the barman and the barman attacks his arrears of wet glasses.

"It's drunk she'd be if I let her," he says, "poor ould divil. . . . Shure I'm sorry for the poor woman."

Moving among the crowds is the pitiful figure of old Bridget.

"For the love av God?" she whispers in a voice as soft as the glow of altar candles.

Farmers, strangely unhappy in their best clothes, move through the crowd. Incredibly ancient brakes and wagonettes have been dragged out to form grand-stands. Their owners pass among the crowds and sell seats on them. Now and then two burly countrymen have a furious row. A crowd forms round them. You expect every second to see one up with his fist and hit his companion on the jaw. Just when the row is most violent, when both men have appealed to the spectators, when reconciliation appears utterly out of the question, the two men come to terms and walk off together arm in arm.

There are shooting galleries, gambling tables, and Aunt Sallies. There is always a crowd round the gambling tables. They toss pennies on various squares and suffer defeat or—win threepence!

On the opposite and privileged side of the course is a grand-stand, a paddock, a lawn, and a room where you can have tea. The paddock and the grand-stand are filled mainly by a masculine crowd. It is a singularly horsy crowd. The staffs of the Curragh stud farms are present in full force.

A more knowing-looking crowd would be impossible to find. You look at it and feel a certain sympathy for the bookmakers. How on earth can they make any money? Their clients are not the usual tipsters who have heard something from the horse's mouth: they *are* the horse's mouth!

What shall I back?

"Wait a while," says a friend, "I'll go and see Johnnie and find out if his horse will win."

He disappears towards the jockeys' and owners' quarters and returns mysteriously, speaking to me from behind his race card in the voice of a conspirator.

"Back Diogenes," he says.

I go to a bookmaker and discover that there are only four horses in the race. Small fields—even three runners—are common in Ireland. I find that Diogenes is the favourite and I only get two to one.

"Did you back Diogenes?" says my friend.

"I did."

"Well, you're right."

"How do you know?"

"I just know. Hullo, here they come!"

Free State cavalry in green ride slowly down the course opposite the grand-stand and clear it of people. The horses come out in long, easy gallops, the little men with the wind in their coloured silk shirts leaning over their withers; and there is a fine sound of hooves thudding quickly on grass as they go to the post.

The crowd is now quieter. The bookies set up a final clamour.

"They're off!"

The crowd is silent. The larks are trilling in the sky. The Dublin and the Wicklow hills look quite near in the sharp light, lying ahead in shadows of blue with the big clouds above them. Riders on the other side of the course go galloping off to follow the race. Part of the crowd trails away to see the horses pass at a distant point in the course. A late jaunting-car far off down the road comes on at a reckless speed in order to be in time for the finish. The driver stands up and urges on his horse; and the horse gallops over the thin brown road. . . .

"Dark Horse wins!" cries men with field-glasses.

But it is not certain.

"He's making the running. . . . He's well away. . . . Hullo! Diogenes! He's coming up on the outside. . . . They're level. . . ."

On they come, neck to neck, the jockeys urging them forward, spending their last ounce of speed; little whips rise and fall above the shining flanks, on they come thudding over the grass, Diogenes and Dark Horse neck to neck, with flecks of white foam at their bridles; then Diogenes seems suddenly to spring forward, a head in front, half a length, a length. . . . Diogenes wins!

I go and collect my winnings.

I find myself among a crowd of expert racing men. They know everything that happens on the Curragh. They know every horse. They know exactly what owner, trainer, and jockey think about them.

"Will your mare win the next race, Bill?"

"No. She's been coughing all the winter. . . . Have you heard what they say about Green Mantle?"

And so it goes on through the afternoon.

*   *   *

In the evening the racecourse is deserted. The larks are coming down out of the sky and the shadows fall over the great limestone plain.

CHAPTER IV

I linger in horsey country towns, hear the angelus in Cahir, and go
on to the glory of Tipperary—Cashel of the Kings

1

A GOOD road runs south from Kilcullen to Carlow.

Towns in this part of Ireland are much the same. You
know when you are approaching one by the ruin of an
R.I.C. barracks burnt out during the Trouble and by
ancient inscriptions in white paint—"De Valera"—now
much faded. Or you see, painted in letters a foot high,
exhortations to men called Duffy or Malone to be up and
doing: "Up, Duffy" and "Up, Malone," say stone walls
and the sides of houses.

Then you enter a peaceful little place which, it seems,
could never have whipped itself into a political frenzy.
The chemist's shop calls itself rather grandly a "Medical
Hall"; and the town clock has stopped at "half-five."

The last excitement in such towns was the Civil War.
The one before that was Oliver Cromwell. Ireland will forget Cromwell only when Wiltshire forgets Judge Jeffreys.
But indignant as men are at the thought of Cromwell, they
half admire him as a relentless but clean fighter and prefer
him to Sir Hamar Greenwood.

There is one straggling street. The houses are small.
The shops are small. The desires of these towns are small
desires. They seem to be, in the main, braces, boots,
aprons, oranges, potatoes, saddles, harness, sticky sweets,
and porter.

Cows come blundering through the street at all hours

of the day; old men wearing decayed hats crouch on the shafts of donkey carts, for the poor donkey expiates his mysterious sin in Ireland as fully as in Egypt; old women, bent with work and rheumatism, pass, wrapped in black shawls and often bearing heavy bundles concealed in sacking; and the only event of outstanding interest in such places is the passing of a racehorse.

When this happens the whole town stops work. The horse is the abiding passion of Ireland. There is not a true-born Irishman, or woman, who does not turn to follow the sight of a nervous steeplechaser, high stepping, his flanks shining with health, his hoofs ringing on the cobbles, the sweetest music to their ears.

If there is a stud farm in the town this horse is a local celebrity. They know his sire and his dam. They know his peculiarities, his virtues, and his defects. The day will come when the whole town will put its shirt on him, as you will read in the English papers the day after he wins the Grand National!

You look through a wide gate in the main street and see a string of horses being led round in a ring.

Young men with horse-like faces and thin legs in well-cut leggings stand round watching the horses with the intensity of a satyr watching a chorus-girl. These young men live in country houses and in farmhouses with pictures of horses, old engravings of horses, photographs of horses. When they are faced with the painful duty of writing a letter they dip their pens into an ink-pot formed from the hoof of a celebrated hunter and mounted in silver. Their favourite literature is *Ruff's Guide to the Turf*, and the catalogues of yearling sales.

When they dream, which I think is not often, they are riding the winner of the Grand National.

No one could know more about horses than these young

men; no one could know less about everything else! They are the perfect specialists.

The atmosphere of a stud farm is compounded of hope and despair. Mares in foal gaze over the half-doors of their boxes. Some will never produce a winner. Some may. Some are expected to, as a matter of course. An Irish farmer will starve himself and his family to mate an indifferent mare with a famous sire.

Who knows? The colt may develop into a famous horse. This is the greatest gamble in the life of the average Irish countryman.

The young men lean over the doors of the horse-boxes and dwell on the chances of their occupants. . . .

That mare from Farmer O'Flanagan ought to be pulling the milk cart instead of taking up room in a stud farm. Now Mr. Leary's black mare, a real good lepper she is—look at her legs and the weight of her—might do something good. She's got a good chance. But, holy Mike, look at Pat O'Brien's Black Diamond! If that mare doesn't produce a flier—well, there's no logic in horse breeding. . . .

So they ruminate as they lean over the stable doors.

They discuss the "visiting mares" and the new arrivals. They discuss the yearling colts. They discuss the fillies. The most enthusiastic matron of a maternity home would be shamed by their solicitude.

That bay filly by Jackdaw out of Lilium Auratum, by the way, three-parts own sister to Brighter London and Jackdaw of Rheims, is a high-class, compact, medium-sized, likely-looking, powerful horse. And what about that fine bay filly by Jackdaw out of Latent? That's an outstanding good quality filly, if you like! The long and low type!

So they go on until a stable-boy leads in the stallion.

The crowd at the gates grows! Men stop their donkey carts and leave them at the side of the road as they crane their necks to see the big black sultan standing there with his head high and his back arched, the sire of winners of over £45,000 in stakes. If there is a stranger at the gates they reel off the sire's accomplishments.

And the men who were bred to breed horses and to ride horses, once their day's work is over, relax over a glass of whisky and—talk about horses until it is time for bed!

2

The charm of Ireland is partly due to the delicious slowness of life. Ireland is a Catholic country, and you feel as in most Catholic countries, but notably in Spain, that the material world is rendered unreal and rather childish because it is overshadowed by the spiritual. The church which abhors secret societies spreads nevertheless through any Catholic country the atmosphere of a secret society; its people belong to something powerful and important which rules their conduct.

Shopkeepers do not seem to be real shopkeepers but to be pretending to be shopkeepers, just as men wheeling barrows along a road appear not to be wheeling them in order to earn money but because they gain some obscure satisfaction in the act. The religion of America, which is conquering England, has of course, no foothold in Ireland. This is the belief in the sanctity of production. It must be almost impossible for a Catholic to believe, as many an American manufacturer does, that in producing a new kind of tooth-paste or safety razor he is conferring a real benefit on the human race. This inability to believe in the spiritual glory of work gives to Ireland a gentle detachment, and necessarily reflects attention on human personalities.

In England, and in all countries where material things are important, we think of a man first as a grocer, an undertaker, a sanitary inspector, and secondly as a fellow human being. It is almost with a shock that we realize on Sunday afternoons that policemen have plain clothes and children. In Ireland it is different. A customs officer is Mr. Casey first and a customs officer a long way after!

If an Irishman wants to accumulate real wealth he must go out of Ireland and shake himself free from an almost oriental detachment. It is this detachment from things that go-ahead nations consider vital, which explains why to some people the Irish never appear serious. Their mental attitude to life is infuriating to the materialist. He calls it laziness. But the Irish are not lazy; they are casual, indolent, and metaphysical. There is a half-sad, half humorous subjectiveness about Irish life which gives to the country a pensive detachment.

The curse of industrial nations is the cruel and cynical subjection of man to machines. Ireland may be poor, but at least her flesh and blood are not humiliated by that tyranny of mechanical things which is inseparable from the production of modern wealth.

One result of Ireland's casual attitude to work is that the country is a place of amusing makeshifts. Objects long past their normal span are pressed into some service for which their inventors never intended them. An old front door will stop a gap in a hedge, bits of string will hold together some antique motor which in some incredible way continues to work; nothing is ever too old or useless to be thrown away. Mechanical inefficiency which is a shame and a disgrace in the modern world is to an Irishman often merely a thoroughly good joke. But, like the child he is in parts, the Irishman will often pretend that a machine is efficient when it is hopelessly defunct. A beautiful story illustrates this in Mr. J. C. Molony's *The Riddle of the Irish*:

"On a cottage by the seaside was exhibited a notice, 'Cassidy salt-water shower baths.' Thither an unsuspecting English lady betook herself. Mr. Cassidy conducted her to the *salle de bain*, and explained the procedure of his establishment. 'Ye pull that sthring, ma'am, an' down comes the wather on top o' yez.' The lady, presumably somewhat undraped, entered the cabinet, and 'pulled the sthring'; a cascade of salt water shot by her, missing her by about a foot. And then from above she heard a voice: 'Sthand over a little aysthe [east], ma'am, av ye plaze,' it said. Mr. Cassidy, his genial face set in a frame of sandy whiskers, gazed benevolently down on her through a trap-door. In his hands he poised a mighty bucket of 'say wather' in readiness for a shot as soon as the bather had been manœuvred into the direct line fire."

As I have tried to say, the Irish have a delightful genius for improvisation!

3

Whenever I think of Kilkenny I shall remember the world's most accomplished snorer. I arrived late at night. The old castle of Kilkenny was lifted against the stars, with the dark river flowing against its walls, and, content with this glimpse of an ancient city, I went to bed dog-weary.

I awakened in the middle of the night with the vague feeling that something unusual was happening. At first, because I was between sleeping and waking, I thought that a great sea was beating against rocks. Or it might have been the tramp of an army. This indecision lasted only for the fraction of a second, because I awakened to the sound of snoring so loud, so remarkable, so vibrant, so sure of itself that had it been produced consciously it would have been the work of a genius.

I detest snorers. I regard snoring as a contemptible and disgraceful thing. I think that a woman married to a snorer should be granted a divorce without any argument. It has always seemed to me a singular reflection on modern science that no silencer has yet been invented for this complaint. During the war, when most of us slept in tents and tin huts, a boot, though primitive, was effective. But no boot could have interrupted the snorer of Kilkenny. He actually shook the air, he filled the universe. I could feel his bass notes in the wall.

How that man made me suffer. His ghastly organ recital was as regular in its devilish rhythm as a saw-mill. Once every half-hour he was seized with a kind of convulsion. I hoped that he was dying. The debasing sounds shuddered to *pianissimo* and ceased, then he gave a violent gasp, a snort, appeared to be choking, grunted, gasped, and got into top gear again.

Every man should be compelled to produce a certificate before marriage to prove that he is free from this horrible malady. I am glad, for the honour of Ireland, to say that he was an English commercial traveller.

He was the king of nightjars, bad cess to him!

Sandy-eyed and nerve-shattered, I was in no mood to enjoy Kilkenny in the morning. I climbed up to the cathedral, which is made of black unpolished marble, where the verger told me, rather ghoulishly I thought, that I was too late for a funeral. An Englishman, from Bedford I think, had, as he put it rather too vividly, "been put under six foot of earth."

I felt that this was going to be one of my bad days!

Kilkenny Cathedral, however, is one of the finest churches in Ireland. It is full of Plantagenet knights lying in full armour holding their swords and gazing upward into eternity. There is an ancient stone seat in which the verger persuades you to sit and wish. Ireland seems more full of wishing-stones and wells than any other part of the earth.

The castle of Kilkenny, which is as feudal looking as any castle I know, contains many fine pictures and the signature of every English king since Henry II.

It was in Kilkenny that a Parliament was summoned by the viceroy, Lionel, Duke of Clarence, in 1367, when one of the landmarks of Irish history—the Statute of Kilkenny—was directed not only at the native Irish but also at those members of the English colony who had "gone native," and were known as "the degenerate English." The object of the Act was to separate the two races: "the Irish enemies," as they were called throughout the Act, and the "degenerate English." As not one Englishman in twenty thousand could probably give an account of this Act it is worth while to outline some of its main points:

Alliance with the Irish by marriage, fosterage (the Irish custom of educating children in the families of another member of the tribe) and gossipred (a baptismal responsibility similar to acting as a godfather) were forbidden as high treason and were to be punished with death.

Any Englishman by birth or blood who took an Irish name, spoke the Irish tongue, wore the Irish dress, or adopted any Irish custom should forfeit his estates.

No Englishman was to allow the Irish to graze cattle on his land, to grant livings to Irish clergy, or to entertain the Irish bards, pipers, or story-tellers.

The necessity for such legislation—which was insisted on 137 years later by Poyning's Law—proves how rapidly a nation was forming in Ireland after the invasion. The fusion of Anglo-Norman and Irish, had it been encouraged instead of suppressed, might have altered the course of Anglo-Irish history.

The streets of Kilkenny are old-fashioned and rather grim. There are beautiful walks beside the river, town walls, and several fine religious ruins; but these did not claim my attention—I wandered about the streets in the hope of seeing a couple of Kilkenny cats fighting!

Strangely enough, Kilkenny is full of dogs! It is so full of them that cats, if they exist, keep prudently within doors.

"Why," I asked a native, "are Kilkenny cats famous as fighters?"

He said that he did not know.

I tried another man who proved to be the usual "stranger" who never knows anything. At length I found an authority:

"That's easy," he said. "There are two stories about it. In the old days there were two towns; one was called Irishtown and one English-town. They fought like cats! The other story is that when Cromwell was here his troopers used to tie a rope across a street, tie two cats together by the tails, sling them over the rope, and watch them fight. Now this was thought cruel, even by Cromwell, which may seem a bit strange; and so an order was given out that no soldier was to amuse himself in this way. . . .

"One day a party of troopers were watching a cat-fight, when two officers were seen approaching. There was no time to separate the cats, so they just cut off their tails! They explained to the officers that the cats had fought until nothing was left but their tails!"

"That is, of course, the Irish version?"
"It is."
I thanked him, and took the road to Tipperary.

4

I like the town of Cahir (they pronounce it Care). I like
to stand at an upstairs window of the excellent, homely
hotel which was once a private house and watch the slow
life of the wide main street.

There is often nothing in it but a few old people mysteriously congregated with their donkey carts, standing
engaged in conversation and earnestly discussing the price
of vegetables. It is a curious, watchful street. Although it
is often empty it is never asleep. It is wide as a parade
ground, and I imagine that anything happening on it is
immediately known all over the town.

Irish country towns vary enormously in atmosphere.
Some seem drenched in a hopeless shabbiness. It would be
impossible to do any work in them. The only thing to do
would be to drink and gloom and make excuses to yourself. But a few miles from such towns are others supris-
ingly different: bright, clean, hopeful, vaguely busy; and
Cahir is like this.

Down the wide street comes a herd of cows. Fine horses
go by with plaited manes and tails and numbered cards on
their flanks. There is a cattle and horse show somewhere
near. A sable priest stands at the corner of the street, and
pauses in his conversation to follow the horseflesh with his
eyes; as in fact everyone does. It is all so peaceful and so
drenched in the sanity of the eighteenth century.

The warm afternoon sunlight falls over the square.
Down the road comes a man leading a great black bull.
There is a ring through its nostrils. Its hide shines like

polished ebony. It sways under the weight of its fat and muscle, placing its feet on the road as deliberately as an elephant, and as it goes by it turns its head now and then and looks with unconscious fierceness round it.

A bell tolls. It is the Angelus.

The man and the bull come to a standstill. The herdsman lifts his shabby hat and bends his head in prayer. The great beast stands rock still beside him. An old man leading a donkey in a cart lifts his cap. Two men who might be commercial travellers or solicitors cross themselves; and the whole town prays.

The moment of the Angelus is, to me, the most touching and the most beautiful in an Irish day. At first a stranger is unaware of the bell. He may be riding in a Dublin tramcar. Suddenly there is a movement. Men and women are making the sign of the cross. Or in a crowded street the man you are talking to becomes silent and lifts his hat. But it is in the lanes and the country towns of Ireland that the Angelus is most beautiful. I do not care how bigoted an anti-Catholic a man may be, how sincerely he believes that all priests are rogues who batten on the superstition of the ignorant, he must, if there is a spark of reverence in him or any feeling for beauty, bare his head at this time and offer up his prayer.

This silent communion with God at morning, noon, and sunset, coming as it does in the midst of life and the business of life, summoning men at work in the fields, in cities and in towns to pause in whatever they may be doing and turn their thoughts to the Throne of God, is an expression of the underlying spirituality of Irish life. This interlocking of the visible and the invisible worlds explains much that is strange and perhaps to a certain type of mind even vaguely uncomfortable in Ireland.

I remember once in Egypt how an old villain who was

trying to cheat me in his shop suddenly wiped me and my affairs out of his mind and without a word turned to the east and, kneeling, placed his forehead in the dust. Then he came back to me and cheated me. Life to him was just a faintly amusing game played to pass the time. And this sense of futility of human affairs steals also into Irish life. Perhaps it explains why the Irish laugh at things which we consider urgent and why they cannot become excited about things which we believe are important. I wonder how many Irishmen have been called "lazy" by Englishmen when in reality they were simply metaphysical.

Cahir Castle is one of the finest buildings of its kind I have seen in Ireland. It lifts its towers above the River Suir beside a pretty bridge. And from its ramparts you look down to a mill dam and a broad sweep of water that reminds me strangely of Stratford on Avon. In the opposite direction you can see the exquisite Suir winding through woodland. There is a bright chequer-work of fields rising to hills that lift themselves against the sky in various subtleties of blue.

There is a perfect hall in this castle which is sometimes used for dances and other functions. If I owned this castle and had the money to indulge a fancy I would restore it and furnish the finer rooms in it with armour and furniture of the period. It is in remarkable condition for a castle that knew the cannon of Cromwell. I believe that if a very little money and thought were spent on it, Cahir Castle could become one of the sights of Ireland.

In the evening I went for a walk beside the river. I came to a ford where a small boy worked a boat by hauling on a rope that was stretched from bank to bank. I walked through a glorious park beside a most tempting bit of water. I would have given anything to have cast a fly into it. The time was just right. There were great deep, black pools in it: a most flyable, tempting stream.

I saw the "big house" on the bank of the river. An old man told me that during the Civil War it was occupied by De Valera:

"An' they behaved like gentlemen," he added. "Whin they were called elsewhere shure they signed the visitors' book. Faith, and what more could they do?"

That night in Cahir I came to read for the first time some poems by Thomas MacDonagh, who was born, I am told, in this part of Ireland. One in particular delighted me. It expressed in some way that I cannot explain a little Irish town like Cahir. Here it is:

> *The fair was just the same as then,*
> *Five years ago to-day,*
> *When first you left the thimble men*
> *And came with me away;*
> *For there again were thimble men*
> *And shooting galleries,*
> *And card-trick men and Maggie men*
> *Of all sort and degrees—*
> *But not a sight of you, John-John,*
> *Was anywhere.*
>
> *I turned my face to home again,*
> *And called myself a fool*
> *To think you'd leave the thimble men*
> *And live again by rule,*
> *And go to mass and keep the fast*
> *And till the little patch:*
> *My wish to have you home was past*
> *Before I raised the latch*
> *And pushed the door and saw you, John,*
> *Sitting down there.*

THE PLAIN OF TIPPERARY

5

So deep a hush lay over the plain of Tipperary that I could hear the dogs barking as far away as Rosegreen and Cahir. The setting sun was almost warm over the plain, and not one whisper of wind moved the grass.

Before me, in the centre of the Golden Vale, rose Cashel of the Kings, that mighty rock, lonely as a great ship at sea, lifted above the flat lands as Ely lifts herself above the fenlands of Cambridgeshire. It is strange that one of Ireland's most sacred relics should have been planted by the devil. Every schoolchild in Tipperary knows that when the devil was flying home (apparently to England) across the plain of Tipperary, he took a savage bite out of the northern hills in passing, but dropped the rocky mouthful in the centre of the Golden Vale.

It is a fact that, if you look in the right direction towards the Slieve Bloom Mountains, you can see the gap in the remote hills which Cashel, it seems, would exactly fit. They call it the Devil's Bit.

The Angelus bell was ringing in the still evening as I took the steep path to the ancient stronghold of the Kings of Munster.

On top of this high rock, surrounded by a stone wall, is all that is left of a royal city of ancient Ireland. The man who unlocks the gate and admits you to a wide space of hummocky grass and the ruins of palace and churches points to a rough stone on which is an ancient cross.

"That," he tells you, "is where St. Patrick baptized King Aengus in the olden days."

In Cashel they still remember the story of the baptism of King Aengus. I like the familiar way people in Ireland talk about the heroes and kings of antiquity. They might just have left them round the bend of a lane. They say that when King Aengus was baptized on the ancient coronation stone of the high kings at Cashel, St. Patrick was old and feeble and in order to support himself he drove the spiked point of his crozier firmly into the earth. When the ceremony was over St. Patrick and those who stood round saw blood in the grass. The crozier had transfixed the foot of the king. The saint asked Aengus why he had not cried out in pain, and the king replied that he had heard so much about the sufferings of our Lord that he would have been proud to bear the agony, even had he not considered it part of the ceremony.

More wonderful than the round tower of Cashel, more interesting than the vague lines of the ancient palace, more beautiful than the roofless shell of the cathedral is King Cormac's Chapel, the most whimsical, the most strange and the most remarkable little chapel in the British Isles.

If you visit Ireland only to see this astonishing building you will not have crossed the sea in vain. It is the strangest sight to one accustomed to Norman churches in England, built by the Normans—apparently with a chisel in one hand and a drawn sword in the other! Durham Cathedral, which is the greatest Norman church in England, holds something of Flambard's sternness in its stones. Even small chapels, like St. John's in the Tower of London and that practically unknown underground chapel in the Black Keep at Newcastle, are essentially grim. They appear to have been designed by architects who had just composed a fortress. But Cormac's Chapel on Cashel is the only piece of gay Norman architecture I have seen. One might almost call it Norman architecture with a sense of humour! There is nothing else quite like it in the world.

What is the explanation? It is the only great piece of

Norman work in the British Isles not built by Normans. It was built half a century before the Normans invaded Ireland by those much-travelled Irish monks who, in the early days, went out from their monasteries to every part of Europe. These monks tried to copy something which they had admired very much in France, but it worked out with a Celtic difference: they put into this chapel—into its rounded dome—toothed arches, something quite original, which you will find only in the Book of Kells and the Shrine of St. Patrick's Bell.

"And do you not see something strange about the chapel?" asked the guide.

I followed his glance, and noticed that it is at a slightly different angle from the nave, symbolizing the drooping of Christ's head on the Cross. This is the earliest declination I remember to have seen.

The guide took me up into a stone room above the chapel which was a library in the days when Cashel was the Tara and the Armagh of the south.

Professor Macalister comments on the diminutive Irish churches in *The Archaeology of Ireland*:

"The small size of the early Irish churches," he writes, "has frequently been commented upon; we all remember how Thackeray in his *Irish Sketch Book* waxes merry over the miniature cathedral at Glendalough. But it must be remembered that the stone buildings, which survive, were in all likelihood the smaller and the poorer structures; and further, that the provision of a building for the reception of the laity as well as the clergy was not necessarily contemplated by the builders. In a large number of cases the people attending Mass remained outside the building, as may still frequently be seen in the country parts of Ireland.'"

Most people who see these churches must be fascinated by the skilful construction of the stone roofs.

"The double roof of the main portion of St. Kevin's Kitchen is an example of an ingenious mode of construction which seems to have been a native Irish invention," says Professor Macalister. "It is also found in the ancient chapel in the cathedral church at Killaloe, in St. Colum Cille's house at Kells, in Cormac's Chapel at Cashel, and in one or two other buildings. It was a device for obtaining a high-pitched sloping roof, such as a rainy climate required, without running the risk of the thrust of the roof pressing the walls outwards and so bringing the whole structure to ruin. After the side walls were erected, a centering of timber was constructed, forming a vault, the extrados of which was covered with timber planking or of brushwood. Upon this centering a stone vault was constructed, and well grouted with liquid mortar, which ran through the joints and accumulated above the brushwood, of which it retained an impression. (There is a fine example of this in the sacristy vault of Clonfert Cathedral.) When the mortar was thoroughly set, the centering was removed: the result was that the church was covered in, as it were, with a solid lid, with flat top and with a vaulted under side. On the upper surface of this 'lid' the sloping roof was erected. There was, in consequence, no outward thrust at all; all the weight of the roof pressed vertically downward; a building of no considerable size could thus be set up without any buttresses. A chamber was formed in the roof, which could be reached with a ladder through an opening left in the vault.

"Professor Baldwin Brown has studied the mechanics of this form of roof and concludes with these words: 'Though they have in most cases been considerably restored in recent times, their vaults seem to have remained firm, and have not been reconstructed, while in no case has any buttressing of the external walls become a necessity. The fact reflects no little credit on the Irish mason, who not only evolved a novel scheme of construction, but carried it out with perfect success into practice.' "

I could return again and again to Cormac's Chapel and never exhaust its singular charm. What, I wonder, would Irish architecture be like if this translation of Romanesque into Gaelic had been allowed to go on? It is, in my opinion, one of the architectural tragedies of the world that the Irish did not, or were not permitted to, develop this style but were forced to adopt the Gothic, which never suited them:

"The Gothic in Ireland differs from that of the neighbouring countries in a remarkable and important circumstance," says Professor Macalister. "Elsewhere the Gothic styles were an organic growth, passing from stage to stage in a natural evolution. In Ireland Gothic was a transplanted sapling, which never became acclimatized.

"To the last the native architects could never master the principle of Gothic; just as they could never master the English language. They forced both to conform to the Celtic idiom. The language spoken throughout Ireland is still Irish, with English words substituted for the corresponding Irish words; and it is on the syntactic anomalies thus produced that the inventor of 'Irish' jokes depends for his livelihood, although his attempts at producing the real idioms of this extremely difficult language are, as a rule, fatuous beyond conception. The architecture practised in Ireland throughout the Middle Ages was, in like manner, Celtic, with a Gothic veneer. In consequence,

we find in Irish mediæval churches an endless succession
of anomalies: churches with the transept longer than the
nave, as at the Black Abbey, Kilkenny; capitals with the
abacus cut into delicate flowers, as at Coromroe, Clare;
arch-mountings twisted into ropes, as at Clonmacnois;
pointed arches with keystones, as in a small church on the
Aran Islands; want of symmetry in groups of window-
lights, as at Glenogra (Limerick) or in a church on Inis
Clothrann in Loch Ree; a chancel roofed with a barrel
vault at right angles to the main axis of the building, as
at Kilmaine (Mayo); there seems to be no limit to the
indifference to the 'rules of the game' which the Irish
architects display when designing Gothic churches. . . .
But just as a foreigner speaking English often hits upon
a phrase which is not English in the least—which would
never enter the head of a native of England to concoct—
and yet which is strikingly expressive, so the Irish architects not infrequently produce a bold stroke of originality
out of their very inexperience and independence of tradition."

If I were an Irishman I would haunt Cashel of the
Kings, for there, and there alone, is visible a link with
the Gaelic Ireland which, subjected to invasion and op-
pression, has stubbornly survived: the Ireland of the
Book of Kells, the Ardagh Chalice, the Cross of Cong,
and the Tara brooch. All these things prove a rich and
imaginative national life which never had the opportunity
to develop. And if the Walter Scott whom Ireland needs so
badly should ever arrive I think it is to Cashel that he
should go for his first book.

"Until important epochs in Irish history have been
given movement, vividness, and depth by a romantic ren-
dering they will remain obscure to us," writes Padraic

Photo. H. V. Morton

CORMAC'S CHAPEL, CASHEL

Colum in *The Road Round Ireland*. "What is wanted is some statement that will resume through a typical figure the great episodes of a certain epoch. And that can be done only by a great artist who possesses racial feeling to the full and who has a sense of the national destiny—in other words, there is need for a writer who will do for Irish history what Gogol did for Cossack history in *Taras Bulba*, and what the writer of *The Glory of Don Ramona* has done for the Spain of the Moorish decadence. Perhaps the reason why this has not been done is that the formal historians have been too occupied in attack and defence to give a picture that is complete and that has in it elements of life that an artist can augment and perpetuate. This state of affairs is changing: Ireland has now historians who are giving us real glimpses into the Irish past.

"One can glimpse a fine story in the sort of life that was here after the wars of the middle of the sixteenth century, when the *duine uasail*, the gentlemen, in this as in other parts of Ireland, took service abroad as soldiers of fortune. Some stayed here, however. It would be a theme for a romantic novelist to trace the career of one or another of these proud Milesians living on the edges of the lands that had passed into the possession of Cromwell's or William's soldiers. Tradition tells us that of an Edmund O'Reilly, a great-grandson of the soldier who had checked Oliver Cromwell's soldiers, and grandson of the soldier who had inflicted defeat on the Williamite army of De Ginkle. He was permitted to settle on a farm of poor land. One day a noble gentleman mounted on a splendid horse visited the neighbourhood in search of him. The peasantry, fearing the stranger meant some injury to him, denied any knowledge of him. 'Edmund on hearing this was much troubled, for he knew it was one of his relatives come from abroad to seek him out. Further tidings of the stranger he never heard. We can see the descendents of the lords who for five hundred years had been paramount in West Breifny, in the words of one of the native historians, "Melt into the peasantry." ' "

Where, I wonder, is the Walter Scott of Ireland? He has a richer store of romance ready for him than ever Scotland gave to the writer who made the whole world love Scotland. It would seem a duty to give to the world the best and the finest qualities of the Irish character: the reckless gallantry, the courage, the humour, the pathos, and the spirituality. It is a task that awaits genius. Let him go to Cashel.

The view from the perilous wall which is on a level with the cone of the round tower is one of the grandest in Ireland. I can compare it only with the view down over the Links of Forth from the height of Stirling Castle. All round is the fat, green country of the Golden Vale: the thin roads crossing running through the fields; the farms; the little belts of woodland and, to the southward, hills.

When it grew dark a great yellow moon swung up over Tipperary plain and hung in the sky above Cashel. The dogs were howling far off in distant farms. Little knots of young men idled and talked at the street corners, laughing and joking and speaking English woven on a Gaelic loom. And on the hill I looked up at the ancient ruins of Cashel of the Kings, rising darkly against the stars. It was silent, empty, and locked for the night, and the moon's light was over it, falling down on it like a green rain.

It rode in moonlight over Tipperary like a haunted ship.

CHAPTER V

I visit the trappists of Mount Melleray, spend a night with them,
   hear a voice in the night and the sequel in the morning, rise
   early, explore the monastery, watch the silent monks at their
   labours and continue my way to Cork, where I hear the bells
   of Shandon and kiss the Blarney Stone

1

THE road that runs due south from Cashel, through
Cahir and Clogheen over the mountains to Lismore is one
of the most beautiful I have ever travelled. You have
the wide Plain of Tipperary round you for miles and
facing you are the Knockmealdown Mountains. Just beyond Clogheen the road rises and you mount quickly into
the wild hills. You come to a hairpin bend, the Devil's
Elbow (his other elbow is in Scotland on the Blairgowrie
road to Braemar!) and, when you can safely do so, stop
and look back.

This is one of the grandest views in the British Isles.
Below you lies the great Plain of Tipperary with the little
white roads criss-crossing through the greenness of fields
and the darker green of woods. West of Cahir are the
Galtee Mountains and on the east is Slieveamon. On a good
day you can see the Rock of Cashel rising up from the
green plain twenty miles to the north.

It is difficult to tear yourself away from such a sight.
But the road goes on and up into mountains, bare and bar
ren and brown; then it falls to one of the sweetest glens in
the world where a laughing stream runs beside you all the
way to Lismore.

101

Here on the banks of the broad, slow Blackwater—a
mighty salmon stream—rises the magnificent Castle of
Lismore which is owned by the Duke of Devonshire—the
Warwick Castle of Ireland. It is not perhaps as fine as
Warwick but the mind immediately connects them, both
majestic, both throned on wooded rocks, both reflected in
water.

The courtyard of this castle is one of its chief beauties.
The view downward from the drawing-room is terrifying.
No wonder that the timid James II, who spent a night at
Lismore during his flight from the Battle of the Boyne,
started back in horror from it when he looked from one of
the windows.

Lismore is delightful, a clean, reserved and dignified
country town. I was pleased to find two kilted pipers wearing Black Watch tartan playing in the streets. When I
hailed them as Scotsmen they answered me in the accents
of Cork!

"It's Irish we are entirely," they said. "Would ye care
to subscribe some little thing, now, to the pipe band of
Cark?"

2

A hundred men who have taken a vow of life-long
silence are living high up in the mountains of Co. Waterford in the Trappist monastery of Mount Melleray. They
are men of a varied experience of life and of many
nationalities. Could they talk to one another they would
probably discover one thing only in common: a weariness
of the world and its ways. Among them, I am told, clothed
in the coarse brown habit of the order and known by the
name which every monk assumes when he leaves the world,
is a once prominent London bookmaker.

It was late when I climbed the steep hill to Mount Melleray. The monks were returning from their rich farmlands. I stopped one and asked him the way to the guesthouse. He placed a finger on his lips and shook his head. He was not allowed to speak, but he pointed with his hand and, following his direction, I turned a corner and came on the guest-house bell.

"Good evening," said a middle-aged, lay brother. "And what can I do for you?"

"You are allowed to speak?"

"I am absolved from my vow while in charge of our guests and"—he added as an afterthought—"the buttery!"

He said it was too late for me to see the monastery. The brothers would be going to bed at 7:30, for they were always up in the chapel at 2 a.m.

"Stay the night here and see the monastery in the morning! Stay a week! Stay a month if you can!"

He smiled at me as if time meant nothing.

The Trappists of Mount Melleray hold open house to the world. Any man—of any faith—may stay there as long as he likes. He is never asked to pay anything, but he is expected to leave a donation in a box if he can afford to do so; if not, well, the brotherhood send him on his way with a blessing just the same.

Mount Melleray is also the only monastery in Ireland which will shelter a woman. If a husband and wife arrive the man sleeps in the guest-house and the woman in a cottage just outside the monastery near the high road. A parish priest in Tipperary told me an amusing story about a honeymoon couple who refused to be separated in the monastery. But that is another story.

"I would like to stay, but I must be in Cork tonight."

"Cork!" echoed the monk, as if I had said San Francisco. "That must be nearly forty miles! How you people dash about. What's the point of it?"

"I have promised to dine with a man there tonight."

"A promise is sacred. You must go. If you want to see our monastery I will show you. Come in. . . ."

In a comfortable room, furnished in greater luxury than the average county town hotel in Ireland, sat a number of men. Some of them had been caught in the hills and had made for the monastery for shelter; some had come there out of curiosity, for the hospitality of the Trappists is well known in Ireland; one was a priest on "retreat"; and one man in smart city clothes smelt (I hope I am not wrong) of whisky!

The monks of Melleray, who live on the most frugal diet and drink only water, have become famous for the curing of dipsomania! Many a young man who has been lifting his elbow too frequently in Dublin is packed off to Melleray for a cure.

"Now, here," said the monk, leading the way into a large building with a hatch at one end, "is the buttery. We give food and drink to any man who asks for it."

"Are you not imposed on?"

The monk turned his pale blue eyes on me. They were amazingly childlike.

"Yes," he said, "now and then. It is my job to weed out the undesirable, but, do you know, when I see them I just close my eyes and—give just the same!"

We were in a long stone passage. A bell overhead began to toll. There was a queer shuffling of feet on the stone. Round the corner towards us came a procession of cowled figures walking with bent heads two by two—first the priests in coarse white gowns, then the lay brothers, in brown habits girdled at the waist with a cord. Not one looked up at us as he passed. They went into the chapel for their evening prayers, and the doors closed silently after them.

I caught sight of many types of men under the cowl. Who were they before they disappeared from their fellows? What had they known of life? No one can say. Once they had names by which the world knew them, now they are Brother Dominic and Brother Paul and Brother Aloysius. Now they are out of life; life to them is merely the antechamber to death.

The silence of Mount Melleray is almost frightening. Cowled figures brush past in dim corridors, quietly like ghosts. Now and then you catch a man's eye, but he quickly avoids you, fearfully, as if you might speak to him. They pass one another in the same quick, fearful way.

"Do they never long to speak? Do they never feel that they will die unless they exchange a thought with a fellow man?"

"Why should they? They are vowed to silence."

Again his pale blue eyes looked at me. They were like ice.

The refectory was set out for a cold collation to be eaten in the grey light of morning.

It was a chilly, bare room with a pulpit in the centre beside one wall. Long wooden tables were set round the room, and at each table a wooden bench. Beside each place were two tin mugs and a plate. Leaning against each plate was a card with the monk's name written on it in large letters—Brother John, Brother Michael, Brother Gabriel, Brother Pius.

There was no need for argument at table, no excuse for talk. Each place was set plainly so that the silent brotherhood could patter in over the cold stones, heads bowed, without a word.

In the library upstairs the monk told me the remarkable history of the monastery. In 1830 a band of Trappist monks expelled from France arrived on the slopes of the barren Knockmealdown Mountains with 1s. 10d. between them! They made some kind of shelter and a little oratory. The peasants came from the hills to do a day's work for them. Their farm-lands grew. They became known for their good works. Rich men made wills in their favour, and so, gradually and within one hundred years, the penniless settlement has grown into a large, prosperous, and obviously wealthy community. Their farm-lands are a tribute to their energy and their knowledge. They have made what was once a wilderness a place of corn and fruit; and grass, where fat cattle graze. They have done in Ireland today what their predecessors did in England in the barren Yorkshire moors and dales, at Fountains, Rievaulx, and Jervaulx, and in many another wild region.

We went out into the garden and into the grounds. There are rows of open graves. At first the visitor does not understand what they are. He has to be told that it is part of a Trappist's duty to dig his own grave. . . .

"Good-bye," said the lay brother. "Pray for me tonight and I will pray for you. If all the world did that how different it might be. . . ."

His blue eyes in a thin, lined face were the eyes of a child.

I went on down the hill in the dusk, haunted by the pattering of sandals and the tomb-like hush of the men who are vowed to silence.

3

I lay awake that night thinking of the monks of Melleray. I promised myself that I would go back and spend the next night as their guest. The friend with whom I dined had told me innumerable stories of their good deeds. He is what is known as a "bad Catholic." He had nothing good to say of the priests. The "blackbirds," as he called them, were maintaining the country in a condition of illiteracy and superstition. But for the Trappists of Melleray he had nothing but extravagant praise. He hunted about in his library and lent me a book on the Order.

To most people in England a Trappist probably suggests *The Garden of Allah* by Robert Hichens. In this novel the emotion of a Trappist who runs away from his monastery and encounters the problems of life have been brilliantly exploited. It is many years since I read this book, but I still remember the horror of that monastery, never described but always suggested, with its silent monks, its harsh denial of the things which we worldly people call happiness. Even my slight glimpse into Melleray told me that the ancient "Peace of the Church" lay over it. It was a sanctuary. It was everything that was good and sincere in the Middle Ages. The uncompromising severity of it frightened me a little. But it also attracted me. I wanted to go back and find out for myself what life was like behind those silent walls.

I opened the book and began to read the fascinating history of the Trappist Order. . . .

In the year A. D. 1140 a number of monks explored the narrow valley of La Trappe in search of some harsh wilderness in which they could retreat from the world. This valley, hidden among the hills in the department of Orme in Normandy, was known as "the trap" because of its remoteness and its inaccessibility. The good monks settled there and soon their abbey buildings humanized the wilderness. Their holiness was that of all Cistercian abbeys of the time. Then came wealth and property. During the wars with France armies plundered La Trappe, and the monks were driven away, homeless and in want.

At the beginning of the sixteenth century the monks returned to their valley; but they were changed men. The austerity and holiness of most monastic orders had, by this time, relaxed. One reason why the discipline of the former centuries had suffered was because by the Concordat of 1526 the king had the power of appointing abbots over monasteries in his kingdom. It is not difficult to guess what happened. Court favourites squandered the rich revenues of the monasteries. Abbots were appointed who were abbots only in name. Their interest was not religious but financial. La Trappe, which, by a chance which reads like fiction, was to establish a name for sanctity and austerity which continues to this day, fell upon evil times. Cynical, worldly men squandered its moneys, and at length monastic life died out and a mere handful of so-called monks inhabited the ruins of their abbey and spent a care-free life, hunting, shooting, and fishing.

About this time—the year 1626—was born a child who was given the fine-sounding name of Armand Jean Bouthillier de Rancé. His father was a court official. Cardinal Richelieu was his godfather. De Rancé was, as an elder son, destined for the army. But a younger brother died and De Rancé took orders absurdly at the age of twelve, receiving with them the revenue of three abbeys and several priories which gave him the sum of 20,000 livres a year. When he was twenty-four years of age his father died, leaving him an estate worth 30,000 livres a year.

This rich young churchman abandoned himself to wealth and pleasure. He kept great state, gave grand banquets and rode out to the hunt followed by a train of friends and hangers-on. There is a rather fine contemporary description of him at this period of his life:

Photo, Thomas Mason, Dublin

TRAPPIST MONKS OF MOUNT MELLERAY

"He wore a light coat of beautiful violet-coloured cloth. His hair hung in long curls down his back and shoulders. He wore two emeralds at the joining of his ruffles, and a large diamond ring upon his finger. When indulging in the pleasures of the chase in the country, he usually laid aside every mark of his profession; wore a sword and had two pistols in his holsters. His dress was fawn-coloured, and he used to wear a black cravat embroidered with gold. In the more serious society which he was sometimes forced to meet he thought himself very clerical indeed when he put on a black velvet coat with buttons of gold."

This was the young exquisite who was fated to make a renunciation not uncommon in the history of Christanity and seek Christ in the wilderness.

Ten years of pleasure sickened him. His conscience awakened and he decided to go into retreat to the Oratorians in Paris; and from this time he became a changed man. He gave up all his rich companions. He sold his estate and gave immense sums to charity. He surrendered his abbeys and priories, keeping only the least significant and the poorest, La Trappe. The final act of renunciation was the determination to sever the last links that bound him to the world and to enter La Trappe as a frocked monk.

He found La Trappe in a deplorable condition. It contained seven worldly monks who regarded his appearance as an outrage. They refused to obey him. They declined to mend their habits. They even threatened to murder him. He decided to appeal to the king, and this apparently frightened them; for they gave way to him and allowed him to introduce into the brotherhood monks of the Strict Observance.

He then entered upon his novitiate like any common man, and when this was over he was invested as abbot of

La Trappe by Patrick Plunkett, the exile bishop of Ardagh. From that time begins the new era in the history of the monastery. His first act was to restore the hard rules of St. Benedict. He revived the vow of silence. He abolished meat, fish, eggs, and wine from the table. He revived the rule of manual labour. His monks slept on hard pallets and rose at 2 a.m. for matins which lasted until 3:30 a.m. Then came private devotion followed at 5:30 a.m. by prime; at 7 a.m. began the successive offices of terce, sext, and none. Everything in the monastery was designed to direct thought on the shortness of human life and the glory of life beyond the grave.

As years went on the holiness of La Trappe resembled that of Clairvaulx and Citeaux in past centuries; the austerity, the purity, and the uncompromising severity of the life led by these silent monks made La Trappe famous throughout France. Men from all parts of the land went there in order that they might repent and die in sanctity. It was to this monastery that James II of England went to pray in his exile. A writer in the *Dublin Review* of 1844 gave a touching description of his visit:

"He was kindly received by the abbot, and after partaking of his hospitality attended evening service in the chapel. After communicating on the following morning, and inspecting the respective occupations of the religious, he visited a recluse that lived some distance up the mountains. His solitude was never interrupted, save by an occasional visit from his abbot, and he spent the greater part of his time in prayer. In the recluse James immediately recognized an officer who had formerly distinguished himself in his army. He asked at what hour in the winter mornings he attended service in the Chapel of the convent, and was answered, at half past three. 'Surely,' said Lord Dumbarton, 'that is impossible. The way is dark and dreary, and at that hour highly dangerous.' 'Ah!' said the old soldier, 'I have served my King in frost and snow by night and day for many a year, and I should blush indeed if I were not to do as much for the Master who has called me to His service now, and whose uniform I wear.' The afflicted monarch turned away his head. His attendants remarked that his eyes were filled with tears. On his departure the following day, he knelt down to receive the abbot's blessing, and on rising he leant for support on the arm of a monk that was near him. On looking to express his thanks, he saw in him another of his followers, the Honourable Robert Graham. He too had been an officer in his army, and lost besides a large fortune in his service. His Majesty spoke a few words of kind recollection. Even the solitudes of La Trappe were filled with the ruins of his greatness."

De Rancé died at the age of seventy-four, broken down in health, suffering the most terrible physical pain, which he bore without a murmur. When he knew that the end was near his face shone with happiness and he cried: "Oh, Eternity, what happiness. Oh, my God, to spend an Eternity with Thee!"

His reforms endured.

Then, nearly a century after his death, came the French Revolution. The Trappists were driven from their monastery. They wandered about Europe, settling here and there, always at the mercy of governments. Napoleon's bright star rose and sank; and still the Trappists were exiled from their home. But after Waterloo they were allowed to return. They bought the ruins of La Trappe for £3,000, and, with an energy which distinguishes their order, had rebuilt and reorganized to such excellent effect that in twelve years no fewer than ten monasteries obeyed their ancient rule.

Today there are about seventy Trappist monasteries in the world. You will find the silent monks in China, in Japan, in America, in Canada. The only English house is that of St. Benedict in Leicestershire.

4

In the early evening I rang the bell of Melleray. The same gentle lay brother came to the door. He smiled, recognizing me.

"You have not been long," he said. "Come in, brother."

I resisted his attempt to carry in for me the small suit-case I had brought, but he insisted.

"It is my duty," he said. "I wish to serve you."

I was standing in the bare hall of the guest-house. There is a definite religious smell, compounded of bare walls, old rugs, stale incense, and furniture polish. It is not an exclusively Catholic smell; I have encountered it in Protestant vestries. I met it again in this monastery.

"Now," said the lay brother, "will you read the list of rules and then sign your name in the visitors' book?"

I cast a quick eye over a printed list of regulations which hung in a frame. I gave them the same swift scrutiny which a man who knows that he is not smuggling gives to the customs officer's list. I signed my name.

"Now," said the monk, "I will show you to your cell."

We mounted the flight of wooden stairs from the hall. On the first landing he opened a door and carried my suit-case into a room. This room surprised me. It was a cell only in name. There was a bed which proved to be much more comfortable than that in the hotel at Lismore. There was a wardrobe, a wash-stand, and a table, all made by the monks. The walls were bare save for a large crucifix, beneath which was a faldstool.

In silence the monk helped me to unpack my vanities: razor, shaving soap, powder, and, rather to my embarrassment, for they seemed so out of place, a pair of violet-red and black silk pyjamas that I had bought some weeks since in Paris. He showed no surprise as he placed them on the pillow, although they symbolized the soft comforts which the Trappist Order has renounced. I thought how tolerant is the Catholic Faith. A Scottish Presbyterian minister in a similar situation would have lectured me about those shameful pyjamas.

"And now," said the monk when we had finished unpacking, "you will examine your conscience for an hour."

He went out, shutting the door. I listened to the only sound in the monastery: the soft shuffle of his sandals along the corridor and down the stairs.

I discovered that my cell was immediately above the porch of the guest-house. I could with a walking-stick have touched the head of anyone standing below. The window was of Gothic design and the panes were small. There was a narrow window-seat, on which I sat looking down into a garden that reminded me of Italy. It was a walled garden enclosed by tall trees. There were several cypress, and against the gloom of their foliage life-sized statues of the Virgin stood out startlingly white.

It was a hot summer's evening. The setting sun filled the garden, falling in bright pools through the trees. The birds were singing. Bees were busy in the flowers. I wanted to go out into the garden. I felt restless. I thought that in London at this time people were dressing for dinner, parties were assembling in the hotels, waiters were obsequiously bending forward with wine-lists bound in morocco, women with naked shoulders were sweeping imperiously to gold chairs, conscious that they were observed and glad of it, actors and actresses were preparing for the play; and the dance of life was going on into the dawn. . . .

I noticed a figure in the garden. A Trappist in a white habit and a black scapular was walking slowly round, his hands held before him but hidden in long sleeves, his head bent on the ground. His walk was monotonous and habitual. I think he was unconscious that he was walking, just as he was unconscious that he was in a garden. When he came near I could see that his lips were moving. He was a lean anchorite who would have been in keeping with the Thebaid. There was something terrible in his concentration. I wondered who he was before he entered this spiritual prison. Was there in the world somewhere a woman who was once his wife? He was a man in the prime of life. Suppose a woman who had once loved him could see him now living only for death, no longer in life but striding with sightless eyes through the beauty of a summer evening in the cold ante-room of Paradise.

Another figure entered the garden. It was that of an aged monk. He walked round in the same attitude of whispered prayer. They passed each other, yet neither glanced up. There was, if anything, a slight—so slight as almost to be unnoticeable—shrinking one from the other as they passed. I watched them, fascinated. They had, through meditation, lifted themselves to another plane.

The history of the Trappist Order is rich in stories which illustrate the inhuman isolation which each monk makes for himself: stories of brothers united at a death-bed who did not know until that moment that they had lived together as Trappists for years, passing one another with downcast eyes as these monks were passing in the garden. Far-fetched as such stories seem when heard in the world of men, they become credible when remembered within the walls of a Trappist monastery; for this

order keeps alive in the modern world that saintly fervour
—or, as some would say, fanaticism—which placed Simon
Stilites on his pillar and led the early saints out into the
Theban desert.

I sat at my little window thinking how strange it was
that in passing through a gate I should have found myself
in the Middle Ages. All my Catholic ancestors rose up in
me and recognized the sacred Peace of the Church; all my
Protestant ancestors rose up and fought them tooth and
nail, so that between them I sat looking into the garden
in a strangely muddled frame of mind, knowing only that
I appreciated from the bottom of my heart the sincerity
and the immortal hunger of these men.

I ached to smoke. I chafed against the hour's meditation. How odd! And these monks spent their lives in silent
meditation. It was the silence of the place that worked on
my nerves: a silence that had soaked itself into the very
stones; a silence of which even the trees seemed conscious;
a silence that was the forerunner of death.

There was a little black book on the table: *The Confes-
sions of St. Augustine.* I turned over the leaves and found
myself in the sweet April of Christianity. But there were
queer, grovelling things scribbled on the leaves by previous occupants of my cell—sentences in hasty, almost
drunken script that trailed off the page. "Blessed Mary,
pray for me!" I read on one; and on another, written in
marking-ink pencil lividly blue in patches, as though the
writer's tears had splashed down on the page: "I am a miserable sinner—pray for me!"

I closed the book with the unpleasant feeling that I had
put my ear to a keyhole.

It was all so silent, the trees standing in a windless evening, a robin singing his lovely elegy to a dying day,
sharp and crystal clear as a fountain in the air, each note

high and rounded like a drop of water flung high and falling back into water. The sun was sinking, but it would be
hours before the dusk fell. I heard the lowing of cattle. I
supposed that the monks were driving their herds from
the pasture to the byre. I leaned from my window in the
hope of seeing them, but the tall trees hid the farm-lands
beyond the garden.

The door opened. The lay brother stood there. The
hour was over.

"Follow me," he said.

He led me downstairs. We left the guest-house and
came into a stone corridor. I could smell incense, and
knew that we were going to the chapel for compline. We
stood back to allow the brotherhood to pass us. They
walked two by two with heads bent. First came the priests
in white robes and black scapulars; men of all ages, men
of all types; scholars and rustics; townsmen and countrymen; all bearded, all wearing the expression of saintly abstraction which reminded me of a fresco by Bellini; and
behind, two by two, followed the lay brothers in coarse
brown habits girdled at the waist with cord.

The chapel was bare and simple. Each monk made a
profound obeisance towards the high altar.

I took my place on a bench reserved for guests. There
were six or seven strangers this night at Melleray, including a young priest, two young fellows on a walking tour,
a young Englishman who was on "retreat," and a shabby
and distraught-looking middle-aged man with thin, wispy
hair turning grey.

When compline was over the monks faced the altar and
sang the Salve Regina. I was anxious to hear this hymn,
which is particularly dear to the Trappists, who sing it
differently from any other order.

It was infinitely touching, full of longing, full of faith,

full of that ache for eternity which runs through the self-imposed hardships of the Trappist. No sooner was the hymn ended than we heard above us a bell ringing the Angelus. Each monk fell on his hands and knees. The brotherhood then said several Our Fathers, Hail Marys, and Glorias, after which there was a pause before they bowed low to the altar and filed out silently with bent heads as they had entered. We followed behind. At the door of the chapel stood the lord abbot holding an aspergillum, with which he sprinkled each one of us with holy water. The monks, like grey ghosts, disappeared down the white corridors to the cells, while we went in silence to the guest-house and were told to prepare ourselves for rest.

It was 8 p.m. by the sun, for Melleray does not recognize the Daylight Saving Act. In the world outside it was 7 p.m., and I was being sent to bed like a child! I sat again at the window looking down into the bright garden. In spite of the comfortable bed I had the feeling that I was about to spend a sleepless night, for the atmosphere of Melleray interested and excited me. The silent, grim routine of worship as decreed centuries ago by St. Benedict was proceeding all round me, and all I would know would be the pattering of feet on stone steps or the ringing of a bell in the night.

A longing to smoke came over me, but the rules said "No smoking," so I put my cigarettes and tobacco at the bottom of my suit-case and tried to forget them. A knock came to the door. It was the lay brother:

"Would you like a drink of water?" he asked. "A drink of milk, then?"

I shook my head and thanked him, thinking that I would really have liked a stiff whisky and soda. He seemed unwilling to go, and I was only too anxious to talk to him. He closed the door and regarded me with a bright, childlike interest, looking me straight in the eyes all the time. He made a perfect picture, standing there with his calm, saintly eyes, his smooth bearded face and his neck rising from the flung-back hood of his rough brown habit. He must have been middle-aged, but he had that curious look which I had noticed on the faces of many of the Trappists —a smooth, youthful, unlined look which reminded me of a young actor in a school dramatic society who is made up with a beard to represent some ancient character.

I have seldom met a man who roused in me a greater curiosity. As I looked at him it occurred to me that the saintly smoothness of the Trappist face is due to the absence of the more evil and powerful emotions which engrave themselves on the face of humanity. Avarice, Envy, Hate, Intemperance, Lust, which are all etched to a greater or a lesser degree on the face of man, are absent from the faces of these monks. They are not simple faces so much as uncomplicated faces. They mirror minds which have thrown over all feeling save only faith, hope, and charity. That perhaps is why they are also rather inhuman, cold, and remote, as faces in a polyptych by Jacobello di Bonomo.

When the lay brother, who had previously spoken to me only in brief sentences, talked with more freedom I realized that he was a Scotsman, or an Irishman from Glasgow. He told me that he was born at Partick, near Glasgow, and that he had entered the monastery twenty-three years ago. In his privileged capacity as lay brother to the guest-house he naturally knew something of the world's events, but he exhibited no interest in them. He had heard that Glasgow had changed in recent years. He astonished me by telling me that there were many monks in the monastery who had never heard of the European War or the formation of the Irish Free State.

I asked him a number of intimate questions about monastic life: how often did a monk find himself mistaken in his vocation? and so forth. He said that to become a Trappist was the final act in a long series of spiritual adventures, and that once a monk always a monk. But I could not understand how young lads—several of the monks were in the twenties—could renounce the world before they had tasted it. I forget his argument. I know it was a good one.

Then, of course, like a good Catholic, he crusaded round me to such good effect that I feared an argument with him. He told me, looking at me with the clear eyes of a child, that he would pray for me every day, and he begged me to accept a little Sacred Heart in which was wax blessed by the Pope.

I described to him how in Rome, only a few weeks previously, I had seen the Pope carried in state into St. Peter's to the sound of drums and trumpets. I never thought to impress anyone so much with a story. He was fascinated with my descriptions. He asked me innumerable questions, then:

"And did you not want to fall on your knees?"

"No," I said. "I stood on a chair like everybody else."

He could not understand it. But I felt that I had achieved a peculiar significance for him because I had been to Rome and attended Pontifical High Mass.

It was after 9 p.m. The brother apologized for keeping me up so late! Before he went he told me that the Trappists who were now lying on their hard beds would rise at 2 a.m. for matins.

"Good-night, and God be with you!"

He closed the door and I heard the patter of his descending feet.

5

I sat at the window unable to compose myself for sleep, and dusk fell; a moon invisible to me cast a silver wash over the garden. Against the cypress trees the white statues glimmered and became real. It must have been midnight when at length I fell asleep.

A cry cut across my muddled dreams. It was repeated. It awakened me. I sat up in bed and listened. A man was groaning in the next cell or in the one above. He was talking to himself like a lunatic. I looked at my watch: it was 3 a.m. Then I heard him cry loudly:

"O Mary, mother of God, I want a drink. . . ."

He repeated this six or seven times, appealing to different saints in a dreadful voice which told me that it was not milk or water he wanted. I shuddered to hear this lonely, agonized voice rising in the dead silence. It was like the despairing cry of someone buried alive.

I knew, of course, that he must be one of the dipsomaniacs who go to Melleray for a cure. Father Brendan, the guest-master, I have been told, is one of the greatest living experts in the treatment of dipsomania. I believe that when a drunkard goes to Melleray he is given the amount of liquor to which he is accustomed, but in reduced quantities every day until, at the end of the cure, he is drinking water. But it is the moral influence of the monastery which pulls him through.

The voice whimpered on for half an hour or so and ended in silly babbling laughter.

6

A noisy bell went down the corridor. The door opened. Brother Gabriel looked in at me smiling, wishing me good-morning, a mug of shaving water in one hand and a bell in the other. It was 6 a.m.

He chided me for neglecting to put my shoes outside the door. I replied that I would not let him clean my shoes. I could rub them up myself. He shook his head at me, and I knew that I had said something wrong. It is the Trappists' creed to serve every stranger, no matter how foul a beggar, as though he were Our Lord; and I realized that I was denying this gentle monk a duty which seemed menial and unworthy to me but to him was a sacred privilege.

I got up, drew the curtains, and the sun leapt into my cell. The garden was beautiful with a silver dew on the grass and the queer early morning shadows over everything. As I looked I saw a lovely sight. A hare came lolloping through the grass leaving a black track in the dew. He sat up below my window and lifted himself up and listened. I thought of St. Francis. I wondered whether the monks had tamed this most timid of all things. He dropped on all fours and ran noiselessly out of sight.

While I was shaving I smelt, almost with horror, certainly with indignant envy, a cigarette. Thin wisps of blue cigarette smoke were blown into my cell. Someone was smoking in the porch beneath my window. I wondered who was breaking the rules. I looked down and saw directly below me a head of wispy hair turning grey. It was the head of the shabby, middle-aged guest. I noticed another thing: the hand that held the cigarette was trembling as with an ague. He could hardly lift the cigarette to his mouth. This, then, was the pitiful creature whose tortured voice had startled me in the night.

While he stood there smoking furtively a monk left the kitchen garden, which lay beyond the monastery garden, and came on down the straight path. It was Father Brendan, the guest-master and the curer of drunkards. As soon as he was seen by the man below the cigarette was hastily crushed against the wall and flung into a bush, and I could tell from the look of the top of his head that my fellow-guest was adopting an innocent expression. I had no idea of eavesdropping. I stayed at the window wondering whether the monk would smell the tobacco smoke and perhaps rebuke the offender. He came up in long strides, the toes of his thick shoes dull with dew.

"Good-morning," he cried heartily; "and how are you this morning?"

"Oh, father," replied the man in a cringing voice, "I'm bad; I'm that bad . . . I had all the divils at me in the night."

"And why didn't ye wake me?" asked the monk sternly. "Sure, I'd have come to ye and calmed ye."

"I was feared to wake ye, father. Ye've been so good to me."

The man raised a dreadful, trembling hand to his head. The monk placed a friendly hand on his shoulder and in the voice of someone trying to comfort a child said:

"Och, well, never mind. . . . Come now and I'll give ye a little drop just to take the cobwebs off your heart."

They went in together and I heard the sound of a key in a cupboard door.

When I had dressed I walked in the garden and beyond through the large perfectly cultivated kitchen garden where the monks grow all their vegetables. Here I encountered my fellow-guests. The silence of the sons of St. Bernard had evidently weighed heavily on them as on me, for we instantly struck up acquaintance and walked round talking rapidly and exchanging impressions. The young English boy and the Irish priest were the only two guests on "retreat"; the rest were travellers like myself—just guests of a night. One of them told me how difficult it was to pay money to the hospitable brothers unless you stayed at least a week. Although there was in the hall an unobtrusive box for offerings, no one was ever asked to contribute, and in fact the guest of a night was soundly rated by the guest-father if he tried to give something for a night's hospitality.

"There was a man once," said a visitor, "who did not believe that any traveller can stay here for nothing. So for a bet he came and stayed a month. He was never asked to give a penny, and off he went at the end of his stay with the blessing of the abbot. He won his bet and sent it with a good cheque to the monastery. . . ."

We heard the sound of the bell summoning us to Mass. It was nearly 7 a.m. We went back and took our places in the chapel. Near me was the slightly less shaky figure of the man with the wispy, grey hair. The wise guest-father had given him a little confidence from a bottle.

The solemn and beautiful Canon of the Mass was celebrated before our eyes. My mind roved down the centuries, seeking a parallel to this wonderful scene: the lit candles, the celebrant and his assistants moving smoothly through the intricate ritual before the altar.

7

Shortly before 8 a.m. we took breakfast in the guest-house. We sat at a long table, and my gentle friend, the guest-brother, waited on us. The priest sat at the head of the table and poured out tea from a gigantic pot. There were eggs, bread and butter, but such marvellous bread and such perfect butter, the produce of the buttery and the bakehouse. We ate in silence. I was ravenous. I was conscious that I had missed my dinner the previous night!

I heard a voice and glanced behind me. A young father,

his face concealed by the hood of his white habit, was sitting in an alcove near the door reading the Imitation. It was a queer, fascinating voice—cold, expressionless—a voice that seemed to come to us reluctantly from some remote region of snow and ice. It was the voice of a scholar. It was also the voice of a man who preferred silence. The priest looked inquiringly round the table. Had we all finished? He struck a bell, and instantly the reading monk stopped; it seemed that he hardly finished the sentence, and when we rose after grace he had slipped silently from the room.

"Now what would you like to do?" asked the guest-father.

The two men on "retreat" had their duties. Others wished to confess; one or two asked to be allowed to examine their consciences in the chapel; but I asked the father to show me round the monastery.

We visited the bakery, the buttery, the carpenters' shops, the piggery; and how strange it was to see Trappists with their habits kirtled busying themselves with expert skill yet never exchanging so much as a glance with the man who worked beside them. In the piggery a fine figure of a monk was busy attending to the needs of a large family of squealing, shrimp-pink piglets. What a picture for a painter! As we watched him another monk came up and made one or two signs with his fingers. The monk in the sty replied with a nod and left his work.

The Trappists, I was told, have a sign language which they employ, never for purposes of conversation but only to impart orders.

When we were walking beside a cornfield my little friend of the early morning, the hare, suddenly sat up in the wheat and looked at us. I expected the father to say something Franciscan about him, but instead he whispered:

"Look at him, the little divil, in the corn!"

He crouched down and stealthily picked up a stone and took excellent aim and threw.

"That'll teach ye, ye rampaging little divil, to come treading the corn down the way ye do!"

He then turned to me the smiling face of a boy.

"I missed him!" he said sadly.

As we went along, the Trappist spoke to me of the routine of the monastery. The monks sleep fully dressed, with the exception that they remove their shoes and put on night-cowls. They retire at 8 p.m. and rising at 2 a.m. go down to the church. The lord abbot intones the Ave Maria, which is followed by the little office of the Blessed Virgin. At 3 a.m. begins the Canonical Office, each monk standing in his stall. Lauds are finished by 4 a.m., and they are followed by Masses served by the lay brothers. The community disperses, the priests after they have said Mass, the lay brothers at about 5.30 a.m., so that the greater part of the night is spent in devotion. The monks meet again in the refectory for the morning collation of coffee with dry bread at 7.15 a.m., after which begins the round of offices in chapel, and work on the farm . . . day after day, week after week, month after month, and year after year until death.

We entered the dormitories. Each monk sleeps in a bare little cell about seven feet long by four feet. The beds are rough wooden couches raised about two feet from the ground, and on each a straw mattress, a blanket, a rug, and a pillow of straw. These cubicles were as bare as prison cells. I expressed sympathy for the hardness of a

Trappist's life, but the priest turned to me a surprised and indignant face.

"Do you think," he said, "any of the pleasures of the material world can compare to the joys of the life spiritual?"

I left the monastery before noon with the blessing of the good priest and the gentle lay brother. They saw me to the gate and waved me on my way. One part of me was sorry to leave them; another part of me was glad to be in the world once more, free. I wanted to run and shout.

A little way down the road I saw the local Ford car which I had engaged to meet me.

"Good-day, sor; and how would ye be after gettin' along wid the monks? Sure, thought I, he's joined up entirely."

Then, as the wheezy machine bumped us towards Lismore, he told me stories of the many people he had taken to Melleray.

"There was wan gintleman given to the dhrink, ye understand, so that he was likely to have delirium tremens at any moment; an' a nice gentleman he was. He was stayin' at a big demesne down the road. Wan day his wife says to the prayst, she says, 'Father,' says she, 'if I could only get him into Mount Melleray maybe they'd cure him,' says she, 'for unless something is done wid him, and quick, there'll be the divil to pay!' So the prayst goes to see the abbot and I dhrive them all to the monastery. Himself goes in as quiet as quiet may be, and the monks see how it is wid him and offer him a glass. Now we go back and stay a little while in Cappoquin, and when we get back to Lismore who do we see in the hotel bar but himself, large as life, standin' up at the counter drinkin' a bottle of champagne to celebrate his escape! Faith, he'd climbed out over the wall! . . ."

8

In the little villages of the south there is always a shop, generally the post office, which exhibits placards showing Atlantic liners forging their way merrily towards a new world. These placards, pasted on boards, lean outside the shops like newspaper contents bills. They are the visible symbol of the tragedy of Ireland: the necessity of going away in order to exist. They make exile seem a pleasant joy-ride. They rather suggest that they are drawn up by the same glib pens which advise rich people to "take a trip round the world" and see the "age-old glories" of this country or that. They promise games-organizers, dances, welfare officials, and Catholic services during the voyage. It sounds attractive.

Above these placards in the crowded, dusty windows is a distinctive feature of all small shops in Ireland—the postcard.

Irish postcards are either sacred or profane. There is the postcard which the tourist buys, heaven knows why, to convince his friends that he is really in a very strange country. This card depicts in brilliant colour the stage Irishman behaving as stage Irishmen are expected to behave and saying things (conveyed to the spectator in little rings from his mouth after the manner of a Rowlandson caricature) which Irishmen are expected to say.

The favourite character is a pug-faced person in a swallow-tail coat, worsted stockings, knee-breeches, a funny hat, who smokes a short clay pipe and twirls a shillelagh as he makes love to a "colleen" with a shawl over her head. Or the same hero is seen driving a jaunting-car over boulders and upsetting tourists into a ditch. Or he is seen leaning over a pigsty, or preparing to fight somebody—this last is the only one with an atom of truth in it!

I wonder if people in England believe in these cards. (But possibly they are made there!)

How different are the real Irish postcards! They are the most touching postcards in the world. You see them propped up in the little jumbled shop windows in white villages; lying among laces and stockings in the country town draper's; stacked in long racks in village post offices. They are designed to cheer the heart of the emigrant.

Their naïve sentimentality and their pathetic sincerity wring the heart. They are an almost too intimate glimpse into the domestic life of Ireland.

There is one, plentifully sprinkled with sprays of shamrock, which shows in a small circle an idealized white cottage against a pink sunset, and with a round tower rising at the back among the fields. The fields, too, are idealized. They are not the rocky fields which helped to drive the emigrant to New York. "The dear little cabin" is the inscription under the cottage. "Fair Land of my Birth" is the general title to the card. Attached to the postcard with gum is a little green packet with these words on it: "A packet of real shamrock seed."

I suppose thousands of these cards go out to sons and daughters on birthdays, St. Patrick's Day, Christmas Day, and other holy days; and I suppose in pots on New York tenement window-sills that little "packet of real shamrock seed" does its best to take into a foreign land something which symbolizes home.

There is in all these cards the fear that the emigrant may forget Ireland. They create an impression of mothers and fathers wondering whether Mike or Bridget, far off in America, is losing touch with home.

"Forget not the land of your birth" is the stern warning on one which shows a little Irish bridge in the circle, much shamrock, and a horseshoe hung the wrong way, which seems usual in Ireland. In England we hang horseshoes with the points up (to keep in the luck), but even Irish stud farms (which need all the luck) hang them the reverse way over the horse-boxes. This card also bears the packet of "real shamrock seed."

So serious is the exportation of shamrock to America that notices are periodically exhibited in all post offices warning people that if the shamrock has roots or is "capable of generation" the American Customs will heave it into the dock.

Side by side with these touching postcards in village shops the steamship posters advertising passages to America are grim or pathetic according to your mood. How strange they would seem in a village street in Wiltshire or Somerset! In villages too small to be marked on the map these bright posters lean against the post office or the draper's showing a great liner far out at sea.

No people are more passionately attached to the land than the Irish. Other nations commit murder for women, but the Irish commit murder for a potato patch.

One of the most amazing sights in this country is the almost crazy courage and industry of the men who scratch a feeble living from a bit of land which no English farmer would dream of tilling. Yet the land they love is too poor to feed large families. Round every open hearth where the great black pot hangs above the turf fire the question comes up at some time: Who shall go to America?

Then the emigrant trains converge on Cork, there is some crying and wailing, the ship sails, and then a mother or a sister goes to the village draper and spends a long time considering the postcard rack:

"Forget not the land of your birth . . . a packet of real shamrock seed."

There is nothing, to my mind, more touching than this in an Irish village.

9

It was a hot, sunny day. The wheels of a donkey cart had parted company in the main street of Cork. The sun poured down on a laughing, animated crowd that would not have seemed out of place in Seville.

I know no other country which sees such humour in the, at times, almost evil intractability of inanimate objects. In England a breakdown in the road is a shameful spectacle. It reflects discredit on the person involved. It is inefficient. The debris is at once rushed to the side and the business of life sweeps on. In England a breakdown is a matter of anger; in Ireland for laughter. This argues a different philosophy of life. Perhaps only nations with a profound spiritual attitude to life can laugh at the occasional failure of material affairs. Or perhaps that is the reflection of a mind becoming tuned-in to the subtlety of Ireland; for no man can live for even a week in Ireland, as in Spain, without looking for a religious explanation to any peculiarity.

The old man to whom this disaster had happened in the main street of Cork was apparently a familiar character. The crowd evidently knew him well. He was so much of an artist that when he saw that his trouble was causing amusement he could not deny himself the pleasure of an audience. He therefore determined to make the most of his misfortunes. He addressed himself in the most droll and idiotic way to the placid donkey, conscious perhaps that his display of emotion heightened the humour of the beast's calm and uncomprehending conduct in a situation with which it had been so intimately concerned. He bewailed the accident with ludicrous lamentations and gave a performance, which, taken together with the donkey's stupid complacence, would have been worth thirty pounds a week to him could he have repeated it twice a night on the English music-hall stage.

Cork was the most foreign city I had seen in Ireland— foreign not in appearance but in atmosphere. One was surprised to hear the crowds talking a high-pitched English. I felt that on a summer's day Cork should be full of vivid striped umbrellas, beneath which the visitor might sit in the shade and sip grenadine.

It was in 1920 that at the height of the madness of the "Trouble" half Cork was burnt down. I felt sorry that Cork has not taken advantage of this disaster to rebuild its streets in a fashion more in keeping with the distinctive character of its people.

Cork is the capital of Munster: if anything should happen to Dublin it would be, obviously, the capital of the Free State. It is built on an island in the centre of the River Lee. A man, who should have known better, told me that it gets its name because it floats like a cork on the water. Cork, however, is derived from an Irish word meaning marsh.

There is a legend in Ireland to the effect that a Cork man can make a fortune where any other man would be applying for outdoor relief. It is certainly true that the people of Cork are different from the people in other parts of Ireland. They have a tradition as aristocratic as that of Dublin. They are clannish. For centuries they intermarried within their own walls, so that a family feeling exists between all men of Cork, which explains why when a Cork man takes over a business, say in Dublin, other men of Cork appear as if by magic in the firm.

Brilliant conversation began in Cork during the eighteenth century, and it is still going on. It is carried on in a quick, high-pitched, musical Welsh accent. (Or have the Welsh a Cork accent?)

They stay up so late in Cork making epigrams that the shops do not open until 9.30 to 10 a.m.

Through the wide streets of Cork, and beside the fine quays, moves a crowd just a pace quicker than any other Irish crowd. Among this gathering are women clothed in black shawls, which they wear over their heads in the manner of the Lancashire mill-girl. They are as distinctive a feature of the streets in Cork as the black-veiled women are in Cairo.

Some of these women are as dark as their shawls. They would look marvellous with tall hair-combs and bright mantillas. There is said to be Spanish blood in the south and in the north of Ireland which dates from the time when Cork, in the south, and Galway, in the west, were important centres of the Spanish wine trade.

Cork owes the most modern shopping street in Ireland to a tragedy of the "Trouble." St. Patrick's Street, which was burned down in 1920, is now rebuilt. Grafton Street, Dublin, is the Bond Street of Ireland; St. Patrick's Street, Cork, is the Regent Street.

There are certain things in all historic cities which tourists and no other people do. They are generally of a nature to confirm local inhabitants in a belief that all tourists are half-witted. In Cork you are supposed to kiss the Blarney Stone and to hear the bells of Shandon.

When I arrived beneath the reddish steeple of Shandon Church, the bellringer was not in, and I became surrounded by an eager and obliging crowd of women wearing black shawls and by barefoot children, all deeply concerned in my affairs and all determined that I should hear the bells of Shandon without delay. Foremost among my assistants was a Mrs. Driscoll, to whose tireless energy, I

SOUTH GATE BRIDGE, CORK

believe, in the end I owed the discovery of Mr. Albert Wellington Meredith, the bellringer of Shandon—"the only Meredith in Cork, sir"—and the owner of a name both historical and political.

We went up into the belfry, where an octave of bell ropes hung down in the ringing gallery. Mr. Albert Wellington Meredith braced himself for the effort, and, swaying his body backwards and forwards like the true virtuoso, shook from the steeple the sound of "The Minstrel Boy."

The bells of Shandon do, indeed, in the famous words of Father Prout, "sound so grand on the pleasant waters of the River Lee." And Cork must know them by heart! Every time a curious visitor enters the belfry Mr. Albert Wellington Meredith treats the city to a concert. He has been doing it for twenty-nine years, and he will tell you that in the summer when Americans dash through Cork on their way to Killarney (which is all they see of Ireland!), the bells of Shandon are never silent all day long.

We had "St. Patrick's Day," "The Harp that Once," "Garryowen," and a wedding peal.

I looked through a window and saw that down below the barefoot children had gathered with financial expressions, glad that the tourist season had opened so hopefully.

Mr. Albert Wellington Meredith then, from force of habit, offered to play me some American melodies, but I felt that Cork had probably had enough.

We talked about the Prince Consort and the Iron Duke, and the British Navy, which Mr. Meredith joined in 1877. He told how he joined the *Revenge* at Queenstown, how he served in distant waters all over the world, how he was once stranded in China, and how he "picked up" the *Cormorant* as she happened to be passing by. . . .

Down below the herd of children clamoured at the gates.

The only thing to do was to hurl a handful of pennies into the air and then run.

10

A few miles from Cork is the saddest spot in Ireland—the port of Queenstown, known now as Cobh, which is pronounced as Cove. When I was there no Atlantic liner waited in deep water for the tenders to come out with the girls and boys who are leaving their country. But that is the characteristic sight of Queenstown.

This place has heard, and will hear again, the keening of mothers lamenting as if for the dead. They say that in the last twenty-five years over three-quarters of a million young Irish men and women have gone away from this port. Queenstown is a wound which Ireland cannot stanch; and from it pours a constant stream of her best and her youngest blood.

I imagine from the accounts I have heard that the departure of an emigrant ship from Queenstown has not altered much since Mr. and Mrs. S. C. Hall described in their weighty work *Ireland* nearly a century ago:

"We stood in the month of June on the quay at Cork to see some emigrants embark in one of the steamers for Falmouth, on the way to Australia. The band of exiles amounted to two hundred, and an immense crowd had gathered to bid them a long and last adieu. The scene was touching to a degree; it was impossible to witness it without heart-pain and tears. Mothers hung upon the necks of their athletic sons; young girls clung to elder sisters; fathers—old white-haired men—fell on their knees, with arms uplifted to heaven, imploring the protecting care of the Almighty on their departing children: 'Och,' exclaimed one aged woman, 'all's gone from me in the wide world when you're gone! Sure you was all I had left!—of seven sons—but you! Oh, Dennis, Dennis, never forget your mother—your mother—don't, avourneen—your poor ould mother, Dennis!' And Dennis, a young man, though the sun was shining on his grey hair, supported 'his mother' in his arms until she fainted, and then he lifted her into a small car that had conveyed his baggage to the vessel, and kissing a weeping young woman who leaned against the horse, he said: 'I'll send home for you both, Peggy, in the rise of next year; and ye'll be child to her from this out, till then, and THEN, avourneen, you'll be my own.' When we looked again the young man was gone, and Peggy had wound her arms round the old woman, while another girl held a broken cup of water to her lips.

"Amid the din, the noise, the turmoil, the people pressing and rolling in vast masses towards the place of embarkation like the waves of the troubled sea, there were many such sad episodes. Men, old men too, embracing each other and crying like children. Several passed bearing most carefully little relics of their homes—the branch of a favourite hawthorn tree, whose sweet blossoms and green leaves were already withered, or a bunch of meadowsweet.

"It is impossible to describe the final parting. Shrieks and prayers, blessings and lamentations mingled in one great cry from those on the quay, and those on shipboard, until a band stationed on the forecastle struck up 'St. Patrick's Day.'

"'Bate the brains out of the big drum, or ye'll not stifle the women's cries,' said one of the sailors to the drummer. . . ."

I think the most poignant description of the departure of a young Irishman and his sister for America is a short story entitled *Going Into Exile* in Liam O'Flaherty's *Spring Sowing*. An all night dance in a cabin is described; at the back of it all is the brooding melancholy of the departure. Dawn comes:

"The father came into the room, dressed in his best clothes. He wore a new frieze waistcoat, with a grey and black front and a white back. He held his soft felt hat in one hand and in the other hand he had a bottle of holy water. He coughed and said in a weak, gentle voice that was strange to him, as he touched his son: 'Come now, it is time.'

"Mary and Michael got to their feet. The father sprinkled them with holy water and they crossed themselves. Then, without looking at their mother, who lay in the chair with her hands clasped on her lap, looking at the ground in a silent, tearless stupor, they left the room. Each hurriedly kissed little Thomas, who was not going to Kilmurrage, and then, hand in hand, they left the house. As Michael was going out of the door he picked a piece of loose whitewash from the wall and put it in his pocket. . . ."

11

When I asked in the hotel for "drisheen" they thought that I was trying to be funny. They treated me to that snobbish amusement which the Ritz would bestow on a man who was honest enough to demand a black pudding or a pound of tripe. However, I was firm, and in dead earnest, so they promised to send out and buy me a length for luncheon.

This drisheen, which looks like a large and poisonous snake, is a native of Cork, although it is imitated with variations in other parts of Ireland. When real Corkers (but Corkonian is, I believe, the accepted word) leave home on business they often take a yard of drisheen with them into less enlightened cities to delight them, and to proclaim an origin of which no Irishman has ever been ashamed. If you see a man in Waterford, Wexford, Galway, Dublin, or Limerick devouring what appears to be a chocolate-coloured python, you can be certain that he comes from Cork.

Now drisheen is a kind of sausage, made, I understand, mainly from sheep's blood and milk. It is the Irish cousin of the Bury pudding. Superior Dubliners pretend that it bites. They make the same wearisome jests about it that men make about Stilton cheese and haggis. But drisheen is above such low comment: one might call it the caviare of Cork.

"I married an English girl twelve years ago, and we were living in London," said a Cork man to me, "and when I had a bad attack of influenza friends in Cork sent me a drisheen. It is the first thing all doctors in Cork give when you are seriously ill, because it is the most nourishing and digestible of all foods. Well, my wife had never seen a drisheen, and when she opened the box it stood up and stretched itself. She screamed and dropped it, thinking it was a snake. . . ."

They brought me the drisheen boiled on a plate. When cut it looked like a firm chocolate blancmange. In a moment of mistaken enthusiasm they poured melted butter on it, but I feel instinctively that drisheen lovers employ a less sickly garnish. It is a peculiar, subtle dish, pleasant and ladylike.

I believe that I would like it better fried.

12

Kissing the Blarney Stone is a difficult and not too pleasant act. It is hard to discover why generations of travellers have endured it, and still more difficult to know why that particular stone, 150 feet above the ground level, achieved its world-wide fame.

The dictionary says that blarney is "to talk over, or

beguile by wheedling speech; flatter; humbug with agreeable talk." When the lift-boy in the hotel heard that I had kissed the Blarney Stone he said, with a grin:

"Och, sir, and now all the young ladies'll be afther ye. . . ."

This represents the cynical local tradition that the Blarney Stone imparts the power of such picturesque deception to the tongue of a man that no woman can resist him. I cannot believe this. As a humble student of human beings I have observed that women, while they on occasion enjoy lies enormously and even at times demand them, can see them sticking up out of a man's conversation like rocks in a sea. Still, the influence of blarney on romance is a fruitful and unexplored subject.

I have formed no ideas on it!

The village of Blarney lies five miles to the north-west of Cork.

In the middle of a pretty wood rise the ruins of Blarney Castle, with rooks cawing round it, moss growing over it, and damp green slime in its dungeons. It is the third castle built on that site. The first was a wooden fortress erected in remote times by Dermot McCarthy, King of South Munster; the second was built about A. D. 1200, and the present tattered shell was constructed in the reign of Queen Elizabeth. It was the strongest castle in that part of Ireland. In it lived the younger branch of the princely McCarthys, lords of Muskerry, barons of Blarney, and earls of Clancarthy.

The word "blarney" entered the language, so they say, when Dermot McCarthy was required to surrender the fortress to Queen Elizabeth as a proof of his loyalty. He said that he would be delighted to do so, but—something always happened at the last moment to prevent the surrender! His excuses became so frequent and were so plausible that the Lord President, Sir George Carew, who was demanding the castle in the name of the Queen, became a joke at Court.

Queen Elizabeth (probably) said, when these excuses were repeated to her: "Odds bodikins, more Blarney talk!"

In any event the term "blarney" invaded the English language, meaning plausible wheedling.

The first question you ask when you enter Blarney Castle is, "Where's the Blarney Stone?"

A caretaker points skywards to the turret of the donjon. You see, 150 feet from the earth, and on the outside of the walls, a large brown stone. Your enthusiasm begins to wane! You go round and round a spiral staircase and emerge on the turret.

In the old days people who kissed the Blarney Stone were hung by the heels over the edge of the parapet. One day a pilgrim broke from the grasp of his friends, and went hurtling into space, and since that time the Blarney Stone has been approached by a different method.

You sit down with your back to a sheer drop of 150 feet. Your guide then sits on your legs, holds your feet, and tells you to lie back over the drop and grasp two iron hand-rails. You are then lying flat on your back with half your body ready for eternity. By wriggling down (and closing your eyes to shut out the distant inverted landscape, you bring yourself to kiss the base of the stone. You then lever yourself up from the abyss, shout: "Are you sure you've got me?" sit up and say, "Well; I did it!"

How did this custom originate?

No one knows. It is the kind of thing a caretaker with a sound knowledge of psychology might invent in a moment of inspiration. Kissing the Blarney Stone was unknown in the eighteenth century.

Since then, I discover, there have been many Blarney Stones. There is, in fact, a dispute on the position of the original rock of Blarney. Some say that it is twenty feet from the top of the tower at its southern angle, and bears the inscription, "Cormac McCarthy fortis mi fieri fecit. A. D. 1446." Others say that it bears a shamrock in relief and is in a position known to few people. It is discouraging to learn this after you have endured the ordeal!

"And what," you say to the guide as you wind downwards to earth through the turret, "will the Blarney Stone do for me?"

He then recites, in the stale tones employed by guides who spend their lives answering the same question, these lines by Father Prout:

> *There is a stone there,*
> *That whoever kisses,*
> *Oh! he never misses*
>   *To grow eloquent.*
> *'Tis he may clamber*
> *To a lady's chamber,*
> *Or become a member*
>   *Of Parliament.*

You go thoughtfully away, comforted by the thought that it is all blarney!

13

I took the western road through Macroom into Kerry, and in Kenmare I found black cows all over the street and a fair day in progress.

Kenmare is as typical a southern Irish country town as you will see in a day's march. It is beautifully placed beside Kenmare River. Its streets are long and wide, the shops are small and dull, but fair day brings life and colour to them.

I was inspired by the air of homely bustle and buying to choose lengths of a particularly attractive loose tweed which is made in this district. It is the colour of porridge. I then did something more difficult. I entered the Convent of Poor Clares where the Mother Superior kindly helped me to choose some of the exquisite lace which the Sisters teach the daughters of Kerry to make.

But Kenmare will be ever memorable to me on account of its hats. Who can ever forget the old hats of Ireland? They are a feature of the landscape. If every countryman were given a new hat Ireland would look strange and ill at ease.

There is the centenarian bowlar, a thing of antique majesty, a creation of storm and tempest, the final sum of infinite experience, disillusioned, heavy with its weight of years, yet somehow light and airy as a puff-ball with a suggestion of imminent dissolution.

This shapeless mass of battered felt with its flattened rim, its bald crown innocent of ribbon sits cocked at a youthful angle over the most impudent of faces. It is often a red face with a bulbous nose, two pale eyes that give nothing away and a funny little mouth that purses itself up and seems to favour words before it projects them into the air.

The Bowlar of Kenmare must be, I think, the senior hat of Ireland. It was worn by an ancient man whose years seemed reduced and rendered almost childish by the antiquity of this hat. It was impossible to believe that it had ever been young and hopeful in a shop window. It was a solemn shade of green. There were various dents and contusions on its surface, and the marks of recent blows, which had succeeded in de-bowlarizing it to such an extent that it gave one a sense of discovery. It was so old that it seemed new and original. I felt that all other less venerable bowlars in Ireland should be doffed in reverence before this patriarch. It was incredible that anywhere in Ireland could be a pretender to the throne of its fantastic antiquity.

I looked with interest and respect at the old ruffian who was wearing it. It was almost like wearing the history of Ireland on his head. When the king assumes a crown which dates only from the Restoration, although it contains older jewels, he does not assume an emblem of national experience so heavy with history as the great Bowlar of Kenmare.

Then there is the soft hat which has lived so long and so vividly that its original shape is lost in the mists of time. It is possible to wear it back to front, or sideways, and no one can tell, because from every angle it looks exactly as if a dirty felt pudding had been poured on the wearer's head. While the decayed bowlar resembles a professional man who has gone downhill owing to "the dhrink" ("You wouldn't believe that he was once a great doctor, now would you?") the desiccated felt hat looks like a ne'er-dowell whose ultimate fate has never been in question.

I adore these old hats. I have always been praised by men and reviled by women for the age of my hats, but I confess myself out-classed in Ireland and for ever beaten. I look with admiration and envy at them and know that I can never hope to own a hat so old even if I put it into training, left it out at night, took to drink and had my hat stamped on and flung down a million stairs. My hat would simply look disreputable. It would swiftly pass that border-line between the comfortable and the unwearable without achieving the air of distinction and personality shown by the rarer vintages in Ireland.

An old hat is a wonderful thing. It absorbs in some un-
explained manner the character, and even the appearance,
of its wearer. You have only to see an old hat hanging on
a peg to know at once whose old hat it is. I have often
thought that if some woman cared sufficiently for me to
ask some token that would bring me vividly before her
during absence I could give nothing more eloquently personal than my oldest hat.

But in Ireland, so powerful is the personality of the
old hats, that a widow, having one lying about the house,
must find it difficult to believe that her husband has renounced it for a halo. These hats can do everything but
speak.

So I lift my hat, in reverence and affection, to the
mighty, the unthinkable veteran, that father of all hats,
the Bowlar of Kenmare.

CHAPTER VI

Describes the pagan magic of Kerry. I explore a house in ruins, meditate on the wall of Pat Flannigan's pigsty, watch a "fair," and take a dangerous drink of poteen

1

KERRY is a magic corner of Ireland. Just as in the Isle of Skye you expect something terrible to rise in the dusk from any boulder, so in Kerry you expect something weird to stand up at any moment beside you on the hills. One day alone in Kerry, away from the roads on mountains that go down sharply to the sea; and you understand why in lonely places the Irish believe in fairies and things not of this earth.

The Kerry villages are poor and small and, many of them, dirty. In small towns there is no apparent social life. There are no book-shops. There are no village institutes; no libraries. There seems to be no public spirit. There are days when a kind of death seems to come to these towns. They might be infected with a plague. The streets are empty. The shopkeepers stand listlessly in their small and often redundant stores. A few loungers lurk at corners holding switches cut from a hedge and looking as if they had lost a herd of cows. The listlessness of these stagnating townships is sometimes almost terrible. But some towns of a size which in England might give a lean living to three solicitors have a sort of lawyers' quarter— a little Temple whose brass plates are like a shining testimony to the pugnacity of the Irish farmer. A law case brings life into them!

Now and again a man comes out of a shop and slowly crosses the empty main street. You are told that he is the local Midas—Mr. Maloney who has twenty thousand pounds in the bank. It is, apparently, always "in the bank"! Mr. Maloney would never think of investing it. He also would never dream of doing anything to enliven or improve life in the town. At regular intervals the chapel bell rings.

In many remote Scottish towns and villages there is always a more or less talkative elderly man who will, when given a glass of whisky, tell you how he *almost* invented something that would have made his fortune, only, alas, just as he was getting it right someone else got in ahead and reaped the benefit! In remote Irish towns his prototype is a genealogist. He will over a glass of porter tell you all about the local ancestors. He stands in Mike Finnigan's drink-shop brooding about parentage. He knows everything about everybody.

"—D'ye see that man now?" he will ask, half turning from the saloon counter and pointing with his pipe to indicate a man in the street. "That's Paddy Milligan, the Sheep Stealer!"

"What?" you ask, surprised. "Does he steal sheep?"

A grim, condemnatory look will come into the man's face and he will tell you solemnly:

"Shure his grandfather was *hanged* for sheep stealing!"

His grandfather! You find it difficult not to laugh! Just because generations ago a man's forebears were barbarously hanged for theft his descendant is condemned to walk about modern Ireland in a sort of reflected villainy! I wonder how much of Ireland's sorrow has been caused by this trick of looking backwards instead of forwards, in nursing old grievances, in putting salt on old wounds. The patriot will say, perhaps, that Ireland never had anything to look forward to and was therefore forced to look backward. Is that just? Surely this habit of living in the past is a common Gaelic habit of mind. The Highlanders of Scotland possess it in a marked degree. It always accompanies a passion for genealogy.

"Even to this day around the mountains of Kerry, there is a regard for the bearers of noble names," writes Padraic Colum in *The Road Round Ireland*. "The shopkeepers in small towns—even they—have a veneration for the old stock. A man who drives his ass into the town will be received with respect by the shopkeeper who could give thousand-pound dowries to his daughters. The man will be one of the old families, an O'Sullivan or a MacGillicuddy, and in his cabin on the mountain he will have the bearing, the manners, and the *hauteur* of an aristocrat. The other evening I was on the road speaking with an old-age pensioner who was leaving the town in an ass cart. A young man came up to us. 'He is one of the oldest stock that comes this road,' he said to me impressively, speaking of the old man. 'Aye, indeed,' cried the pensioner. 'I am one of the old stock. I can trace my family back for three hundred years—aye, and beyond three hundred years. Seumas Ua Mongain—that's my name in Irish.'"

The hollows of the hills fill with blue shadows. Just before the sun sets there is a silence, a suspended excitement in the air, and in the silence no bird sings and no creature moves, only the clouds change colour and the wind cries among the stones. It seems, even to a stranger and a foreigner, that the whole world is waiting for the blowing of horns that would shatter the silence of the dusk for it seems that the old gods of Ireland might come striding down the hill.

Although the Angelus bell may be ringing in the village this sadness on the hills at evening is a pagan sadness, something right from the very roots of a nation's consciousness, and you look at the queerly shaped stones, like men lying in the half light, thinking that if some spell were spoken they might move and, rising heavily, march down armed with spears; and men would recognize Cuchullain and the Red Branch Knights, Keltar of the Battles, Fergus Mac Roig, and the three great sons of Usna. . . .

Down in the darkening town there is nothing but the sound of the chapel bell. There is nothing to do but to drink and to look up at the pagan hills and—think backward.

2

I would go day after day to read among the ruins of the big house beside the road. It was quiet and mysterious. The weeds had made a riot of the garden, but roses still flowered. All I knew about the big house was that at some time during the "Trouble" the owners were turned out and the place fired by the Irregulars. There was not far from the house, in a shrubbery, the remains of an ancient wall and tower, all that was left of a fortress. The place had evidently been occupied for centuries.

The dead house began to fascinate me. I would prowl about in the ruins looking at the blackened walls and the faded wall-paper, the places where pictures had hung, the staring windows, doors which led nowhere, stairs that ended in mid-air; and I would wonder what kind of people lived there and what they had done to deserve this.

I asked questions about it and bit by bit pieced together its history; and in the story of that piece of land was also the history of Ireland.

When in the year A. D. 1171 Henry II became Ireland's first absentee landlord, he left behind him a Norman baron (Welsh on his mother's side, like so many of the original invaders) in possession of this estate. The six-foot thick boundary wall in the shrubbery is all that remains of the castle built by this settler.

This Norman family settled down and developed along that line of least resistance which had it not violently conflicted with the ideas of England's rules might have solved the "Irish Question" centuries ago. In the course of a few generations this family became, to all appearances, Irish. It spoke Irish, intermarried with Irish families, observed the Brehon Law, adopted the Irish system of fosterage, and changed its name to—say—MacFerris. Such union between the English and the Irish was hateful to Westminster. Such families were known as the "degenerate English." The Statute of Kilkenny was launched against them in 1367, forbidding them on pain of high treason to intermarry with the Irish, speak Irish, or adopt the speech or dress or customs of the Irish. The MacFerris family, however, managed to weather the storms of three centuries, until a bright light of burning in the sky announced the arrival of Cromwell on his war of extermination. Then the MacFerris family was driven into the hills. That was in the year A. D. 1653.

The new owner of this estate was one of Cromwell's Puritan followers, a soldier named—say—Buckley. He took the MacFerris demesne, built himself a suitable house, and established himself on the land. He weathered the Stuart storms as successfully as his predecessor had weathered those of Plantagenet times.

The Georgian age found these Buckley's no longer
humble ex-service men of Cromwell's but distinguished
country gentlemen with Gainsborough's and Romney's on
their walls, good wine in the cellar, and a stable full of
noble horses. The house of their ancestors had made way
for an austere square mansion with a portico upheld by
Corinthian columns. They were, by comparison with others,
good landlords and well liked. They disappeared for long
periods into England, where their rents were sent to them.
Here the process of Irishing which had penalized the Plantagenet settlers was a kind of social charm. The Buckley's
when in England were considered to be delightfully
Irish. They were expected to do and say funny things
and to be generally a bit mad. But they could not speak
Gaelic and they were staunch Protestants. (When they
returned to Ireland their tenants thought of them as
English.)

They sent sons into the Army and the Church. A
Buckley distinguished himself in Crimea. Another became
an English Bishop. In Victoria's resign—so glorious and
well-fed for England, so miserable and starved for Ireland—the Buckleys heard the first faint rumble of rebellion, but they rode to hounds right through it. They
served in the South African War, and a Buckley commanded an English yeomanry regiment during the war
with Germany.

This was the Colonel Buckley who had come over to see
his agent in 1922. He discovered that the warning rumble
of Fenianism through which his great-grandfather and his
grandfather had hunted now swept with the force of a
gale through Ireland. The young men on his estate seemed
to belong to a secret society. He saw strange slogans
chalked up on the walls. His tenants had the appearance
of spies. One night, he was sitting at dinner in the big

Georgian room, congratulating himself, perhaps, that the good deeds of his ancestors had preserved his Irish fortunes, when there was a tramp of feet as a band of Irregulars walked in, tough young men with caps pulled over their eyes. He had time to notice among them the sons of one or two of his tenants.

"You've got your rosary?" one began from force of habit; then, remembering that the colonel was a Protestant he smiled grimly and said: "Come on now to the top of the hill."

The Buckleys, like most of the unfortunate Anglo-Irish, may at times have been stupid but they were never cowardly. The Colonel, knowing at once that he was about to be murdered, and knowing too that argument was pointless, asked to be allowed to find a hat. They marched him to the top of his own hill in the dark. Here a huge young man stood over him.

"Who does that demesne belong to, Colonel Buckley?" he asked.

"It belongs to me," said the Colonel.

"Oh; it does?" replied the young man with deep irony. "Well, now, take a good look at me while you can! that demesne belonged to me before you came over with Cromwell. My name's MacFerris! Now down with ye on your knees. . . ."

But the Colonel was not shot. At the last moment the men, becoming alarmed by a scouting-party of Free State troops, fled, leaving the middle-aged Anglo-Irishman kneeling on the grass without the slightest idea that Cromwellian had met Plantagenet. As the Colonel rose he looked down and saw that his house was on fire. He then and there swore never to set foot on Irish soil; and he kept his vow. He retired to an English cathedral city.

So I go day after day to read among the ruins of the
house beside the road. There is something as inevitable as
Greek tragedy in the thought of a MacFerris, probably a
farm-labourer, swooping down with the indignation of
centuries behind him to snatch a brief vengeance at the
pistol's point. If this long memory is not nationalism,
what is it?

There is not a great estate in Ireland owned by one of
Cromwell's settlers which has not always had a ghostly
other owner in the memory of the common people. He may
be only a legend or he may be somebody living "up in the
hills"; but he is not forgotten.

It all proves that in Ireland there is no ancient history:
all history is contemporary. It also suggests a number of
other things.

3

There is one sign that a writer is beginning to enjoy
Ireland: he stops writing. There is another: he disappears.
This generally happens when he enters Kerry.

People in England, becoming anxious about him, post
letters which are returned; then, becoming angry, they
fire off telegrams which are not delivered. And all the time
the man who is supposed to be working sits, wrapped in a
kind of Oriental lethargy, smoking his pipe on the wall
that goes round Pat Flannigan's pigsty.

No one in England could possibly understand that
sense of the futility of effort which falls over a man in
Ireland. England is not a contemplative nation, and any
cessation of effort is considered to be pure laziness,
whereas it is often what the Catholic Church calls "examination of conscience," which is confoundedly hard work.
There is something in the air of Ireland, something that
rises from the peat bogs or falls from the hills, which

drenches the spirit in a calm which a philosopher would probably call the true value of life; at times this Irishness is a rather pleasant melancholy; at other times it is just a comfortable detachment. I now realize that unless you feel this you can never hope to know Ireland.

I have been sitting on the pigsty wall for a week, confessing my sins and my stupidities to Pat Flannigan's old sow who, at the moment at the very pinnacle of maternity, is, I consider, a sympathetic companion. She has nine little swine the colour of boiled shrimps and the size of fox-terriers.

All round us the enchanted hills of Kerry lift their fantastic ridges to the sky, the big yellow clouds move softly over them, and the evening turns them purple. The white road curves through the valley, and the hills, sloping away from it on either side, lift themselves upward past a bright checquer-work of fields sown with corn and vegetables to harsh, uncultivated summits where grey rocks thrust themselves through the grass.

Nothing ever comes over the road but little vermilion carts drawn by donkeys and loaded with turf like bricks of dark chocolate. Old men, or old women with their heads in black shawls, crouch above the shafts. Sometimes an incredible tramp comes along wearing garments which suggest a riot in a rag-shop, and as I see him I wonder whether he was a writer who came to Ireland forgotten years ago to produce a book about the country.

And the whole scene—green hills, white roads, yellow clouds—has a kind of jewel-like sharpness which compels complete attention.

Mike O'Brien, who delivers letters all over the mountain on a bicycle, came to me as I sat on the pigsty wall, and said:

"Faith, ye must know a divil of a lot of friends, for me back's broke wid carryin' this up to you."

And he placed in my hands a bundle of letters redirected from London.

"Mike," I said, "it's a dusty road."

"There was dust on ut the day after the Flood," said Mike.

"Which suggests that a glass of stout might not be out of place."

"It might not," said Mike.

So we left the pigsty wall and entered the dark, evil, yeast-smelling drink-shop which all over Ireland does duty as the village bar. Why Ireland, the most friendly, the most talkative, the most convivial of all countries, has not developed the lovely inn parlours which for centuries have been, and will remain while there is a man left on earth, one of the great glories of England, passes my understanding.

The cat was asleep on the counter; a dried pig's face, the colour of a bad lemon, with salt caked in its ears, gave us a horrible squashed kind of leer from the top of a barrel, and the place smelt of spilt drink and foul tobacco.

"Mike, I've got to do some work."

"Is that so?" said Mike, politely interested.

"You, although you don't know it, are the messenger from another world, and these letters recall me to duty. I seem to remember that I was going to write a book about Ireland, but I shall never do it."

"There's no harm done!" said Mike rather crudely. "And who the blazes wid want to read it?"

"That's exactly how I feel about it! Ireland does that to you. Who in blazes would?"

"Did you ever hear the story," asked Mike, "of the tiger that died on Duffy, the circus man?"

His stocky figure in the blue uniform became suddenly important. A funny story in Ireland is as important as a board meeting in England. And here, I thought, is the whole thing in a nutshell! No sooner does a man recall himself to duty than this confounded, insinuating country takes him by the arm and tells him a story that drives everything but good nature out of his head. . . .

"Wait now while I tell you," said Mike. "When the tiger died on him, Duffy didn't know what to do at all, at all. 'It's ruined I'll be,' sez he, 'for I cannot open the circus widout a tiger.' 'I'll tell ye what ye'll do,' sez Pat Dempsey, who came from Cork, and was up to all kinds of diviltry and deception. 'What's to prevent me being the tiger,' sez he, 'for wid his skin on me and a glass of whisky inside of me to give me a grand roar, it's a fine baste I'll be and no mistake,' sez he. Wait now while I tell you. . . .

"Pat skinned the tiger and got inside the skin, and whin the circus opened ivery wan sez that niver was such a savage, roarin', snarlin' baste seen before. Faith—for I was there at the toime and saw it—Pat was the most evil-timpered murtherin' divil of a tiger ye ever saw! Wait now while I tell you. . . ."

Mike lifted his glass, drank, moved the back of his hand over his mouth, edged a bit closer, fixing me all the time with a dancing eye:

"Whiles he was caperin' and roarin' and trying to get at the audience a little door opens and what should walk into the cage wid him, quiet and aisy-going, but the most ferocious-looking baste of a lion that iver walked the earth! Pat gave one look and knew that his last hour had come! The lion let out a blood-curdlin' roar and came prowlin' round wid his tail hitting the ground. Pat saw him and the whisky died out of him, and 'For the love o'

Mike,' sez he, 'let me out o' this.' and he made a run for the door, but the lion was afther him! 'Saints above!' hollered Pat, 'open the door! Let me out o' this!' But the lion sprang on him and a voice inside sez: 'Go aisy, Pat, it's all right Pat—*I'm from Cork too.*' . . .

"Nor did ye ever hear the story of Mrs. Mulligan goin' to see the prayst? . . . Well, wait now while I tell you. . . ."

Back on the wall of Pat's pigsty I sit idly, with my arms full of correspondence, watching the hollows of the Kerry hills fill with mists the colour of violets. Their queer, fretted ridges are jet black against a sky that, glowing with incandescent light, is almost pale green. High up on the hillside the small cabins shine as if built of snow. There is a reek of peat from nowhere and the distant creak of a cart grinding the dust of the road, then silence deep as the ocean—the silence of enchanted hills, the silence of the sky.

And London is only a few hours away from Kerry. It seems impossible. Some day tired people will know this and will come here to let the peace of Ireland sink into their weary bones; and they will become more tired and more tired, content just to sit on the wall of Pat's pigsty watching the hills change colour and listening for the little bell which ends each day with a prayer for the beauty of God's earth.

4

If your bedroom is in the front of a house in Kerry you will be awakened while it is still dark by a queer, insistent pattering on the road outside. You look at your watch. It is 5 a.m. When you pull the blind aside you see herds of cattle going past in the moonlight. The drovers walk behind, bent over their sticks, and as they smoke their pipes

they call now and then in early morning voices to the sub-
dued dogs who skirmish on the fringes of the herd.

There is an interval, then along the empty roads walks
a man driving a cow and her calf. He melts into the darkness. There comes a little cart drawn by a sleepy donkey.
It contains a litter of pigs. There are more herds, then a
donkey burdened like Atlas—just four thin, knock-kneed
little legs beneath a great stack of hay. He patters off, to
be followed by a donkey carrying brown squares of dry
turf packed in two wicker baskets slung on either side of
him.

You have seen enough to know that the whole countryside is awake for miles around. It is market day. (It is
always market day somewhere in Ireland!) Women have
been awake at 3 and 4 a.m. in hundreds of little white
cabins far off in the hills, getting their husbands and sons
off to market, preparing food while the men, outside in the
dark, round up the cattle and pack the pigs in the donkey
cart. . . .

And all the time, as this strange procession of hill men
and their beasts passes beneath your window, the moon
sinks, growing paler every minute, the little chill winds
that run before the sun bend the grass, and the air grows
grey; and you feel that you have seen something from an
Irish fairy-tale or something from the very beginning of
history, something older than agriculture—the migra-
tion of herdsmen and their herds.

In the course of a day's motoring in Ireland you can see
perhaps twenty market days, known, goodness knows
why, as "fairs."

Some are in the abnormally wide streets of French-
looking towns; others are in towns more physically attractive; others are held in mere villages; but the market day
as we understand it in rural England does not exist, at

FAIR DAY

least in the south of Ireland. Consider a market day in Wiltshire with the sheep pens overflowing and the fat cattle lowing in the market, while the farmers lean over the pens and make jokes and troop into the "Nag's Head" to drink beer. Their daughters are buying silk stockings, their sons are buying a new wireless, their wives are packing brown paper parcels into a Ford motor-car. There is a robust family joviality about it.

In the little villages of Kerry market day means hundreds of tousled, mud splashed black cows standing with dazed expressions all over the main street, some on the pavement, some in the middle of the road. Now and then an indignant gombeen man comes out and smacks a cow out of his shop.

Attached by bonds of self-interest to each cow is a man who adopts the same casual attitude. He is a tall, wild-looking fellow from the hills, leaning on a stick, his clothes are ragged, and his hat was once a bowlar. Sometimes the man leaves his cow and joins a group of men, but how he discovers his cow again in that queer mix-up of cows, all small and all black, is beyond my understanding.

The queer thing about these men—and this, I think, holds good throughout the country —is that if you picked the most bedraggled, the most villainous-looking, the wildest, the one who lost his razor in 1800, and the owner of a hat which is obviously the hero of a hundred tavern brawls, and spoke to him, you would find him worth talking to. This was the first lesson I learnt when I left Dublin. At first I talked down to moth-eaten characters beside the road as one would suit words to the understanding of an English yokel; but—they invariably replied like orators!

There is a fine touch of good breeding and an almost disconcerting air of culture about most of the tattered men who trudge the roads of Ireland.

To return to our market. . . .

Donkeys chased by small boys, skip about among the melancholy cows. Many of these donkeys are too young to work which is the only brief happiness a donkey ever enjoys. At the side of the street are rows of small donkey carts, their bodies painted blue, their shafts bright saffron. Inside are slumbering pigs, maternal sows, and nurseries of pigeens.

The cow, the pig and the donkey are the props of the Irish countryside.

Such a market, spread haphazardly against the background of the white village street, a few tiny shops, and a public-house, is an expression of country life at its barest. That man has walked fifteen hard miles from the peat bog with five shillings' worth of turf; another has tramped for many miles through the dawn with ten shillings' worth of hay.

These people scratch the barest living from a hard land, and their wealth is counted in pennies. Yet there is not one of them who would not rather drive his cow back again to the distant hills than accept less than he means to get for it. The Irish cannot compromise.

But they can argue! Watch a man who is anxious to buy a pig. He makes a careful survey of all the pigs on view, he prods them through the bars of the cart until they squeal and leap up; then, when his heart is settled on one surpassing pig, he approaches the owner and says:

"Good-morning. And it's fine weather we've been having, glory be to God."

"It is."

They talk about everything but pigs for twenty minutes. Meanwhile other candidates for the pig assemble furtively in the background. It is not etiquette for a buyer to break in on a conversation of this kind. Many a nose has been broken in Ireland because a man has not waited for another man to conclude his conversation with a pig-owner.

Eventually the would-be purchaser mentions airily, as if it had just come into his head, that a certain little pig in the cart is a good pig and might fatten well; and how much, he wonders, just as a matter of curiosity, might that little pig be worth?

He then decides to "play tough." That is to say, he lets it be known that he would buy the pig for five shillings less than the price named, and when the dealer has exhibited a polite indifference he moves off; and the next would-be buyer swoops down!

So the pig carts on market day are surrounded by a ring of men, all politely holding off until an argument has ended, all distrustful of each other, all anxious to buy the pig, all holding out, all "playing tough."

The pig is sold by a process of contraction and expansion in the generosity of buyer and seller. Frequently when they have reached the last argumentative fence a third party—the peacemaker—is called in to help them over. They pledge themselves to accept his decision. He hears the details of the transaction, splits the sixpence, and— the pig changes carts!

Most extraordinary in these markets is the absence of women. That is why they look such dull assemblies. Hundreds of men in black coats, hundreds of black cows. The women, of course, are miles away in the hills. They have no butter to sell, no eggs, no honey, no clotted cream, no cheese like the women of Somerset and Devon.

They wait at home on the bare hill-side for the man to come home with silver in his pocket. But sometimes he comes back with the sow or the pig, angry, independent, uncompromising.

I hope that sometimes he takes her back something from the village, but looking round the village shops I wonder what on earth he could take her! A pair of boots? A few yards of flannel? That is not the kind of present to take to a woman who waits for you in the hills all day! I think the only beautiful thing he could take to her from an Irish village shop is a little coloured picture of Our Lady.

5

It is odd that Ireland should have the reputation of a gay and rollicking country. I suppose the hard-drinking, hard-riding Anglo-Irish of the Georgian age are responsible for this legend.

As the road goes on into Kerry I came across stretches of country from which melancholy seems to ooze from the hard soil. There is a sadness and a disillusion in the air. The very rain weeps rather than falls over the land and the wind is a sigh. I compare such places with happy countrysides: the fat orchard lands of Herefordshire; Kent with the hops ripening in tall battalions; the vineyards of Burgundy; the silver plain round Avignon; the saintly country about Siena; the plump cloudy dairy-lands of Holland.

There can be nothing in the world like the sadness of some parts of Ireland. The rain might be the tears of exiles; the wind might be the crying of those forced to die in foreign lands. It is an atmosphere which speaks of centuries of hunger, eviction, and emigration.

Ireland is as moody as its people. Just as an Irishman will follow a mood of laughter with one almost of tears, so this country changes in a few miles from a cheerful, quiet, knowing region which might be the land of Slipper and Flurry Knox to a dreary, sorrowful, neglected area of

depression which has, so far as I know, never been described
in fiction. If some writer with E. Œ. Somerville's gift
of humour and John Galsworthy's gift of pity had in some
way combined these two atmospheric extremes we might
have had a true novel of Ireland. It seems to me that the
pictures of Irish life are desperately incomplete. Behind
all the laughter, the horsecoping, the steeplechasing, the
drinking, the intrigue is a character who never appears,
but one who has proved himself the most important in
modern Irish history: the sullen countryman with a pitch-
fork. He stands behind a stone wall watching the hunt go
by, a member of an inferior race but, in his own imagination, the descendant of saints and kings.

And in these sad parts of Ireland it seems that his long
memory has filled the air with a hard resentment, and perhaps the pathos has been put into it by women who have
seen their children go hungry to bed. . . .

This may be fantastic. Ireland encourages fantastic
thought. Any true book on Ireland must be full of contra-
dictions and thoughts that may be only half true.

6

"If you want a taste of poteen," said my friend, "go to
the place I'm telling you of and say, 'Mike O'Flaherty's
black cow has died on him.' "

"And is it safe?"

"It is not."

"Will I get a taste of poteen?"

"You will. But," he added "for the love of Mike, if you
write about it, disguise it well. You understand why. . . ."

"Poteen" is the most mysterious word in the country
places of Ireland. It is never spoken: it is always whispered. This illicit firewater, which is distilled in the dead

of night, or on misty days which hide the smoke from the still, has always been made in the lonely hills of Ireland. It is made today under conditions of extreme danger (which appeal like a challenge to the Irish temperament) because the Free State Government is determined to stamp out the evil traffic.

Hundreds of enterprising young Civic Guards roam the roads of Ireland, or lie up in the hills with binoculars, bent only on raiding the stills and bringing the poteen gangs to prison.

That is why country people lower their voices when they mention this subject and refer mysteriously to "the stuff."

I had been walking for over an hour along a road that was barely a sheep-track. It was a dangerously clear day, with great yellow clouds rising up over the rim of the hills. The valley was desolate and rocky, without a house, lacking even sufficient grass for the little black Kerry cows, which seem able to live on next to nothing.

As I went on the rocks gave way to large tracts of snuff-brown bog, soggy with dark water, showing in places a seam of turf laid bare, the sides of the bank, firm and chocolate-coloured, bearing the marks of the turf-cutter's little spade.

Turning a corner I saw, lying in a hollow of the bog and built on a ledge of rock, a small white cabin, and, sure enough, sitting on a pile of stones some distance from this cabin, was a little old man.

When I approached him and looked at him I knew that every nerve in his body was taunt with apprehension. I admired the way he concealed this. Who was I? Was the game up? Those questions were running round and round his brain, yet he smiled and said:

"Good evening. . . ."

We agreed that it was a rare and beautiful day and quite warm in the sun.

He was old and undersized, and his grey eyebrows came down over his eyes like a screen, but I could see his eyes very bright and alive, looking not at me, but round the hills restlessly all the time.

"I'd like a drink of the stuff," I said.

He replied that once, when he was a nipper, he had tasted it, but it had not been made in those hills for years. Now that we had come to grips he was completely master of himself. I told him that I was a traveller in Ireland, and wanted to be able to say that I had tasted poteen in the hills. No; not for years had he set eyes on a drop of the stuff! Now, in Connemara . . . a tinker had told him once. . . .

"Have you heard," I said, "that Mike O'Flaherty's black cow has died on him?"

"And in the name of —— why didn't you tell me that at the first?"

Without a change of expression he got up from the stones and walked slowly to the white cabin with his hands in the pockets of his patched trousers.

Things then happened with quiet efficiency.

Two strapping girls, one about sixteen and the other perhaps eighteen, wild black hair flying and bunchy black skirts flapping against their bare legs, ran from the cabin over the rocks. The younger ran up and stood on the crest of the hill; her sister slipped like a setter into the turf bog. The old poteen man slouched down from the cabin to me, his hands still in his pockets and his eyes behind their grey screen searching the hills all round.

"It's grand weather entirely," he said, adding that times were as hard as the very divil himself. Even when he was lighting his pipe his restless eyes were moving over the hills. . . .

A girl came running through the turf bog. She looked magnificent, with the wind blowing her short skirt back against her and her white legs stained with the brown peat water. She grasped a bottle. There was peat sticking to it. She had pulled it from the turf, which was probably stiff with poteen. Hardly stopping in her run, she bent down, placed the bottle beside a stone wall, and leapt like a mountain goat up the sharp rocks and into the cabin.

The poteen man walked casually away smoking his pipe, the most innocent old man you ever saw, leaving me alone with a bottle of white poison and a small tin mug beside a stone wall.

Poteen is a foul, stupefying drink. It can send men mad. It can put them in a trance that lasts for days. Under its influence a man can commit any crime. I treated it with great respect. I poured out just enough to fill a liqueur glass and I drank it neat.

It was like fire with the smoke in it. It was white in colour, it burned the throat, a crude, coarse, violent raw spirit. I hid the bottle in the grass at the base of the wall and joined the old poteen man. He said it was real good stuff. He called it "mountain dew"!

And was it a bottle I'd be taking away with me, or maybe half a bottle? It was dear these days! "They," he said mysteriously, kept putting up "their" prices. "They" found it hard to make with the young devils in blue coats coming on "them" day and night over the hills. He could, as a favour, let me have a bottle—here his eyes left the hills and rested on me keenly—for, let him see now, nine shillings.

I thanked him and said no. He went on to talk about "them." I felt that these mysterious unknown were really

"I" and "me"! I could see him in my imagination slipping off in the dead of night, or in the mist of a wet day in the hills; and again I admired his nerve, for he seemed to get nothing out of this furtive traffic.

I went on down the road, leaving a gentle old man sitting on a pile of stones smoking his pipe, while a girl with the wind in her hair ran like a setter into the turf bog holding something. A white cottage on the ledge of rock with little black, uncurtained windows seemed to be sightless, or were its blank windows searching the hills and pretending to be blind?

I went on by the lovely coast road round Bantry Bay and came to rest in a heavenly place called Glengariff. (There I developed a stunning headache which lasted until bedtime. It served me right!)

7

It is difficult to believe in London. It is possible that crowds at this moment are moving along Piccadilly, that a line of traffic halts on Ludgate Hill, that men are seriously worried about catching a train to Manchester or Bradford? In Glengariff such thoughts are grotesque. Here nothing has happened since the police barracks were burned down in the "Trouble." There is nothing else to burn down, so one can venture to say that nothing is likely to happen here again. . . .

Old Mick and I potter about on a frail little boat over the creeks and baylets as men might potter round a garden, nosing our way over still waters, round tiny islands, listening to the silence—a silence so deep that the splash of a careless oar is like a cough in church.

Small things here are enormously important. I give my

whole attention—and so does Old Mick—to the flight of gulls and to the seals which bob about in the sea round the outer islands. The gannets are interesting. They cruise high overhead, slowly, deliberately, then, having spotted a fish, they just drop through the air beak first like white darts and cleave the sea with the splash of a small calibre shell. They remain under the water for some time and reappear in an unexpected direction looking satisfied.

Mick says they often do a six-foot dive in pursuit of their prey. He combines a rare love of natural beauty with the countryman's carelessness for animal life. He wants to show me how easy it is to kill gannets. All you have to do is to place a fish on the gunwale of the boat. The gannets dive to it and break their necks; which is stupid of them. Mick cannot understand why I threaten to beat him about his venerable head with an oar if he attempts to do this!

There are guillemots, like little penguins, who sit up in the sea and wave their tiny wings; there are kittiwakes, there are sea-parrots with red beaks, oyster-catchers, and wild geese. Occasionally a blue heron lifts himself from the rushes and flaps his way slowly to a new island.

In still little bays the water is the colour of pale jade. The bed of the sea is studded with stones like jewels and shellfish of queer and attractive design.

Old Mick tells me that he has brought up a family of twelve children on potatoes, buttermilk, fish, and an occasional egg. They are healthy children, and the three in America are doing well.

"They're in the next village," says Old Mick, waggishly, nodding his head towards the Atlantic.

He has never been to Dublin. The City of Cork has seen him once or twice. London is to him a mere abstraction, as remote as Moscow. America, however, is a reality. His ragged pockets are stuffed with American newspaper cuttings sent home by the exiles. He knows all about New York.

"Aye, it's a hard life entirely," says Old Mick. "It's a very divil of a life when young children are growing, but you can't starve with the sea full of fish and the rocks covered with mussels as big as duck eggs; and you can't freeze with turf in the bog. . . . I'm thinking there's some in the cities have a harder time, and they with money in a bank. . . ."

Och, sure now, he wouldn't change places with the king of England!

We were cruising one morning near the islands which lie like ships at anchor in the bay. All round us were mountains washed in every unlikely tint of blue, from the grey blue of a Colmar grape to the deep blue of the violet. The woods marched down to the water's edge, and there was no sign of man or land on sea. This is the Riviera of Ireland!

"That's the view Mr. Bernard Shaw thinks the finest view in all the countries of the earth," said Old Mick suddenly and surprisingly.

"And who is Mr. Bernard Shaw?" I asked him.

"Och, sure, he's a nice quiet man with a beard on him. And he's written a lot of his pomes on the island there. Pomes just spring from um as he's walking round Garinish Island. . . . He comes from London, but they do say he's a Dublin man. . . ."

I tried to reconcile the restless personality of G.B.S.— the famous poet!—with the serenity of Garinish Island, which we approached over a placid sea. When we rounded the point we saw a boat-house and a steam-launch on the beach. We disembarked under the scrutiny of an ancient man like a leprechaun, who, instead of hopping away into the bushes, advanced and told us that the garden gate was open.

Garinish Island is part of the magic of Glengariff. It has no right to be there! It is an affront to one's sense of probability! Such things happen only in fairy-tales.

Here, facing the Atlantic Ocean, marooned in the wildest and most primitive portion of Southern Ireland, is a perfect Italian garden with pergolas, rock gardens, a marble pond full of gold-fish, Roman statues on marble pedestals, sombre, cone-shaped cypress-trees, and every conceivable flower and flowering shrub. It might have been blown over from the hills round Florence on the wings of some magic gale.

Old Mick told me how Mr. Bryce, the brother of the late Viscount Bryce, bought the island because his wife fell in love with it, and how together they set themselves to make a Garden of Eden from a wilderness. There is a story that every bit of earth had to be carted from the mainland, but Old Mick says that is all blarney. Mr. Bryce died, and his widow lives there alone, on Garinish Island, in a small cottage. The great house that was to be erected on the island was never built.

The island is an astonishing labour of love. When the sun falls over the marble pillars, over the wide pavements by the fish-pond, over the white stone balustrade that runs round the edge of the rock, the garden shines. It is a poem in the sea.

"What a spot for a love-story, Mick!" I said.

"Thousands it costs," said Mick. "Thousands."

CHAPTER VII

*I come through a wild gorge to the Lakes of Killarney. Here I fall
into a coma and listen to tall stories. I ride through the Gap
of Dunloe*

1

THE solitude is deathlike. There is no sound but the cries
of wild birds and the bleating of black-faced sheep. There
is no movement but the clouds which steam gently over the
crests of the mountains. The road to Killarney winds
round and up through a gorge as destitute of life as the
Valley of the Dead in Egypt.

When I turned a corner I saw approaching slowly over
the mountain path a coffin lying in a motor-car. Behind
were three cars full of women with white, tear-stained
faces. A mourner ran beside the coffin tightening the ropes
that held it in position. This funeral might have been a
vision called up by the grim spirit of the hills.

So I went on for twenty miles into a wilder solitude,
watching the cloud-shadows racing down the hill-sides,
watching the clouds dip down into the valleys to float
suspended there, watching the flight of some wild-bird as
it launched itself into space. This pass is drenched in the
uncanny mystery of all high places; over it is the watchful
hush of hills and sky. Then— Windy Gap!

Is there a greater surprise in the British Isles? With
a suddenness that takes the breath away you are faced by
one of the grandest views in Europe! There is no warning.
You emerge from the wilderness as suddenly as a man

169

leaving a dark tunnel comes into the light of day. You do not expect it! You can hardly believe it! Behind you the abomination of desolation; below you an earthly paradise —the three blue Lakes of Killarney.

I rested on a stone wall and stayed in a kind of dream, gazing down at the amazing bird's-eye view of the lakes, the blue mountains, and the green woods. It was a warm, sunny day. The lakes were the colour of the sky and as still as glass. A boat smaller than a leaf moved slowly over the water, and I could see men pulling at a salmon net.

Every graciousness and softness that nature has denied the mountains have been poured out into the rich Valley of Killarney. It is almost too good to be true; almost too opulent to be quite credible. You feel, as you look down on it, that it might at any moment dissolve into mist, leaving you in the stern reality of the hills. . . .

A man rested his horse and came over to the stone wall. He pointed out the tall crests of Macgillicuddy's Reeks; and, turning to the left, indicated the mountain of Mangerton, an extinct volcano of which the crater is a lake so deep that its water looks like black ink. The wildest storm never ruffles the Devil's Punch Bowl; the hottest summer day never varies its icy temperature. They say that it is 700 feet deep; and they believe that if a childless woman who longs for a child climbs Mangerton and drinks the icy water of this lake she will gain her wish.

"It's been proved time and again!" said the man, giving me the names of two English Peers who, said he, owe their existence to the magic of Mangerton!

I suggested that it must be a wonderful thing to live under the influence of such scenery. He turned his back on the lakes and, gazing over the wild hills, said that strange people lived in the "black valley." He told me of queer, hidden places which no man really knows, and of a shy, hostile race, different from ordinary Kerry folk, who live by poaching and mix only with their own kind.

He went his way, and I dipped down into the almost tropical luxuriance of Killarney.

In the early morning the lakes are covered with a white mist which curls over them in a thousand strange, suggestive shapes. This is the time when you can see the O'Donoghue of the Glens riding over the water on his white horse.

When the sun is strong the hills become blue and purple and mauve. You can spend days in the woods and thickets marvelling at the incredible richness of the soil. (I believe they could grow date palms in Killarney!) There is a touch of jungle vegetation about it. Tall palm-trees lift their spiky heads against the blue sky. Kerry is warmer in winter than any other part of the British Isles. In the month of February, I am told, spring is already in Killarney moving through the hedge and woodland, the gorse is in full bloom, the chestnut buds are unfolding.

In summer Killarney is a botanist's paradise. Here grow cedars of Lebanon, arbutus, wild fuchsia, the Mediterranean strawberry-tree, which is unknown elsewhere in the British Isles, the scented orchid, which grows along the Mediterranean coast and in Asia Minor, the great butterwort, which is a native of Spain, the "blue-eyed grass," which you will see only in Canada.

The boatmen and the jarveys of Killarney are expert at feeling your pulse. They have a genius for telling you what you expect them to tell you! They sum you up in ten seconds. A silent Scotsman who has been fishing at Killarney for three years assured me that he had the services of the ideal guide. He had barely spoken one word a year! (I learned afterwards that the guide is famous as the most garrulous old man in Kerry!)

"Are there any leprechauns in Killarney?" I asked a jarvey.

"Leprechauns?" he said, taking a good look at me. "Why, this is the most terrible place in all Ireland for them! You could not stir a foot in the old days for them. . . ."

Then he told me a story about a wicked land agent and a hunchback farmer. (The land agent is always the villain in Irish fairy-tales!) The leprechauns, in order to reward the hunchback farmer for refusing to level the fort in which they lived, moved his hump to the land agent!

The sun sinks behind the mountains, mists like grey veils lie in the hollow of the hills, the lake water is silver white, the chill wind of evening blows through the ruined garden, and the first star burns over the entrancing loveliness of Killarney.

2

Cracking stones on the roadside, stoking a furnace or breaking in wild horses are simple recreations compared with the savage and intolerable effort of trying to write in Killarney.

Killarney is not a holiday resort: it is an opium den. Bath, which I once considered the apex of the world's pyramid of ease and somnolence, is in comparison with Killarney wide awake.

The only desire left in the vacant mind is to drift slowly about the lakes in a boat, appalled by thoughts of the volcanic energy which produced so many blue hills and purple mountains. I am too lazy even to row. I just droop, as Ulysses might have drooped during his famous rest cure, dabbling my hands in lake water, and observing, half in admiration and half in pity, the energy of jumping trout.

Photo. F. Frith & Co., Ltd., Reigate

MIDDLE LAKE, KILLARNEY

The lakes of Killarney are a vast cradle; sleep has come for ever to the sunny hills, to the woods, and the high-banked lanes. Why has no one gone into literary hysterics about the lanes of Killarney? They are as lovely as the lakes. They are the most luscious I have ever seen; they are Warwickshire transferred to the tropics.

Flowers pile themselves on the grey stone walls; great hedges of fuchsia hang their blood-red tassels over battalions of six-foot foxgloves, trim and stalwart as grenadiers, and there are Canterbury bells by the million; snapdragons; pale, pink sheets of wild roses ashake with bees; tropic palms and flowers whose names I am too tired to remember. . . .

If England contained the kingdom of Kerry it would become a kind of Riviera, and it would, of course, be rich, but ruined. The temperature of Killarney in January is identical with that of Nice. This is due to the fact that a hundred miles from the Kerry coast the sea-bed plunges suddenly into oceanic depths, and warm currents give to this part of Ireland a semitropic winter temperature.

I have no energy to fight the beauty of Killarney. On the way here I hoped to be able to find some fault with it, because professional beauty encourages a mood of faint resentment.

The vanity of a beautiful woman is often pitiful because her beauty is such a short-lived condition, but the vanity of a landscape is eternal. Most people who know Killarney will agree that she has every right to an eternal vanity. Nature has in this place made a paradise. Windermere and Loch Lomond are almost the suburbs of cities, but Killarney is over the hills and far away, for ever lonely, for ever sunk in peace.

And I lie in a boat on the sunlit lakes watching the lines of mountains against the blue sky: Macgillicuddy's Reeks to the west, and to the south Mangerton with its Devil's Punch Bowl.

"The wather's so deep in ut," says the boatman, telling the famous Irish lake story, "that there's no end to it at all. Two young men wint up the mountain to bathe, and afther a while one of thim noticed that the other was missing. 'Now what shall I do,' sez he, 'for he's surely gone and drowned himself?' So down the mountain he runs, and a rescue party goes up with ropes, and they drag the Punch Bowl for a week, includin' Sunday. But divil a bottom can they find to it! Three weeks afther comes a postcayrd from Australia from the drowned man sayin' he'd arrived quite safe, and would they please send his clothes. That's how deep it is. . . ."

On the edge of Lough Leane rises the ivy-covered keep of Ross Castle. The boatman will tell you that in ancient times, when the O'Donoghue owned all this country, he made his exit from the world from the ramparts of Ross Castle. He dived into the lake and disappeared, entering that Land of Eternal Youth which, as everyone knows, lies beneath Killarney.

"And when the boatmen reach the age of sixty," explains the boatman with his eye on the American girls, "we push thim in the lake, and, bedad, they come back to us at the age of eighteen! Mike, here, came back last week. . . ."

"Well, now, you don't say!" laugh the American girls. "If that isn't too cute. . . ."

When the Halls visited Killarney a century ago they heard a lot of good yarns, including the story of Thady Connor's Bagpipes:

"Ye see, yer honours, Thady Connor (who was own brother of Maurice Connor, that had the wonderful tune,

by the manes of which he married the grand sea lady at
Trafraska), was the greatest piper in these parts, and
taught Mr. Grandsey a power of fine music; and the both
of them, as well as Maurice, were stone blind. Well,
Thady's pipes war ould and cracked, and had a squeak in
'em that bate the Mullinavat pig hollow; and the gentry
war mighty fond of him, and many a time said something
about the new pipes they intinded for him; but somehow
they ever and always remembered to forget, and the dick-
ens a dacent pair Thady would ever have had, but for
the grate O'Donoghue that gave them to him in the ind.
And the way of it was this: Thady, like his brother, loved
a drop—and a big one—and two drops better nor one.
And one night he spint at a wake, and wint off airly, on
account of a weddin' he had to be at, the morrow morning,
a long way off among the Reeks. So to be sure he was over-
taken wid a wakefulness, and an imprission about his heart.
'Arrah, what's this?' says he; 'sure it can't be the liquor,
and I after dhrinking no more than sixteen tumblers, to
keep myself sober!' Wid that he sits down by the roadside
and begins to play to keep himself from sleeping; and
then, all of a suddent, he hears a troop of horsemen ridin'
past him. 'A pretty set of boys ye must be,' says Thady,
'to be out at this time o' night,' says he; 'fitter for ye to be
in your dacent beds,' says he, 'than gambolling about the
country; I'll go bail ye're all drunk,' says he. Well, wid
that, up comes one of 'em, and says, 'Here's a piper, let's
have him wid us.' 'Couldn't ye say by yer lave?' says
Thady. 'Well, then, by yer lave,' says the horseman. 'And
that ye won't have, seeing I must be at Tim Mahoney's
wedding by daybrake,' says Thady, 'or I'll lose my good
seven thirteens.' So widout a word they claps him upon a
horse's back, and one of 'em lays hould of him by the scruff
of his neck, and away they rode like the March wind—aye,
or faster. After a while they stopped. 'And where am I at
all, at all?' says Thady. 'Open yer eyes and see,' says a
voice. And so he did—the dark man that never saw the

sun till that blessed night; and, millia murther! if there
wasn't troops of fine gintlemen and ladies, with swoords,
and feathers, and spurs of goold, and lashins of mate and
drink, upon tables of solid diamonds, and everything
grand that the world contained since the world was a
world. 'Ye're welcim,' says the voice, 'to the castle of the
grate O'Donoghue.' 'I often heerd talk of it,' says Thady,
nothing danted; 'and is the Prence to the fore?' 'I'm here,'
says the Prence, coming for'ards; and a fine portly man
he was, sure enough, wid a cocked hat and a coat of mail.
'And here's yer health, Mr. Connor, and the health of all
my descendants, grate and small,' says he; 'and when
they're tired of the sod, they'll know where to get the best
entertainment for man and baste,' says he, 'every one that
ever owned the name.' If Thady passed the bottle, yer
honours, 'twas the first time and the last. Well, to continue:
the dance began, and didn't Thady play for the dear life
'Jog Polthoge' and 'Planxty Moriarty' and all the jigs
that ever war invinted by man or mortial. And the gintlemen and ladies dances wid their hearts in their toes.
'Twas all very well till the ould ancient harper of the
O'Donoghues asked for a thrial agin Thady, to see
wouldn't he get louder music out of a handful o' catguts;
and Thady bate him to smithereens; when the blaguard
that was bet comes behind Thady and wid an ould knife
they called a skeen cuts the bag of his pipes and lets out
the wind that makes the music. 'I'm done now,' says Thady;
but first he hits my fine harper a rap on the head that sent
him reeling along the flure; and all the company set up a
loud ullagone that the dancing was over and Thady might
go home. 'And who'll pay for my pipes?' says Thady,
'that war as good as new,' says he—for he was a cunning
boy and wouldn't be crying down his own lawful property—'that war as good as new,' says he, 'and that aren't
worth minding,' says he. 'Fair exchange is no robbery,'
says the Prence, 'and here's a pair that'll make yer fortune; so be off as fast as ye can, for the harper is bringing

up his faction and he'll sarve you as he did yer pipes.'
Well, Thady makes a spring; and there was a wizzing in
his ears, and the waters rushed into his eyes, blinding him
agin; and he hears a voice after him that he thought was
the harper's—only it wasn't; but it was his wife Biddy,
that was waking him, and he asleep under the very hedge
where the O'Donoghue found him over night. . . . No-
body misbelieved the story he tould the neighbours, because, ye see, the bran'-new pipes were to the fore; there he
had 'em under his arm, and how ud he get 'em, if it wasn't
from the O'Donoghue himself?"

That is a pretty good example of the yarns which the
Killarney boatmen present for visitors. It is done well and
in the best tradition.

They are a peculiar type. In fifty years' time archæ-
ological societies from Dublin will travel down to study
them, to make gramophone records of their patter, and to
write papers on "Interesting Survival of the English Conception of the Native Irish," for these desperate hu-
morists, who catch salmon in the non-touring season, do
from June to September live up to a racy tradition.

I must say that it comes naturally to them. The apparent spontaneity which they bring to the telling of tales
almost as ancient as Carn Tual is a tribute to the eternal
artistry of the Celt.

3

There was once a Frenchman, I am told, who said that
Ireland was the jewel of the West, that Kerry was the
jewel of Ireland, that Killarney was the jewel of Kerry,
and that the little uninhabited Isle of Innisfallen was the
jewel of Killarney. I have nothing to add to this.

In the centre of the Lower Lake is this enchanted island.

I wandered there for two days, never meeting a living
soul, listening to the lapping of lake water and the wind in
the trees.

Half-hidden by shrubs is the grey ghost of Innisfallen
Abbey, where in the old days Brian Boru was educated.
This abbey, like the churches at Glendalough, Cormac's
Chapel on the Rock of Cashel, and the ruins on the Skellig
Rocks, goes back to the days of the saints. It is one of the
many homes of early Christianity in the West, and in it
Christ was worshipped when England lay storm-tossed in
those centuries of paganism which followed the end of the
Roman occupation.

I would like to see the shrubs uprooted from it. The ivy
should be pulled from its walls. It seems to me to demand
this as surely as Cormac's Chapel, the most magnificent
piece of architecture in Ireland and the finest example of
Romanesque work in the British Isles, demands protection
from the deadly green damp that will some day ruin it.

I know of no more perfect place than Innisfallen in
which to spend a summer day. It is a country in miniature: it has its hills and valleys, its little green pasture-
lands, its dark woods, its creeks and its bays. There is a
holy peace over it; and a man, parting the thick bushes,
comes on the old grey ruin almost fearfully, thinking as he
stands before the altar whose cloth is a green moss that if
a saint wished to show himself to men this is the place
where he might shine a moment, his sandals deep in summer flowers.

4

There are in Killarney a number of picturesque arch-
ways which lead to narrow lanes with houses on either side
of them. I took some photographs of them, one of which is
reproduced here. Most people when asked to guess what

AN ARCHWAY IN KILLARNEY

part of the world they depict have said Spain or Italy. One traveller even recognized a street in Algiers.

I think their foreign atmosphere will be generally admitted. They are singularly southern; and at night when a lamp is hung in the archway and a few lights shine in the lanes they might be anywhere but in the British Isles.

In Tipperary and in Kerry there are dancing platforms at the cross-roads. Many of them are made of concrete and must be very hard on the feet of the dancers.

There is one just outside Killarney, over the bridge towards Muckross. I went there one Sunday night, which is the great dance night, in the hope of seeing a few jigs. I found about twelve hulking youths sitting on the stone wall near the platform, but not one girl. The segregation of the sexes is a remarkable feature of the Irish countryside. The girls go about together and the boys loiter in glum groups at street corners or the end of lanes; and both seem a bit sad about it.

One of the boys had a fiddle and another had a concertina. When I spoke to them they became shy as colts. The girls, they said, were a bit late for the dance, and if they did not turn up soon they would have to give up the idea of dancing.

They kept looking up the road in search of the reluctant maidens. The fiddler sat on the wall and played a marvellous jig. He said the name was "Job of Journey Work." Still the itchy music charmed no partners to the dance. I felt sorry for the youths who were dying to step out on the concrete.

They noticed, with a brightening of the eye and a smoothing of tousled hair, a number of girls coming

slowly towards them down the lane. Here were the partners! But the girls walked right past, and the boys just
nodded and smiled at them in a sheepish way. No one suggested that they should join the dance. Then a priest
cycled past and they all took off their caps. I wondered
whether the priest's presence had stopped the dance; but
that was not likely, because I have been told that most
priests approve of cross-road dancing.

The boys cast a miserable glance in the direction of
the departing girls, the fiddler put away his instrument,
the other musician closed his concertina, and sadly the
group melted away.

There was nothing to do but lean over the bridge and
watch the trout rising.

5

For several days I have led the life of an American
tourist. I have sailed over Killarney's lakes, I have visited
beautiful Muckross Abbey, I have climbed to the Torc
Waterfall, I have watched the sunset from Aghadoe, and
I have made that most famous of all Killarney excursions,
the pony ride through the awful Gap of Dunloe.

Killarney is a friendly spot. I know few places which
extend a warmer welcome to the stranger. You have not
been there long before some radiant American girl comes
up and says to you:

"Say, we're planning to take that trip through the Gap
of Dunloe tomorrow, and we kinder wondered if you'd
care to join in on it. . . ."

Most men dash chairs out of the way and kick down
intervening tables as they leap at the idea. They are then
led to a little dried-up man in horn-rimmed spectacles.

who sits smoking a cigar in a corner with an air which
suggests that he is expiating some mysterious sin.

"This is Dad."

"Glad to know you," says Dad sadly.

In the morning a Victorian wagonette pulls up at the
hotel with a canopy over it fringed with tassels. The
beauty chorus come twittering down the steps hung about
with cameras.

"Well, I'll say this is quaint enough. . . ."

"Say, Gracie, how long is it since we took a buggy
ride?"

Sallow fathers, richly upholstered matrons, and their
magazine-cover daughters mount, the driver flicks his
whip, and two horses set off at a brisk trot, the brake
sliding on, a little square of shadow through the blinding
brilliance of Killarney's lanes. And so on for ten miles.

About seventy good-looking ponies stand crowded together in the mountain gorge. They recall that part of a
Wild West film when the sheriff rounds up the "boys"
and sets off after the villain and his gang. The ponies are
saddled, standing with their heads to a stone wall. Wagonettes and motor-cars from all the hotels in Killarney dis-
charge their passengers. Some regard the horseflesh
doubtfully; others examine Kate Karney's cottage. (Kate
is, like the Colleen Bawn, one of the vague and unconvinc-
ing deities of the district.)

The crowd which now approaches the ponies is an extraordinary assembly for a mountain pass. There are fifty
or sixty men and women, youths and maids; some can
ride; others have never sat astride a saddle; some are
heaved into position like sacks of potatoes; others leap
nimbly up and apply their heels and go off.

After an astonishing display of silk stockings and gar-

ters the beauty chorus mounts, and the line of slightly
cynical ponies plods on up the pass. It is all rather reminiscent of the morning departure from the west bank of
the Nile for the Valley of the Dead at Luxor.

But a more varied pilgrimage has never set out since
the time of Chaucer! A pony of a go-ahead disposition
jogs along, overtaking his more leisurely companions and
bringing his rider into touch for five minutes with various
characters. He will walk for a few minutes beside a pony
burdened with a Japanese professor who announces that
he is interested in Gaelic!

He will then trot a bit and anchor himself to the pony
of an American matron who confesses that her son, way
back in Ohio, has bought an airplane and that she has sent
him a week-end cable demanding an explanation; another
trot and he paces beside the steed of a young wife from
St. Louis, who says that she is pining for an infant
daughter left behind in the Middle West; another spurt
and he is in touch with the pony of a beautiful girl who
believes that she has seen England in a fortnight; and so,
via a man from Manchester who talks about Manchester,
up the line to the head of the procession, where a girl from
California, careless of her silk knees, has made her pony
canter for long and reckless intervals.

The riders have not been long in the gorge before the
bandits of Dunloe appear.

The first, who really earns his money, steps out from
behind a rock holding a cornet. The obedient ponies, who
know him well, stop immediately and look bored. He lifts
the cornet to his lips and blows a long and melancholy
toot; then, pausing, cap in hand, he waits for the echo, as
if he had created it himself. The toot comes back magni-
fied from various directions. The whole gap echoes it;
it goes rolling from valley to valley, it is tossed about

from ravines, and flung downward from the great grey cliffs.

The valley, which is as grim and terrible as the famous Pass of Glencoe in Scotland, is soon discovered to be inhabited by people who credit the cavalcade with an unquenchable thirst for milk. Little girls and ancient dames emerge from rocks and pace beside the ponies imploring men and women to drink. Some even whisper to the more dashing tourists that there is a "dhrap o' poteen" in the bottle; but this is not true. I am told that recently two innocent-looking tourists, authentically horn-rimmed, rode up the Gap, and, having tasted the "milk" offered by a certain dame, took her into custody. They were police bent on the Free State's anti-poteen crusade.

But the Japanese professor is seen to be in grave difficulties with the bandits. They surround him and shake their heads. He is, it appears, talking Gaelic with a Tokyo accent. An old lady, who announces that she is the beautiful Colleen Bawn, clutches his shilling, and, chuckling at his pedantic complaint that he is drinking neat milk, leaps nimbly over a rock with a careless laugh, and tries to sell an apple to a Wall Street broker.

She knows perfectly well that the Japanese professor is not a cavalry man, and is doomed to be carried with his indignation onward into the gloomy hills.

And the gloom of these hills casts a hush over the strung-out cavalcade. Conversation ceases. There is no sound but the sharp click of the stones under the feet of the ponies and the voices of the guides pointing out the great wall of mountains on the right, MacGillicuddy's Reeks, and the Purple Mountain on the left. Even the bandits have ceased their hold-ups, and the desolation is such that the pilgrims might be traversing the mountains of the moon.

Suddenly round the shoulder of the Purple Mountain, far off and to the left, shines a gleam of lake water, and gradually the Lakes of Killarney, blue and faint in a heat haze, gleam like the Promised Land.

This is undoubtedly one of the greatest views in the British Isles. It is certainly the finest view of the Lakes of Killarney, and I have heard it said by confirmed pedestrians that it has amply compensated for a breakfast eaten from a mantel-piece.

So the riders, strung out now like some weary steeple-chase, dip down into trees and gentle country. Here are a few "drink more milk" fanatics and women who run beside a pony for a hundred yards holding an orange, saying:

"Come now, Captain, and take an orange from me; shure it'll bring ye luck, and yourself such a grand-lookin' handsome man. . . ."

Such a snare is Irish flattery, and so deep is man's vanity, that elderly, extremely sore men with Big Business jaws sometimes pull up and buy an orange.

At the lakeside wait a number of boats with attendant boatmen ready to burst into legend during the long four-hour pull back to Ross Castle. Each boat has a big picnic basket in it. I am sure, too, that many a man has realized the full beauty of Killarney during this voyage, for it nearly always happens that some divine maiden fixes on him eyes as blue as Carn Tual on a summer evening, and, holding up a cheese sandwich, says:

"Say, now, would anyone care to trade this for cake?"

This is one of Killarney's beautiful moments. And like a voice in a dream is the brogue of the boatman telling stories of the giant's leap, O'Donoghue's Library, or the island of enchanted white mice.

Photo. by courtesy of the Office of the High Commissioner, Irish Free State

A ROAD IN THE SOUTH

6

If anyone doubts that flowers grow more luxuriantly and more swiftly in Killarney than elsewhere let him visit the great red-brick ruin of the Earl of Kenmare's house, which was burnt down before the war. This has now become one of the sights of Killarney.

This great mansion was built in the Tudor style a generation or two ago, and its size and beauties have become almost legendary. Seventeen years ago a fire started in a nursery and the place was gutted.

It is inconceivable that seventeen years could have cast such a jungle over it. It looks today as ancient as Kenilworth Castle. Its gardens, which sloped down to the lakeside and looked out over a view of water and purple mountain lovely beyond description, have been untouched since the day of the fire.

To wander in them is like walking in the gardens of the Sleeping Beauty.

You can trace here and there under masses of wild flowers and wilder shrubs the faint lines of borders, of paths, and of hedges that once were clipped and shaped like men and birds. People treat this place as if it were an ancient ruin. Those who leave their names behind them everywhere have signed a great slab of plaster which is now the visitors' book.

One man who evidently believed that the house was destroyed during the "Trouble," has written:

"A monument to the fanatics of Ireland."

A later comer has added:

"He that wrote the tripe above betrays himself a monument of ignorance."

So what might have been quite a promising fight came to nothing!

CHAPTER VIII

Describes the "Treaty Stone" and the Shannon scheme at Limerick, where men have harnessed a river. I lunch in the Eighteenth Century and go on to the grey town of Galway. Here I find a village that dates from the Norman conquest. I am shown the Claddagh and its folk. In the morning I lean over Galway Bridge and watch the salmon coming up from the sea

1

I LEFT Killarney in a mist that developed into rain along the road to Tralee. How it can rain in Ireland! With what exaggerated enthusiasm it falls in straight sheets hour after hour. I passed through drenched villages and towns that stood helpless in the downpour, the rain dripping from their roofs, splashing upward from the roads, gurgling in the gutters, blowing round corners; and there was hardly a soul to be seen but some daring person with a sack over his shoulders making a run for it from door to door. Tralee, Listowel, Athea and Rathkeale, all looked much the same, equally grey, deserted and abandoned to the rain.

Suddenly it grew thinner and ceased; and I came, by one of those unbelievable transitions not uncommon in Ireland, into an improbable place called Adare. I think Adare is the happiest looking village in Ireland. It looks cosy, comfortable, prosperous, its wide road is flanked by model houses, and there are even flowers in the gardens.

Everything about Adare spoke of some presiding genius. Someone loved the place, spent money on it and made the

best of it and enjoyed doing it. I learnt that behind the long
wall beside the tall trees against the road was the seat of the
Earls of Dunraven, and the Earls of Dunraven, I was told,
had created Adare.

I was much tempted to spend the night in the charming
hotel which bears their name, but I tore myself away from
this lucky village and splashed on in the direction of
Limerick.

Limerick is a big, sprawling city that, like Edinburgh,
re-created itself during the eighteenth century. Just as Edinburgh marched down from the rock and built that Georgian district whose backbone is Prince's Street, so Limerick
at much the same time built a rectangular district called
Newton Perry, after Mr. Saxton Perry who became Lord
Glentworth, a title now merged in that of the Earl of
Limerick. This new town of Mr. Perry's is modern Limerick; but Old Limerick still exists in English Town and
Irish Town, those inevitable and eloquent components of
Anglo-Irish civic life, which correspond to the Canongate
of Edinburgh. Those ancient districts face one another
over a narrow piece of water. English Town had the best
of it. It is built on an island and had a good castle to defend
it; Irish Town had none of these advantages although
later on in history the walls of Limerick enclosed it.

The memory of Limerick that I, and I suppose everyone,
takes away is that of a fine bridge over the Shannon which
at this point is a wide and splendid river. At one end of
this bridge rise the massive rounded towers of an ancient
castle; at the other end is one of the sights of Ireland: a big,
rough boulder now much chipped by souvenir hunters
which stands mounted on a plinth. This is the famous
"Treaty Stone."

Ireland's heroes are unknown in the wide sense of the
word to all except those of Irish blood. How many English-

men could give an account of Red Hugh O'Donnell, Sarsfield, Lord Edward Fitzgerald, Robert Emmet or Daniel O'Connell; yet where is the Englishman to whom Wallace, Bruce, John Knox, Mary Stuart, Montrose and Prince Charles Edward are not as familiar as the heroes of his own country?

Scotland has flung the veil of romance over her history. She has made her national story admired and beloved all over the world; but Ireland has been too busy making heroes to achieve that mood of detachment in which great historical romances are written. But the time will come.

Ireland's heroes are magnificent. They stand out against the sombre background of their times with the elemental splendour of all who, defying fearful odds, are willing to pay for defiance with their lives. The time cannot be far off, let us hope, when the Walter Scott whom Ireland deserves and needs will take her heroes from Sarsfield to Collins and breathing the breath of life into them, will show the world the soul of Ireland.

When a man stands at the Treaty Stone of Limerick he remembers a hero whom any nation would be proud to honour: Patrick Sarsfield.

It is the first of July 1690.

A horseman is riding to Dublin through the summer night. He makes for the house of Lord Tyrconnel, the Lord Lieutenant of Ireland. Those who see him know that the Jacobite cause is lost. He is that futile and unfortunate man, King James II. "Our good king James is an excellent and worthy man," once said the Duchess of Orleans, "but the most foolish person I have ever encountered. Piety has made him positively stupid."

This night he has much to occupy him. He is flying for his life. He tells Lady Tyrconnel how he was beaten by

his son-in-law, William III, at Boyne Water. He tells her
bitterly that his Irish army ran away:

"But," replies her ladyship, "your majesty won the
race."

The next day he rides to Kinsale where a French man-
o'-war takes him and his ruined hopes into exile.

But the struggle continues. It is really three struggles
wrapped up as one. It is the struggle of a Stuart king to
regain the throne of his fathers. It is the struggle of Britain and her Protestant allies to oppose the ascendancy in
Europe of Catholic France. It is the struggle of the Protestant Anglo-Scots and the Catholic Irish for the leader-
ship of Ireland.

The Irish forces mass on the west coast. Tyrconnel, who
was as incompetent as James, follows his master to France
and the commander of the Jacobite forces is Patrick Sarsfield. He is an Anglo-Irishman, a brooding, melancholy,
modest man, a great patriot and fearless. He had learnt
his soldiering as an officer in the English army. He decides
to put Limerick in a condition to stand a siege. He has with
him 20,000 foot and 3,500 horse.

The garrison work day and night to strengthen the walls
of the city, to mount cannon and to store munitions, and
hardly have they done so before King William and his army
arrive and seize all passages over the Shannon north of
the city. One man from the royalist army finds his way into
Limerick and seeks out Sarsfield. He is a Huguenot de-
serter. He tells Sarsfield that King William has summoned
a siege train from Dublin that is already on its way with
quantities of gunpowder, cannon and pontoons. Sarsfield
determines on the gallant and reckless venture of intercept-
ing and destroying the convoy.

That night while Limerick is snatching its uneasy sleep,
and as the sentinels watch the camp fires of the enemy, five

hundred horsemen steal out of the beleaguered city on the stroke of midnight. Patrick Sarsfield leads them and with him is a daring soldier, Galloping O'Hogan, a man who knows every inch of the countryside.

They ride cautiously through the darkness, moving to the north, taking a wide sweep to avoid the enemy outpost, and they cross the Shannon at Killaloe. They dare not be seen in daylight. In the few hours of darkness left to them they gain the glens of Keeper Hill. There they hide all that day while a few scouts are sent out to report the route of the convoy.

When night falls again the five hundred horsemen saddle and mount, taking the road to Ballyneety, only seventeen miles from Limerick, where the convoy has halted for the night. As they go through the darkness Sarsfield learns with grim enjoyment that the enemy have chosen his own name as the night's pass-word!

As they approach the camp a sentry challenges:

"Halt! Give the pass-word."

"Sarsfield!" replies Sarsfield.

"All's well. Pass on!"

The five hundred horsemen ride through the sentry-lines until in a loud voice comes the cry from the Irish commander, "Sarsfield is the word and Sarsfield is the man!" And five hundred sabres are drawn, as the horsemen charge down on the sleeping convoy. It is all over in a few moments. The pontoons are smashed. The guns are filled with gunpowder, placed muzzle down in the earth, the wagons are piled in a circle round them, a train of gunpowder is set to them and the five hundred horsemen withdraw to watch the end of Willam's siege train.

With a flash and an explosion that awakens the villages for miles arounds, and is seen even in William's camp, the convoy is blown sky-high. In a few hours Sarsfield is welcomed back within the walls of Limerick.

But, alas, all Sarsfield's adventures were not to be so easy or so fortunate. William procured another siege train from Waterford. He broke the walls of Limerick near St. John's Gate and sent ten thousand storm troops into the breach. The story of this fight is still told and sung in Ireland and it will never die. Wives and daughters joined their men-folk in the fight and beat back the enemy with anything that came to hand. Tradesmen snatched the muskets from the hands of wounded soldiers and carried on. Butchers leapt into the fight stabbing with their long knives. Sticks, stones, scythes—anything that could be used to maim or kill—were used with deadly effect and for two terrible hours the fight swayed back and forth through the streets of Limerick. In the midst of the fighting a terrible explosion shook the city. William's Brandenburghers, a crack Prussian foot regiment, had been blown up in the powder magazine which they had captured. Three times the royalist armies flung themselves on Limerick; three times they were sent reeling back from the city walls. When night fell 2,000 of William's troops lay dead or dying.

That was the first siege of Limerick. Three days later William sailed for England. But the war in Ireland still went on.

There was that heroic battle on the bridge at Athlone. The royalist troops were attempting to ford the river.

"Are there ten men here who will die with me for Ireland?" cried Sergeant Costume of Maxwell's Irish Dragoons.

Ten men led by Costume sprang from their barricade and hacked at the pontoons with axes until one by one they fell under a hail of bullets. While these gallant men were dying another hero cried for volunteers and again eleven men rushed out and hacked at the beams. Only two of these got back to their trenches.

On August 25, the second siege of Limerick opened with a terrible cannonade from the Williamite forces. Limerick was now the last city in Ireland held by the Jacobites. Sarsfield was in command with the remnants of the Irish army. The city was surrounded, but it held out all through September. On October 3 an honourable peace was agreed on and the gallant defenders of Limerick surrendered. It was on the large slab of stone at the bridge head that Patrick Sarsfield signed the famous Treaty of Limerick. The Irish were by this Treaty to enjoy full civil and religious liberty and all Irish soldiers who had fought for James were to be given a free passage to France.

Only a few days after the Truce was signed French reinforcements appeared in the Shannon: 3,000 trained troops and 10,000 arms with ammunition and provisions. But too late! General Ginkel, the head of the Williamite forces, was fearful lest Sarsfield would tear up the Treaty and resume the fight. He had nothing to fear:

"We have pledged our honour and the honour of Ireland," said Sarsfield.

With drums beating and colours flying, the Irish forces marched out of Limerick into the great meadow on the Clare bank of the Shannon. King William, who was a soldier and knew troops when he met them, was anxious to enlist as many of Sarsfield's men as possible. Proclamations offering service in the English ranks were passed from hand to hand. There were 14,000 on this sad parade. Only 1,046 joined the English forces, 2,000 decided to retire to their farms and 11,000 with Sarsfield as their leader, lined up beneath the flag of France.

They had no sooner left the shores of Ireland than the Treaty was violated. King William was perhaps no more to blame for it than he was for the Massacre of Glencoe. The English Parliament had wrested from him the chief share in the domestic government of the country. Had Ireland's fate depended on the Crown and not on the Parliament it would have gone differently, for King William was an honourable soldier. Out of this gallant Irish sacrifice came only more Penal Laws directed against Catholics and the deliberate ruin of the Irish woollen trade. . . .

Meanwhile the "Wild Geese" were flying over the world. Wherever England's enemies were to be found Irish soldiers of misfortune would be in the front rank with them. It is said that from the time of the Treaty of Limerick in 1691 to the Battle of Fontenoy in 1745 no fewer than 450,000 Irishmen died in the service of France. The Irish Brigade is the most unnatural event in the military history of the world. The Irish Catholics took their revenge for Limerick at Fontenoy; the Irish Protestants took their revenge for the wool embargo at the Battle of Bunker Hill. Peace be upon this great and splendid army which although it fell upon foreign soil and in foreign quarrels knew that it died for Ireland.

Sarsfield was killed at the moment of victory during the battle of Landen on July 20, 1693. He was struck from his horse by a musket ball. As he lay wounded he heard the orders to advance. He knew that the English were falling back. He placed his hand on his breast and withdrew it wet with his blood. He looked at it and made one of the most splendid remarks in history:

"Oh," he said sorrowfully, "that this were for Ireland!"

But it was for Ireland. Sarsfield filled a place in Irish history comparable with that of William Wallace in the history of Scotland. He was not a tribal chieftain. The clans had been crushed and their leaders driven into the hills. But a new Ireland was arming herself for the fight; and he was its first leader.

In his last cry we seem to see clearly for the first time that Ireland of the Sorrows for whom so many brave men have suffered and died. He is one of the deathless characters in the history of nationalism: a great soldier, a man cast in the unhappy heroic mould, a noble patriot and a man of honour.

No land on earth has borne a nobler son than Patrick Sarsfield.

2

Ireland might be compared to a mediæval castle which is being modernized and fitted with electricity. Half the rooms are unoccupied, and many of the turrets have not been entered for centuries, but—there must be an electric switch in each one of them! Will electricity bring the old castle to life again and fill it with paying guests?

That, briefly, is the problem of Ireland's mighty £5,-000,000 Shannon power scheme, which is now making its electricity. The most mediæval country in Europe owns the most up-to-date electrical equipment in the world. Over the land of the small farmer, whose methods are those of ancient Babylon, now flashes the power of milking cows by electricity; over the white cabin whose inhabitants have never seen a bath is the possibility of heating water by pressing a button.

Everywhere you go in Ireland you see, springing unexpectedly from rock and field, forty feet high steel standards which ring the territory of the Free State in concentric circles. From these a kind of spider's web of overhead wires will take to large cities the most remote huts in the Bog of Allen electricity made at Limerick by dynamos worked by the waters of the Shannon.

Everyone who desires to see Ireland a peaceful and prosperous nation will pray for the success of the Shannon scheme, because the future of Ireland is bound up with it. There are, of course, as usual in Ireland, two points of view. Some Irishmen say that cheap electricity broadcast over the land will in a few years make Ireland another Denmark; others say that the Irish farmer will not employ the power! Some say that an electric Ireland will develop thousands of new industries; others say that nothing will ever make Ireland an industrial nation! Some say that the power will be so cheap that no one can afford to do without it. The Shannon scheme, if it is to pay, must double the present use of electricity in the Free State.

A German engineer in a Norfolk jacket and tweed cycling knickers explained the scheme to me. The Shannon is being harnessed by German brains and Irish muscle. About 300 German engineers and foremen, and 4,000 Irish labourers, had been working on it since 1925.

As we stood above the power-station at Ardnacrusha I looked down at the most spectacular engineering sight in the British Isles. It is a terrific undertaking! A twelve-mile long artificial bed has been excavated for the mighty waters of the Shannon. Imagine what a new bed for the Thames would look like running straight from Battersea to Greenwich!

The river, flowing over this new bed, will be trained over an artificial Niagara where the flow is transformed by turbines into electric power. The water will then run through a tail-race to its old channel.

We looked down into a mighty excavation—an artificial valley in which men the size of flies swarmed over a

rocky bed or stood on ledges working, tending strange
bucket excavators and all manner of uncanny machines
which moved on caterpillar wheels. The valley was criss-
crossed by railway lines. German engines and German
trucks full of rock moved busily down there. Across the entrance was the huge concrete dam. Underneath lie the
giant turbines which will be worked when the river flowing
down the head canal empties itself into space at this point.

The ground level, too, was scarred by machinery and
railway lines. All round us cranes moved blindly against
the sky, lifting tons of earth and clay. Little locomotives,
with a blond German face in the engine cab, puffed along
loosely laid tracks, taking concrete and rock to their appointed places. Beyond, very remote, were the blue hills of
Clare.

The engineer, with the German's love of big machines,
gazed over the immediate landscape—just like a mining
camp at the height of a gold-rush—and told me, with a
wealth of statistics, how much top soil per hour the seven
caterpillar multiple bucket excavators can move, how
much earth the queer, tank-like monsters fitted with elec-
trically driven shovels can pick up, how easily the two
great transporters, each weighing 250 tons and with the
sinister name of Krupp on them, build up an embankment
by dropping earth from a height sufficient to ram it in
and then let fall on it a stream of water to tighten it. He
told me, with pride, that everything had come from Germany—30,000 tons of machinery, 40,000 tons of coal,
8,000 tons of oil, 3,000 tons of iron, 400 tons of explosives
for blasting the rock.

He gazed with pride over the amazing scene. We could
hear the throbbing of dynamos in the temporary station.
They light the Shannon Valley from Killaloe and drive all
the nightmare machines. . . .

"And what," I asked, "is Ireland to get out of this?"

"Foreign industry!" he replied instantly.

"You mean to say that there will be an invasion of foreign capital?"

"Well, why not? It will mean employment. It will reduce taxation. German factories will spring up. Belgian factories. Perhaps American factories. . . ."

"Poor Ireland!" I said. "Can she never be alone?"

He looked at me as if I were mad. (The Shannon, by the way, has often been the main route for invasions of Ireland.)

"And the Irish farmer?" I asked.

"The Irish farmer?" he repeated, shrugging his shoulders.

"How much is the power to cost?"

"It is not known."

"Irishmen tell me that the cost of the scheme will be more like ten millions than five."

"That I cannot say."

"During Armageddon, which Irish legend says is to be fought on the Curragh, one bomb on that barrage would put the Free State in darkness, wouldn't it?"

He looked at me with a faint respect.

"It would," he replied. "One bomb."

Two hutment towns have grown up near the power station; one is German Town and the other is Irish Town.

German Town is an extraordinary place. There are, of course, delicatessen stores in which you can buy liver sausage and *Sauerkraut*. Big blonde women gaze from the windows. Little boys with cropped hair, and small ringleted frauleins, return from the German school with satchels full of German grammars and German history books.

I returned to "Limerick of the Ships" impressed by the magnificent energy which has expressed itself in the valley of the Shannon, admiring the courage behind such a gigantic venture, and hoping that the new Ireland, which it prophesies, will be a happier and a more prosperous Ireland.

But will the scheme pay? Will it bring new life to Ireland? Will it stem the sad river of emigration? No man can say. I have heard Irishmen argue for and against it. It must not be forgotten that a population of eight millions has sunk to three millions. There is room in Ireland for ten times her present population, and, given the markets and the enterprise, there should be work for at least twelve millions. It may be that the Shannon scheme, developing all Ireland's potentialities, will open the way to new industries and will keep the young Irishman and Irishwoman on this side of the ocean. It will not be easy, and it will take time.

On the road to Limerick I met a man driving cows, with a pig following behind in a donkey cart. I suppose he, and thousands like him, are the first potential customers. It occurred to me that the first move of the publicity campaign will be to kill, if possible, the rather fine motto of rural Ireland: "We're well as we are!"

In English this means: "What was good enough for Dad is good enough for us, and you can go to blazes!"

3

What is the charm of Ireland?

It is the charm of a country that is still living, spiritually, in the eighteenth century. Ireland, unlike England, France, or Italy, is a country that has no real pride in machinery. Motor-cars that in any other country would have been flung on the scrap-heap still explode unwillingly over the Irish countryside. Railway engines and carriages that would have been banished ages ago by English public

opinion still roll on over the main lines of Ireland and give
to travel what Americans call an "old-world air." But what
horses you see in the fields! What possible Grand National
winners graze in every other meadow!

The poorest farmer in Kerry will find enough money to
paint his cart; but many a well-to-do garage proprietor
thinks it no shame to drive a Ford car whose mudguards
are held to the main body by string! ("Shure, the thing's
only a machine!") If a new Rolls-Royce came into an Irish
town at the same time as an old racehorse no one would stop
to admire the motor-car.

I find this mental attitude refreshing, as any man must
who comes to it out of a country which is machine-mad and
speed-mad.

We go to Christie's and we pay enormous sums of money
for chairs made by Chippendale, Hepplewhite, and Sheraton. We go to Sotheby's and pay enormous sums of money
for calf-bound books of the eighteenth century and for
sporting prints of the same period which show the hunt in
full cry, the mail-coaches racing on the Great North Road,
the bustle outside inns as the horses were changed, and all
the other scenes of that red-faced, hearty age. It is a truism
that every age sentimentalizes the age that went before.
We are at the moment becoming sentimental about the
reign of Queen Victoria; and in all this is, I believe, a kind
sadness for the good, leisurely days that are gone for ever
—the days when our forefathers, no matter what their
faults and their stuffy hypocrisies, were closer to the
eternal soil.

In Ireland this time has not passed away. In Ireland the
candles of the eighteenth century are not burnt out. It is
a country of horsemen and herdsmen. If Squire Weston,
Jorrocks, Tony Lumpkin, or Dr. Syntax came back to life,
Ireland is perhaps the only country in which they would

feel quite happy. And the wonderful thing about Ireland is that a more ancient and a more eccentric cavalier than any of these would also be at home in Ireland, because no one would be ill-mannered enough to call him mad—Don Quixote.

There is in the country of Limerick a house behind a wall. There are two lodges at each end of this wall, but you could hammer and shout until Domesday and no gate-keeper would come and let you in. The lodges are unten-anted and the window-panes—those that are not broken—have not been cleaned for many a year. But appearances in Ireland mean nothing.

The drive curves round through ancient trees conceal-ing until the last moment a long, low mansion with a pil-lared portico and a door with a fanlight over it. There are stables, with a fire-bell above them in a little belfry, and various barns and farm-buildings.

I rang the bell. Dogs of various calibre set up a frantic protest. The door was opened by a slim, horse-faced man of middle age clothed in riding breeches, leggings, and a rough coat of Kerry tweed reinforced at the wrists and on the shoulders with strips of leather. He presented a threat-ening appearance as he stood there looking at me with the cold eyes which Ireland reserves for the rate-collector. Six or seven dogs of various breeds all furiously barking at me did not make my welcome appear warmer.

"Who is it," he asked at the top of his voice, while cer-tain of the dogs rushed down the steps and cut off my re-treat. A peculiarly savage hound that even in my moment of trial reminded me of Sir Oliver Lodge, barked and snarled savagely, advancing in an unpleasant manner to gaze in a reflective manner at my calves and then retreat-ing, as if choosing a better objective.

"Whist, now will ye, Pat!" cried the man; "or must I take a whip to ye? Come off wid ye, Bell; down there, Red Maid. . . . Who is it, if ye please?"

I mentioned that I had a letter to him from a friend.

"Ye're a friend of Mike's?" he cried. "Come in, come in. . . ."

His manner changed. He smiled like a boy. His cold scrutiny changed into extravagant affability. A friend of Mike's! Fancy that! He took the letter of introduction and pushed it into the pocket of his jacket unopened. And how was the ould divil? His mare Kathleen made a bad show on the Curragh! Did I see the race? I did?

All the time we were shaking hands and walking about the hall, and I had the feeling, so common when you meet someone for the first time in Ireland, that we were bosom friends reunited after many years.

"Mary," he shouted up the stairs, "will ye come down now and meet a friend of Mike's? What's your name?" he asked in a stage whisper. "Mr. Horton's come to see us; yes, a friend of Mike's. . . ."

And in spite of frequent corrections on my part, Mr. Horton I remained to the end of my visit!

We entered a room which had not altered in one particular for over two centuries. It was my host's library, that is to say, it was the room in which he wrote his cheques, kept his pedigrees, and maintained touch with the stock breeding world. An elderly man, the image of my host, gazed down at us from a gold frame. He wore a bag wig, a snuff-brown coat, and a light-coloured waistcoat. His nose suggested that he liked a bottle of port in the evening. There was a Sheraton bookcase filled with brown books in full calf, an untidy desk with a mass of tumbled papers on it, and an oval mahogany table set for luncheon.

"Sherry or a glass of whisky?" he asked.

He poured out two enormous whiskies, added a teaspoonful of water, and we smiled at one another over the glasses and sat down. The Irish have a way when they meet anyone to whom they wish to be friendly of creating the impression that their arrival has cast the normal routine of life into the shade, that nothing on earth matters but this glorious meeting. It is an infectious attitude. The most misanthropic temperament must respond to it.

So we talked rapidly about Mike—Mike's racehorses, Mike's English wife, Mike's father and his more famous grandfather, the Government, Mr. Cosgrave, the betting-tax, the Totalisator, Michael Collins, his life, his death, his place in history, the Shannon scheme, Empire Free Trade, Irish agriculture, and the condition of the horse-breeding industry. Then more Mike.

At this moment in came my host's wife, Mary. She was one of those vivid little Irishwomen, dark-haired, blue-eyed, who always remain youthful and superbly competent to handle men. You look at them and admire their frankness, their humour, their lack of convention, their trick of talking as man to man; and behind them you seem to see a crowd of brothers all on horseback!

She swept me into the family with a gesture, and then said that it was just like Mike to send his friend on a day when the cook had gone off to visit her old mother at Clonmel and when there was nothing for lunch but a cold pie. Would we go into the garden now and pull lettuce and things for a salad? We would; and we did!

The Irish have no middle-class pretences. The English middle class, which is always flattered and praised by Press and politicians because they know that it is too "respectable," too snobbish, and too stupid to revolt against the fantastic financial burdens placed upon it, is riddled with all sorts of silly social fetishism. It would never do to call

like this on strangers in England, because if the larder
happened to be low the wife would feel humiliated. But in
Ireland there is a sound and, I think, aristocratic carelessness about such things. "Take us as we are or—go to the
devil!"

I like that enormously. Most men do.

So while Mrs. O'M—— was busy getting out the pie and
making the salad, I went with her husband over his farm,
admired his cows, and came at length to a paddock in which
a wild stampede of colts took place. They went galloping
off, their manes and long tails flying in the wind. In the
next field we found the usual potential Grand National
winner.

I asked him how he fared during the Rebellion and the
Civil War. During the Rebellion he was serving with the
British armies in France. After the War he returned to his
estate. I could not discover whether he was in sympathy
with the Rebellion or not; but I think from things he said
about the treatment of the enormous Irish army in France
—"Here come the Shinners!" and so forth—that a mind
that had been quite content to accept the old social and
political system now welcomed the new. He was that rare
thing in a country house: an Irishman of the old blood. His
neighbour—Lord X—— whose lands marched side by side
with his on the south, had been driven from the country. He
was one of those unfortunate Anglo-Irishmen occupying an
estate granted to him in the time of Cromwell. He replaced
an old Irish family that had been driven "to Hell or Connaught," and the people never forgave him for it. He was,
like all his class, regarded as an Englishman when in Ireland and as an Irishman when in England. They burnt him
out.

But my friend passed through the Civil War without any
trouble. Sometimes, he said, the Free State troops would

come and billet themselves on him; at other times it was the Republicans. They were both very civil, and apart from the blowing up of local bridges, which had inconvenienced him a bit, the birth pangs of Ireland had not affected him.

"Come along!" cried Mrs. O'M—— from a window; and in we went.

It is really marvellous how in Ireland the fretful centuries slip off and you discover yourself like a dreamer in another age. This meal was like every meal that had taken place in that room for two hundred years. We were back in the candle-light of George II. If my host had suddenly turned to me to ask what I thought of Prince Charles Edward's rebellion in Scotland I would not have been very surprised; such a question would have been in keeping with the house, the room, the meal, and the general tone in which our talk was pitched. It would have been merely like an echo of the old house: some ancient whisper coming from a dark corner.

The dogs pushed their damp noses into our hands, and now and then my host would give them a bone. They would creep off with it and soon in every corner of the room was a dog gnawing and pausing only to gaze up at his master with respect and adoration.

The talk rattled on as Irish talk does, leaping and jumping about like a leprechaun on a hill.

My friend was indignant at the treatment meted out to many of the Anglo-Irish land-owning families during "the change." He said that the innocent had suffered with the guilty. Many a good man whose heart was in the country had gone down with that curse of Ireland—the absentee landlord. But you cannot have a revolution without injustice somewhere. I realized for the first time how bitter must have been the Revolution for the man Irish born, educated in England, full of English prejudices, yet full also of Irish loyalties, who found suddenly, over-night, as it were, that the son of one of his tenants was holding a pistol to his head. Would the remaining Anglo-Irish left in the country ever form an aristocracy again? I asked him.

He thought not.

"Ireland today," he said, "is a country without an aristocracy. A new aristocracy may form in time. General So-and-So, the son of a shopkeeper, will join a hunt and ride to hounds, and the country may look the same some day with different people in the saddle. Whatever happens let us keep hunting going. . . ."

And although I had come to lunch it was dusk when at last I tore myself away.

"What's the hurry? Stay the night," said Mrs. O'M——.

I looked back at the walled house. That wall protected a few acres of the eighteenth century.

4

I came over the mountains of Clare into the grey town of Galway as men were lighting lamps in the harbour. An unearthly afterglow lingered in the sky, a dull red haze hung over the hills like the dust flung from chariot wheels, and the edges of the Atlantic were washed in a colour so strange and so vivid, almost a pale green, that melted marvellously into the blue of the dusk. And as the light was drawn out of the sky a few stars hung over the grape-blue heights of Connemara.

Such a velvet softness pervaded Galway, and in those first moments I felt, as one feels sometimes on meeting a stranger, that a new loyalty had come into life. Galway did not seem to belong to any part of Ireland that I had seen; it seemed to belong only to itself.

I know now that the strange beauty that flies like dust through Galway to the spirit of Gaelic Ireland, something that is a defiance to time, something that is like a declaration of faith. Galway must be almost too beautiful to an Irishman. He must feel about it as an Englishman would feel if, in an England conquered for centuries, and speaking a foreign tongue, he came one night to a little town in Somerset and heard men talking English.

When the hotel porter was unloading my luggage he drove away a determined old woman shrouded in a black shawl who was trying to tell me something. I went after her and asked her what she wanted. Her husband was out of work and her sons were out of work. She was a gentle old creature, and when I placed a shilling in her hand she said:

"May the Virgin bless you and bring you safe home."

I encountered her twice during my first walk round Galway, and each time she repeated her blessing with a gratitude out of all proportion to the miserable gift, so that I felt that my first steps in the west were taken in sanctity. . . .

I went through many a narrow street, past a ruined Spanish house, for Galway reflects Spain in the eyes of its people, and, here and there, in a square house with a central courtyard and a gate flush with the street. The drapers' shops of Galway introduce you to the gorgeous colour of the west. Outside are stacked piles of scarlet flannel, which the fisherwomen—though the fashion is dying—make in to wide, brilliant skirts.

But what a town of yesterday! The curse of Cromwell lies heavier on Galway than on any other Irish town. It is a town of dead factories and great houses brought to decay. In the Middle Ages Galway was the Bristol of Ireland. Its very name has the ring of a great city in it—London, York,

Bristol, Dublin, Galway; there is something high and authoritative about such names.

The fourteen Anglo-Norman families of Galway, who gained for their town the title of "Galway of the Tribes," were the most exclusive families in Ireland. I believe that they intermarried for so long that special dispensation had more than once to be obtained to establish canonical legality. They founded the fortunes of the town. The quays were stacked with the wine casks of Spain. The galleons of Galway were as accustomed to the ports of Spain as they were to Irish waters. During the Civil War, Galway remained loyal to Charles, but Cromwell had his way with it in the end, and Galway has never recovered.

Its inhabitants a hundred years ago numbered 40,000: today the population of this once mighty seaport is reduced to that of a small English country town. Only 14,000 people live here among the ruins of past endeavour.

I met an Irishman in the hotel who told me this story: "During the war a German submarine appeared in the bay and the captain gave orders to bombard Galway. A young officer who was making a reconnaissance sent down the message: 'Galway *has* been bombarded, sir.' "

My friend thought this was a screamingly funny story; but I could not laugh at it.

I was lucky enough to meet a little pink-faced, middle-aged Irishman known to everyone as Michael John. If you have ever fished in Galway you will know him well!

We went round the town together, to the Church of St. Nicholas, patron saint of children, sailors (and thieves!), where a bell hangs taken (no one knows how or why) from an abbey in France; we went to gaze at an old Spanish house in which the term "lynching" and "lynch law" originated; and Michael John told me the grim story.

In 1493 John Lynch FitzStephen, Mayor of Galway,

went over to Spain to improve trade relations between that country and Galway. He was entertained by a rich merchant name Gomez, whose son, a handsome young Spaniard, returned to Ireland as his guest. Lynch had a son named Walter, and the two young men became friends. Walter Lynch was in love with a girl named Agnes, whose father, a merchant of Galway, spoke Spanish perfectly, and was delighted to welcome the young Spaniard to his house. Walter Lynch became madly jealous, and one day, in the height of his passion, he stabbed the Spaniard and threw his body in the sea.

Walter Lynch was arrested and confessed his guilt. His father, as mayor, pronounced the death sentence. But no man in Galway would execute the boy! The mob attempted a rescue, but before this could be made, and in sight of the crowds, Lynch hanged his own son.

"I suppose he felt he had to do it," said Michael John, "for the honour of Galway. His son had not only committed murder, he had violated the laws of hospitality. After the hanging Lynch went to his home, and was never seen again by living man. . . ."

It is by the strangest perversion of meaning that "Lynch law" means today the vengeance by a mob on a criminal.

We went to the salmon weir on Galway River, which Michael John knows as a man knows his own land.

"A little later in the year," he said, "this is the most surprising sight in Ireland. You can look down from the bridge and see great salmon, thirty and forty pounders, packed as tight as sardines in a tin! You wouldn't believe it unless you saw it! Back to back they are, waiting like a great crowd at a ticket office to get up to the lakes from the sea. . . ."

This narrow river is the only entrance from the sea to 1,200 miles of lakes.

I suppose the river by Galway Weir is the anglers' paradise. They tell a story of a fisherman who died from excitement here, but they do not end the story with the funniest part of it. The local paper after reporting the event said: "Our readers will be glad to learn that the rod which Mr. —— dropped was immediately taken up by our esteemed townsman, Mr. ——, who found the fish still on, and after ten minutes' play succeeded in landing it—a fine, clean-run salmon of fifteen pounds."

That, I am sure, is the perfect epitaph!

We went over the dangerous wooden weir above the rushing water, and were just in time to see a man with a boat-hook murder an amazing salmon which turned the scale at forty-two pounds! He was as big as a shark and thick. Two nets are out for salmon, but a clear passage must be left by law. A fish gets caught by sheer bad luck or natural foolishness. Every week-end the nets are lifted, also by law, so that a sensible salmon should come up from the sea on a Sunday.

"What do you do with salmon?" I said to the man who was weighing the monster.

"London," he replied briefly.

5

The Claddagh at Galway is one of the most remarkable sights in Europe. I find it almost inconceivable to realize that a man can breakfast in London and lunch the next day within sight of this Gaelic village.

Nothing is more picturesque in the British Isles than this astonishing fishing village of neat, whitewashed, thatched cottages planted at haphazard angles with no regular roads running to them. If you took three hundred little toy cottages and jumbled them up on a nursery floor you would have something like the Claddagh. It is a triumph of unconscious beauty. The houses have been planted at all kinds of odd angles, one man's back door opening on to the front door of his neighbour.

"How on earth did this happen?"

"When Galway was the City of the Tribes," said Michael John, "the native Irish had to live outside the walls. They formed this little town. They were as proud as the Tribes."

Outside every Anglo-Norman town there grew up one of these "Irish towns." The Claddagh is the only one that survives. Michael John can remember the last "king" of the Claddagh; for this community has for centuries observed an unwritten law, administered, until recently, by a chief, a fisherman like the rest, whose verdicts were never questioned.

When the Halls wrote their book on Ireland nearly a century ago the king was still a power in the Claddagh:

"This singular community are still governed by a king elected annually, and a number of by-laws of their own; at one time this king was absolute—as powerful as a veritable despot; but his power yielded, like all despotic powers, to the times, and now he is, as one of his subjects informed us, 'nothing more than the Lord Mayor of Dublin or any other city.' He has still, however, much influence, and sacrifices himself, literally without fee or reward, for 'the good of the people'; he is constantly occupied hearing and deciding causes and quarrels, for his people never by any chance appeal to a higher tribunal. Even when a Galway person offends, who is not a Claddagh man, he is punished by their law; for instance, a gentleman complained of the price of a cod he had bought from one of the singular community; it was in his estimation too dear by 'a tester,' and he refused to pay at all; he told the fisherman to summon him, which would have been contrary to Claddagh law, and so was not done; he thought he had conquered. Requiring

THE CLADDAGH, GALWAY

Photo. by courtesy of Independent Newspapers, Ltd., Dublin

some fish for a dinner-party a day or two after, he went to
order some of another fisherman in a different part of the
Claddagh. 'No, sir,' was the reply. 'I can't serve you
until you have paid So and So for the cod.' 'And what is
that to you?' was the inquiry. 'I will pay *you*.' 'Not until
you have paid him. We Claddagh men stand by each
other.' "

The Halls then go on to describe a visit paid by them to
the king's cabin:

"His majesty, however, was at sea; but we were introduced to his royal family—a group of children and grandchildren who for ruddy health might have been coveted by
any monarch in Christendom."

Mr. Stephen Gwynn has some interesting things to say
about the Claddagh folk in *A Holiday in Connemara*, now
out of print, which was published in 1909. He was once a
Parliamentary candidate in this district:

"My own opinion is," he writes, "that we have here the
descendants not of Spain but of that older Irish race who
built the great dun of Aran—the Firbolgs, 'men of the
leathern wallet,' whom the taller, stronger Milesian breed
drove back into the outlying mountains and islands. When
one sees fair hair in this community it is such as one finds—
in the south. . . .

"Election times show up curiously the separateness of
this community. The borough area of Galway comprises
two outlying parishes, with a crowded population of small
labouring farmers—Irish speakers to a man. These people
come in cheerfully to support the Nationalist party with
voice and vote (and not with voice and vote only) because
they are part of Ireland and the issues which interest Ire-

land generally interest them also. But to the Claddagh man you can only talk about the Claddagh; Ireland has no appeal to him. The land question does not touch him, for he has no land; the revival of fisheries along the coast has done him no good, for he was catching fish before, and had his own sufficient market. . . .

"Of one thing I am convinced—that to argue with the Claddagh you must speak in Irish. I went down there to make acquaintance with the men at a time when I was not looking for votes, and was directed to get into talk with an oldish fisherman who stood apart from the rather voluble group surrounding me. He would not answer a word until I tried him in Irish, and then he discoursed freely and fairly. We fell into talk of technical matters relating to boats, and soon I was out of my depth, and told him so; whereupon he continued in excellent English. When he had finished, 'Why would you not speak English to me at first?' I asked. 'Ah,' he said, relapsing into Irish, 'if we talked English you would be a wiser man than I; in Irish it is not that way the story is.' "

Mr. Gwynn goes on to give a fascinating glimpse of the Claddagh. I would give anything to have been with him at this time:

"A few days later," he writes, "I had to go through the whole village, house by house, and it was odd enough at three or four in the afternoon to find strong young men rising up between the blankets in a corner of the dark little house. That, of course, is natural in any fishing community, whose work is mostly done by night. But a thing struck me which I have never seen elsewhere in Ireland, where generally men have a prejudice against handling babies or doing anything else that is taken to be women's work. But here, in at least a dozen houses, I found the woman bustling about while the man stood or sat with an infant on his arm—and holding it as a woman does, the arm making the same soft line where it supported the infant as a hammock holds a sleeper. It was curious to see, and very pretty—natural enough, too, when one considered; for the women must be out most of the day hawking their fish at the street corners. Yet more than anything it stamped on my mind that feeling of distinctness and aloofness in the Claddagh and its people. I have never found any other community in Ireland so alien, so shy, and so hard to know."

I walked through the Claddagh late one afternoon. The fishers were out, for I saw only very old men standing at the corners smoking their pipes. There was one who might have stepped from a Spanish galleon. There was nothing of the Firbolg about him; he was pure Spanish: tall, thin, sallow, long headed, with fierce dark eyes, a pointed beard, and in either ear a thin gold ring.

It is a pity that the Claddagh has attracted the attention of sanitary authorities. Many of the lovely white houses have been pulled down and in their place have come the most hideous little modern houses I have seen—worse and more hateful to the eye even than the atrocious bungalows of Sussex.

I saw a sight typical of the modern Claddagh. From a primitive thatched house came a smart young girl in a fashionable felt hat, blue tailor-made costume, and flesh-coloured silk stockings. Her mother accompanied her to the door. The older woman belonged to a different generation—almost, so it seemed, to a different world. She wore the wide red skirt of a fisherwoman; her feet were bare, and with one hand she held a grey shawl over her shoulders.

"That's it, you see," said Michael John. "The girls change from their working clothes and put on their finery to go out at night. Some of the smartest girls you'll see in Galway go home to a Claddagh cabin. . . ."

There came towards us a girl who walked like a queen— in men's boots! She bore on her head the big round wickerwork basket in which the Galway women sell fish. She was a beauty of the dark kind. She was going home to put on stockings, high-heeled shoes, and a tight little black felt hat! I was, I felt, somehow unfortunate that after resisting the world for so long the Claddagh should have capitulated to Mr. Selfridge.

"In the old days the Claddagh never married outside itself," said Michael John. "But now that's over. A Claddagh girl will marry a Galway boy."

6

At night the Claddagh is most beautiful. There are no street lamps. You find your way through the maze of houses by the light that falls through windows and open doors. The path of earth has been beaten hard by the feet of generations going back to the Norman conquest of Ireland. The limewashed houses with the peat reek coming from their chimneys shine in the half light. The children who in daylight play on the squares of beaten earth and before the cabin doors have been put to bed. It is quiet and watchful and full of the chirping of crickets. Figures of men stand in little groups in the dusk talking in the Gaelic. Sometimes they pause and cry out softly:

"Goot night."

Lights shine in the small windows. Through open doors you see little rooms with low ceilings. They are warm, clean, and comfortable; but so small. You wonder how certain of these long-limbed Gaels can live in them and move about. It seems strange that the Gael, who hates the feeling of walls, has not developed a more roomy domestic architecture. It is odd, here and also in the Highlands of Scotland, to see giants with their heads bent in case they might hit the ceiling. Perhaps the Gael has never bothered to build himself real rooms, because he would be just as miserable within big walls as small ones.

Beyond every little open door you see, sharp as an interior by Peter de Hooch, a woman bent above some task, sometimes with the fine colour of scarlet on her; now and again an infant cries and a woman's tender voice soothes it, singing an Irish lullaby like little waves falling on a shore; and in those rooms, warm with the peat fires and loud with crickets piping in the ashes, a red light is burning before the Sacred Heart.

7

The parapet of Galway bridge is worn smooth as glass by the arms of those who lean over it when the salmon come up from salt water. This is one of the sights of Ireland.

At first when I looked down into Galway River I could see nothing. Then something which I took to be weed moved strangely; and I realized that I was looking down on the backs of hundreds of salmon. I have never seen anything like this great crowd of fresh-run fish with the sea-lice still on them lying still, fanning themselves with their noses towards the sweet lakes. Could I have dropped a brick into the river I must have hit at least ten eighteen-pounders; for they lay side by side, apparently touching, edged together in one incredible queue.

Now and then some monster would seem to become impatient, and he would, with a muscular movement, urge himself forward; but so tight were his companions pressed about him that he would make no progress and be forced to fall back into his place.

There were three earnest salmon fishermen on the bank below me. I watched them casting for at least an hour and —not a rise did they get! One man constantly hit the water immediately above at least thirty mighty fish, but not one of them took the slightest interest in the fly!

Yet men must catch fish in this place or they would not pay two pounds a day for it, and on the condition that they keep only one in three.

Stephen Gwynn, a great fisherman, has said that one man killed a ton of salmon in about three months' fishing. So thick are the salmon in Galway River that I find it difficult to understand how it is that if you do not hook a fish in the orthodox manner you do not hook him in a fin or in his tail!

In the early morning you will lean over the bridge and see that the salmon have moved up in the night. There are only two or perhaps three left. One morning I saw for the first time that fish which killed an English king—the lamprey. He was a curious fellow, half fish and half eel, lying low down against the stones of the river-bed and swaying with the stream.

CHAPTER IX

Tells how the world ends on the stone walls of Connemara. I go into a bare land of beauty, hear the music of the Gaelic and talk with a barelegged girl on the edge of the Atlantic

1

I KNOW now where the world ends.

It is a grey land, and the gold clouds ride up over the edge of it, shouldering one another, slow as a herd of steers. The land is as grey and speckled as a piece of home-spun tweed. It is grey with hundreds and thousands of little stone walls. They run up to the edge of the sky, and they fall into dips and hollows, criss-crossing like the lines of your hand. These grey walls guard the smallest "fields" in the world. They are not real fields: they are just bits of rocks sprinkled with soil. Some of them are no larger than a dining-table, some of them are oblong, some square, some almost circular, some triangular; and to everyone is its own little breast-high wall, so that the land, silver-grey wherever you look, is, as I say, just like a big piece of the tweed that they weave in the hills.

The white road twists like a snake between the grey walls, and over it walk strong, barelegged girls, wearing scarlet skirts and Titian-blue aprons. They swing from the hips as they walk with the grace of those who have never known shoe leather, and they carry on their backs great loads of brown seaweed in wicker baskets. Or they ride, sitting sideways with their bare legs to the road, above the tails of placid donkeys, over whose backs are slung baskets piled with peat.

217

If you speak to them they shake their tangled heads, and say something, which sounds pretty, in Irish. They are shy as fawns with a stranger; but when you have gone on they burst into peals of laughter. . . .

Behind the grey land, moving round in a solemn dance as you go over the twisting road, are blue hills—hills blue as the sea at Capri—with the biggest and the most golden clouds on earth like haloes over their heads. Among the blue hills and the grey fields, and beside the blue waters of little loughs and on the edges of sudden peat bogs, stand small cabins, incredibly poor and marvellously white, with hens round the door pecking round fat black pots.

And the sound of this land is the click of a donkey's hoofs on the road and the ring of a spade like a crowbar which men drive into the rocky soil. When the sun goes out this place is as grey as a ghost.

Connemara. . . .

How can it exist in the modern world! In years of travel I have seen nothing like it. It begins suddenly as soon as you leave Galway due west by the coast road through Spiddal to Clifden. It is a part of the earth in which Progress—whatever we mean by it—has broken in vain against grey walls; it has been arrested by high hills and deep lakes to the east and by the sea on the west. These people have been locked away for centuries by geography and poverty. I have been into the tomb of Tutankhamen in Egypt, but entering Connemara gave me a finer feeling of discovery and a greater sense of remoteness from modern life!

They are so poor that no one has ever tried to exploit them; their land is so poor that no one has ever tried to steal it. There are no railways, no shops, no motor-cars,

CINDERELLA IN CONNEMARA

no telegraph poles. There are three things only: the Catholic Faith, Nature, and work.

Connemara could not be more astonishing than the discovery in England of a forgotten country in which men spoke the language of Bede or Alfred the Great, wore Saxon clothes, and prayed to Saxon saints. Connemara is the most surprising thing in the British Isles. It is nearer to St. Patrick than it is to Dublin.

As I went on in a kind of stunned astonishment I realized that I was an impertinence. Connemara is not used to motor-cars! Cows lowered their heads before me, backed away with glazed eyes and distended nostrils, exposed a flank to an imaginary death, and retreated up the road with every sign of terror. Dogs ran barking furiously after me. Girls riding donkeys leapt off with a flash of bare legs and a flurry of scarlet skirts and held the noses of their steeds away from me; long-haired sheep fought madly together for the gap in the stone wall; geese lengthened their necks towards me like serpents and made vague oathful noises as I went by; hens, who all the world over are an excitable, suicidal people, flung themselves into an ecstasy of panic and performed mysteries of self-preservation beneath my careful wheels.

In fact, the whole Gaelic countryside said, in a variety of mooings, bleatings, brayings, gabblings, yelpings, and cluckings: "Look out! Here is something quite horrible and deadly from the outside world!"

Near the coast I saw, drawn up outside cabins or leaning against grey walls, the queer canoes, called curraghs, in which the fishermen of Connemara dare the perils of the ocean; and dare must be the right and only word! They are light as feathers, and made of skins or canvas stretched over a wooden frame. They are exactly the same as the coracles used by the Ancient Britons in the time of Cæsar.

I stopped before one cabin and asked if I might examine the curragh drawn up near their manure heap. A young girl and an old woman were inside, both wearing those beautiful scarlet skirts, the girl washing potatoes and the woman tending a black pot which hung above a turf fire burning in an open hearth. The cabin was bare except for a chair and table and a wooden bench standing on the hard earth floor. On the wall hung two bright pictures of the Holy Family.

"Can I look at your boat?" I asked with a broad grin. There is no country in which a broad grin is more useful!

"You can," said the girl.

The old woman, who was deaf, asked the girl in Irish what I wanted; she replied in Irish, then the old woman smiled and nodded.

While I was examining the flimsy boat a sturdy young man lounged over to me. There was nothing of a peasant's boorishness about him. He smiled, said the boat was not much good now because it was old. He employed it to get seaweed to manure the potato patch. From the pocket of his homespun sleeved jacket peeped a copy of a New York morning paper! Somehow that brought me to earth! It was rather like meeting Brian Boru with a cigar in his mouth!

His three brothers, he said, were in America! He would like to go too, but he was the eldest son and had to look after the "land." I looked towards the "land," and my heart sank for this firstborn. New York must be a great place, he said. It was, I felt, nearer to him than Galway.

A few miles farther on I saw a man making a "field"! The mystery of the stone walls was solved! They are not so much a sign of ownership as a necessary preliminary to a "field." The whole of Connemara in ancient times must have been subjected to a fall of stones the size of a man's head. A "field" is made by gathering up these stones and making a wall of them round the rock from which they have been removed! (Do any people on earth scratch a living from more villainous soil?)

While I watched him a big, dark girl sprang over a stone wall and walked over the sharp rocks in her bare feet with a basket of earth on her back. This she poured on the cleared rock, laughed a moment with the man, and, taking up her basket, leapt over the wall again like a deer.

I went on down the road. Grey walls; white cabins; little chapels, so small, many of them, that when the people tramp in for miles on Sunday morning the priests celebrate Mass in the open. But always grey walls and little poor fields spread with seaweed. I saw a lovely thing on a hill. Children poured out of a small corrugated iron school. The hill rang with laughter. They danced round in a circle, their little bare legs flashing in the sunlight, and in the centre of them, wind-blown, tall, slim, was a young girl, the teacher.

So I came at length to a kind of hotel; and in it was a fisherman from the city. He knew Connemara.

"Happy?" he said. "I wish I was as happy as these people. They are, of course, always discontented, their land is bad, they are poor, the young people have their minds on America—the real capital of Connemara is New York—but they do not know real unhappiness! They are outside the world!"

"How do they live?"

"Hundreds of the white cabins you see are kept on dollars. The sons and daughters in America send home money every week, or when they can. You notice how good-looking the people are. There is nothing mean about them.

They are real men and women. They are the real Irish.
They have been driven into this wild land, some say by
Cromwell, but that's all nonsense! It must have begun
centuries ago, before the Normans came, perhaps. They
are the real Milesians. You could not evolve a type like
that in a few generations. They are as old as the hills; and
as strong. . . ."

I watched the sun sink into the sea at evening, and I
saw night fall over the grey land at the world's end. And
I knew then the strangeness that blows through the town
of Galway like dust.

That town is half in the world and half out of it. It is a
frontier post, and the winds from the end of the world blow
into it day and night.

2

"There is no 'land' in Connemara," wrote Patrick
Kelly in *The Dublin Magazine* of March 1925. "Mountains there are, and beautiful lakes, and swiftly flowing
streams, and deep, narrow creeping streams and swamps
and stones, and little patches of more or less sheltered
ground where the meagre crops are grown—but there is
no 'land'; that is to say, Connemara—or at least the
greater part of Connemara—has no farms. And it follows
from this that all the theory of all the theorists concern-
ing agriculture and so-called 'Improved methods of culti-
vation' might as well be preached to the Man in the Moon
as to the inhabitants of Connemara. Why, the poor tiller in
that great lone country, working on tradition, is able to
get a better return from his miserable nine or ten acres of
indescribable soil than would the best Professsor of Agriculture in Europe, were he to condescend, spade in hand,

to try his luck and test his skill beyond the hills of Maam. . . .

" 'Under what possible conditions will the people of Ireland in Connemara be thoroughly satisfied?' a fly-fishing tourist once asked. He was what is called a 'practical man' and 'practical men' have never accomplished anything worthy of note in the world. However, the question is a good one and very easily answered.

"The people of Connemara will be thoroughly satisfied when the climate of Ireland accepts responsibility as its guiding principle, when America is the America of the Irishman's dream, when immigration, so far as Ireland is concerned, is no longer restricted by the authorities at Washington, and when poteen is manufactured from barley and rye (three parts barley and one part rye) and not from chemicals, as it is.

"Connemara is over populated, and that's the truth, sad or otherwise. It has been said that an attempt will be made by the Government to remove some of the people to the rich lands of Leinster. The people of Connemara will not leave their beloved home, with all its strange charms and strong traditions, for Leinster, or any other part of Ireland, if they can possibly help it. Either Connemara or America. There is no third place within the range of their vision.

"It has been said by ardent admirers of the people of Connemara that they have no faults. This is wrong: they have more than one fault. They are inclined to depend too much upon the supposed omnipotence of the Government. They might of themselves, and at very small cost, improve their homes and make them more comfortable. They might with profit pay a little more attention to drainage. They might, also with profit, study the great virtue of that

simple combination called soap-and-water. They might
show a little more love for the poetry of flowers. . . . But
what can you expect? The young have their eyes fixed on
America and the old upon heaven.

"America! In that single word lies the solution of the
dislike now openly expressed in Connemara of the Irish
language, or, rather, of the teaching of Irish in the schools.
They say—and who can answer them to their satisfaction?
'Why are our children taught so much Irish at school?—
what wonder if I *was* Irish! It is English they want. They
must go to America to earn their living, and English is of
use to them in America and Irish is not.' And then with a
shake of the head they will tell you the story of the girl
who was sent back from the office of the American Consul
in Dublin because she failed the English test. She returned
to Connemara in tears. America, the land of her waking
dreams, and perhaps of the dreams of her sleep, was lost to
her for ever. . . ."

A true and tragic thing is said in this same article:

"Connemara is a strange country, a country of contra-
dictions. Its nominal capital is Clifden, but its real capital
is Boston in the United States of America."

3

I am walking along a road in Connemara. It is a narrow white road that runs between sloping fields cut across
by breast-high boundary walls. A thin rain ceases and the
sun shines. Now and then to my left I get a glimpse of the
sea coming into a creek that is edged with saffron-coloured
weed, but as I go on the shoulders of the hills cut off this
view and I am again surrounded by small hills, by sudden

miniature bogs where stacks of peat are drying; and over the crests of these hills and on their inhospitable flanks are set small limewashed cabins, rudely thatched and surrounded by a queer assembly of things: an old barrel at the door; felled tree trunks, a stack of turf, an odd little hayrick bound by rope and propped up by poles. A fishing-net is nailed to dry against the side of a cabin. Sometimes a hen, making busy ruminating noises, will walk out of a cabin and stand a moment in the sunlight on the threshold, looking round with one foot lifted rather like a man-about-town putting on his gloves on the steps of his club.

In the centre of the "field" a piece of ground higher than the rest has never been levelled. A thorn bush grows on its summit. The farmer who owns this useless and heart-breaking land has cultivated all round the tiny hill, leaving the hillock to sprout weeds and thorns. The reason why he has done this is simple and well known. The high ground is a fort or rath. The people say that such forts were built by the Danes. Some people think that this word is a corrupted form of De Danann, the mysterious people called Tuatha de Danann—"the tribes of the Goddess Danu." They are said to have conquered Ireland by virtue of great magic. But the druids of the people of Mil were too strong for them; and magic meeting magic, Tuatha de Danann were forced to fly and take refuge in the fairy mounds.

Every countryman in the west of Ireland knows that these places are haunted. It is on record that a labourer gave up the land which he had secured under the Labourers Act and upon which a well-disposed district council was willing to build him a house because, as he wrote to the council, "on no account would he interfere with the fairies' home."

That is why in the west you see so many raths with their trees waving above them, the standards of an invisible world; and all round the meagre crops are growing but never intruding on the territory that belongs to fairy-land.

"What are the fairies?" Padraic Colum asked a blind man whom he met on a west of Ireland road.

His face filled with an intensity of conviction.

"The fairies," he said. "I will tell you who the fairies are. God moved from His seat, and when He turned round Lucifer was in it. Then Hell was made in a minute. God moved His hand and swept away thousands of angels. And it was in His mind to sweep away thousands more. 'O God Almighty, stop!' said Angel Gabriel. 'Heaven will be swept clean out.' 'I'll stop,' said God Almighty; 'them that are in Heaven, let them remain in Heaven; them that are in Hell, let them remain in Hell; and them that are between Heaven and Hell, let them remain in the air. And the Angels that remained between Heaven and Hell are the Fairies.' "

What he said was as true to the man as one of the Gospels.

Saxon fairies are naughty children like Puck, who loved to turn the milk sour and knock fat women from their milking stools. In Scotland the fairies are sinister and terrible. I have talked to men who have seen Highland fairies. I know a young man who drives the village hearse in a loch-side village in the far north. He sees fairies and "ghost lights" before anyone dies, and, being a practical youth, he at once cleans up the hearse! But these Scottish fairies are mostly terrible. A Scotsman would kill a fairy as he would kill a stoat.

MARKET DAY IN CONNEMARA

Mr. Yeats has commented on this. He attributes it to the stern theological character of the Scot, which has made "even the devil religious." But in Ireland the people have settled down in kindly tolerance side by side with their old gods, which is, of course, what all fairies are.

"Our Irish fairy terrors have about them something of makebelieve," writes W. B. Yeats. "When a peasant strays into an enchanted hovel, and is made to turn a corpse all night on a spit before the fire, we do not feel anxious; we know he will wake in the midst of a green field, the dew on his old coat."

This graciousness to fairies is, I think, all part of the aristocratic hospitality of Ireland. Only mean and low-born people are ungracious to a guest. In the old days when heroes walked the world disguised as common men— just as Ulysses came home from his wanderings—you never knew for whom you poured wine or broke bread. Your common harper might rise up and, casting off his rags, become a god.

And on the roads of Connemara I feel as though I am in Ancient Greece, and that men know that a stranger with all the mystery and potentialities of a stranger is abroad upon the roads. They look at me with a gentle yet searching interest, as though I might be an old god playing a trick in a tweed coat.

If this were so, and a wandering god from the old times came to them and proved himself, they would not, I think, betray him to the priest. They would take him in, sorry for him and vaguely proud of him also; and they would give him milk and kill a fowl for him and go short of potatoes in order to feed him. Not until he was far off down the road beyond the wrath of men would they, I am sure, go to confession!

4

As I go along the road I meet an old woman driving a black calf. She wears a wide scarlet petticoat. Her feet are bare. The calf is small and long-legged, lean and dung-spattered. To the left the hungry land lifts itself in a lace-work of stone walls; to the right the sea runs in to a fretwork of estuaries, the black rock slippery with sea-weed.

The scene is one ready made for a painter, and one that has been painted again and again by the younger school of Irish artists. When I have seen these canvases hanging on the walls of a Bond Street gallery during some annual show of Irish art I have admired the composition, the sincerity, but I have doubted the colouring.

In Connemara, on fine summer days, the hills are an intense blue and the sky behind them is sometimes almost a fine pale green. Just behind the outline of a hill the sky is often a lighter colour, a pale incandescent greenish-blue, that flings the hill out in a heroic manner; the light almost trembles behind it.

There is something heroic about Connemara. I do not mean the heroism of the men and women who till stony ground or the heroism of women who bring up big families on a few shillings a year: there is something deeper than this, something that goes back beyond written history; something that will not be caught in a net of words.

And against the grape-blue hills and the green sky an old barefoot woman in a red skirt drives a black calf.

I sit down on a stone and think about her for a long time. Why did she seem important?

5

I talked to a young fisherman who had brought ashore
a pot full of blue lobsters.

"Will you sell one to me?" I asked.

I had an idea that I might take the lobster to my next
hotel and ask them to cook it, not as a test of Irish manners, but because I can seldom resist lobster.

The young man replied that he would like to sell me a
lobster, but he was not at liberty to do so. He worked for
a man who sold all the lobsters caught in the neighbourhood so that they did not belong to him but to his master.

"To whom does he sell them?"

He said that French trawlers called for them at regular
intervals.

I stood there on a slippery rock wondering how many
times I have sat in a Paris hotel, a string orchestra playing and a *maître d'hotel* leaning forward with a religious
expression and a poised pencil, saying:

"The lobsters are—magnificent!"

I could not help laughing.

The young man looked hurt and embarrassed, so that
I hastened to explain.

"I think it rather funny that I should have to go to
Paris to eat one of your lobsters."

He did not think it at all funny, because it meant nothing at all to him; but he flung back his head and laughed
as a compliment to my sense of humour.

But it is rather odd. I shall never eat lobster in Paris
again but I shall see the Atlantic sweeping into the fretted
coast of Connemara, a little cloud sitting on the head of a
blue hill, and I shall hear in imagination the young fisherman's voice and the sound of yellow sea-weed popping in
the warm sun.

Connemara to Paris. . . .

It is hardly possible to believe that two such places could have any traffic one with the other, or even that they can exist in the same world.

6

I hear men and women of Connemara singing in the fields. Sounds go a long way in this still country. I hear the click of spade against stones and a voice lifted in some old Gaelic song. I would give anything to understand it. I have never wished to understand a foreign tongue so much. I remember hearing Arabs sing in the desert at night, but I was quite content to be told what they were singing. I have heard the Moorish Spaniards of the Balearic Islands making up long, loud songs on the mountains; but I was quite happy to be told that the man was singing "I am a man and I love you, look at my fine brown arms and the muscle on me," while the woman replied, "I am young and beautiful but not for the like of you."

But in Connemara, although these songs are just as foreign in sound, I feel drawn to them in a way impossible to explain so that it is almost pain to be for ever in ignorance of them. I would love to fling back a verse over a stone wall as I go on.

The manner in which these Irish peasants have kept alive the traditional literature of the Gael is one of the wonders of the world. They are not yokels in the English meaning of the word. I never meet a good specimen of a Connemara man without wondering what fine blood runs in his veins; for among these people are the O's and the Mac's of the ancient nobility.

"It has been said," writes Padraic Colum in *The Road Round Ireland*, "that in England the country people have a vocabulary of from 300 to 500 words. Doctor Pedersen took down 2,500 words of the vocabulary of Irish speakers in the Aran Islands. Doctor Douglas Hyde wrote down a vocabulary of 3,000 words from people in Roscommon who could neither read nor write, and he thinks he fell short by 1,000 words of the vocabulary in actual use. He suggests that in Munster—especially in Kerry—the average vocabulary in use amongst Irish speakers is probably between 5,000 and 6,000 words."

Stephen Gwynn has finely sketched this hidden side of the Irish peasant's life in *Irish Books and Irish People:*

"There is nothing better known about Ireland," he writes, "than this fact; that illiteracy is more frequent among the Irish Catholic peasantry than in any other class of the British population; and that especially upon the Irish-speaking peasant does the stigma lie. Yet it is perhaps as well to inquire a little more precisely what is meant by an illiterate. If to be literate is to possess a knowledge of the language, literature, and historical traditions of a man's own country—and this is no very unreasonable application of the word—then this Irish-speaking peasantry has a better claim to the title than can be shown by most bodies of men. I have heard the existence of an Irish literature denied by a roomful of prosperous educated gentlemen; and, within a week, I have heard, in the same county, the classics of that literature recited by an Irish peasant who could neither write nor read. On which part should the stigma of illiteracy set the uglier brand?

"'The Gaelic revival sends many of us to school in Irish-speaking districts, and, if it did nothing else, at least would have sent us to school in pleasant places among the most lovable preceptors. It was a blessed change from London to a valley among the hills that look over the Atlantic, with its brown streams tearing down among boulders, and its healthy banks, where the keen fragrance of bog-myrtle rose as you brushed through in the morning on your way to the head of a pool. Here was indeed a desirable academy, and my preceptor matched it. A big, loose-jointed old man, rough, brownish-grey all over, clothes, hair, and face; his cheeks were half hidden by the traditional close-cropped whisker, and the rest was an ill-shorn stubble. Traditional, too, was the small, deep-set blue eye, the large, kindly mouth, uttering English with a soft brogue, which, as is always the case among those whose real tongue is Irish, had no trace of vulgarity. Indeed, it would have been strange that vulgarity of any sort should show in one who had perfect manners, and the instinct of a scholar, for this preceptor was not even technically illiterate. He could read and write English, and Irish too, which is by no means so common; and I have not often seen a man happier than he was over Douglas Hyde's collection of Connacht love-songs, which I had fortunately brought with me. But his main interest was in history—that history which had been rigorously excluded from his school training, the history of Ireland. I would go on ahead to fish a pool, and leave him poring over Hyde's book; but when he picked me up, conversation went on where it broke off—somewhere among the fortunes of Desmonds and Burkes, O'Neills and O'Donnells. And when one had hooked a large sea-trout, on a singularly bad day, in a place where no sea-trout was expected, it was a little disappointing to find that Charlie's only remark, as he swept the net under my capture was: 'The Clancartys was great men too. Is there any of them living?' The scholar in him had completely got the better of the sportsman.

"Beyond his historic lore (which was really considerable, and by no means inaccurate) he had many songs by
heart, some of them made by Carolan, some by nameless
poets, written in the Irish which is spoken to-day. I wrote
down a couple of Charlie's lyrics which had evidently a
local origin; but what I sought was one of the Shanachies
who had carried in his memory the classic literature of Ireland, the epics or ballads of an older day. Charlie was
familiar, of course, with the matter of this 'Ossianic'
literature, as we are all, for example, with the story of
Ulysses. He knew how Oisin dared to go with a fairy
woman to her own land; how he returned in defiance of her
warning; how he found himself lonely and broken in a
changed land; and how, in the end, he gave in to the
teaching of St. Patrick ('Sure, how would he stand up
against it?' said Charlie), and was converted to Christ.
But all the mass of rhymed verse which relates the dia-
logues between Oisin and Patrick, the tales of Finn and his
heroes which Oisin told to the Saint, the fierce answers with
which the old warrior met the Gospel arguments—all this
was only vaguely familiar to him. I was looking for the
man who had it by heart. . . ."

Mr. Gwynn then describes how he journeys on, coming
at length to a man called James Kelly, who knew many
songs written "in very hard Irish, full of 'ould strong
words.' "

"I should like to send a literary Irishman of my acquaintance," he continues, "one by one to converse with
James Kelly as a salutary discipline. He was perfectly
courteous, but through his courtesy there pierced a kind
of toleration that carried home to one's mind a profound

conviction of ignorance. People talk about the servility of the Irish peasant. Here was a man who professed his inability to read or write, but stood perfectly secure in his sense of superior education. His respect for me grew evidently when he found me familiar with the details of more stories than he had expected. I was raised to the level of a hopeful pupil. They had been put into English, I told him. "Oh, aye, they would be, in a sort of a way," said James, with a fine scorn. Soon we broke new ground, for James had by heart not only the Fenian or Ossianic cycle, but also the older sagas of Cuchulain. He confused the cycles, it is true, taking the Red Branch heroes for contemporaries of the Fianna, which is as much as if one should make Heracles meet Odysseus or Achilles in battle; but he had these legends by heart, a race requirement among the Shanachies of to-day. Here then was a type of the Irish illiterate. . . . When I find an English workman who can stand up and repeat the works of Chaucer by heart, then, and not till then, I shall see an equivalent for James Kelly."

When darkness falls over Connemara I cannot look at the glow from turf fires shining high on the hill-side in cabin windows without wondering how many old stories from the fresh youth of the world are remembered over the white ash.

7

She was perhaps eighteen years of age, slim, tall, and her fine legs were bare. A scratch near her right knee had dried in a thin line to her ankle. It matched her skirt, which was blood-red. Her feet were black with sea-slime, and she stood on an overhanging ledge of rock grasping a long, primitive rake with which she lifted great bunches of dripping sea-weed from the edge of the lagoon. There was a soggy pile of it, waist-high, beside her.

She was in that part of the Connemara coast where the Atlantic, running in between tall hills, spreads out, contracts, and pushes itself towards the land in wide, blue lagoons, in thin creeks and rivulets, which, heavy with a brown fringe of sea-weed, lap gently against the rocks. The men in this part of the world scratch the hard soil with spades like crowbars, while the young girls go down to the edge of the sea and bear up on their broad shoulders baskets of sea-weed with which to encourage the reluctant earth. . . .

When I sat on a rock near her and lit a pipe she took no notice of me. Curlews were crying, gulls were sweeping in low, wild circles, and the sun was almost warm.

I would not call her pretty, but she was sensational in her complete unconsciousness of sex. Here, within twenty-four hours of London, was a primitive woman. She was more primitive than Eve, who was obviously a completely sophisticated person. This girl did not know that she was a woman. She had no idea that she was cast in the same mould as Helen of Troy. It had never occurred to her that she might be beautiful, because the traditions of her tribe, which go back to remote ages, tell her that the man she will marry demands not beauty but strength of hip and shoulder and arm, and the ability to carry baskets of sea-weed from the shore to the potato-patch.

I looked at her and wondered at what period in history women became vain.

Artists invariably paint primitive women gazing at their beauty in pools of water, combing long and lovely hair, and exhibiting an æsthetic pleasure in their own persons. But is this true? Did woman believe that she was beautiful until man had time to tear himself away from the potato-patch and make up a few poems? Surely that began all the trouble. Before that time woman was, it occurred to me as I watched her, just a convenient fetcher and carrier, uncombed, unwashed, devoid of vanity, unconscious that she was anything to brag about, because no man had told her! Perhaps the beauty of woman is a comparatively recent discovery!

The girl grubbed up great gobs of sea-weed and splashed them on the salty pile. Now and then her tangled hair fell into her eyes, and she shook it upward with a bare arm. She had never wanted any of the things for which her sisters (separated from her physically by a few hills, but actually by exciting centuries) sacrifice their digestions and their peace of mind.

Those fine legs had never known, or wished to know, the feel of silk. From the look of her head she had never owned a comb. Possibly she had never seen herself, except such portions of her that became reflected by chance in a still pool beside the sea. She had never experienced a complete bath.

Yet, in spite of it all, she was attractive. She pleased the eyes. I longed to be able to paint her or to cut her in marble as she stood, strong and poised, above the sea, her feet gripping the slippery rock, her toes curved and muscular, like the toes of a savage. Then she, perhaps sensing my interest, turned to me a pair of enormous empty dark eyes.

She was not pretty, but—she might so easily have been beautiful.

I pondered a number of problematical things as I admired the magnificent, efficient movement of her arms regularly forking up the weed and splashing it on the pile. She would never know romance as other women know it.

Men do not marry for love in agricultural tribes. They marry land or cows or sheep or the potato-patch that runs next to theirs, whichever seems to them the best dowry. There is a proverb in rural Ireland that it is unlucky to marry for love. Scots have a proverb: "As loveless as an Irishman."

But, suppose some man from the outside world fell in love with her, a man in flight from the artificiality of sophisticated women, a man who loved her simplicity and her primitiveness, and her magnificent ignorance, what would happen to her? Suppose he took her to a city and tried to fit her into his way of life? From Connemara to Curzon Street?

There was a fineness about her, characteristic of all the Connemara peasants, and a queer smothered nobility. That also is typical of men and women here. She looked in fact better bred than most of the women in a fashionable hotel in London or Paris. What would a bath and a Paris gown do to her?

And such girls do enter the modern world. They go in their blood-red skirts to the emigrant ships, weeping and sobbing, to step out with an astounding adaptability into the life of America. . . .

She filled the basket to the brim with sea-weed, and, bending one shoulder slightly, swung it up with one quick movement of her arm to her back. Then, stepping like a goat over the jagged rocks, she went towards the land.

I saw her later outside a white cabin talking to an elderly woman over the half-door.

"May I take your photograph?" I asked.

She looked at me with her great Spanish eyes, then she placed her chin on her shoulder and blushed with a kind of hoydenish coyness. I was confused and ashamed for her.

She lost her vague queenliness and became a stupid country wench. I asked her name, and she became silly again and shook herself like a little girl of six.

" 'Grania,' she's called," said the woman.

"You have lived in cities?" I said to the woman.

"Yes, I was a servant to Lord X——"

"Has Grania ever been to a city?"

"She has not."

"She has never wanted silk stockings, cinemas, lipsticks, face-powder, and cigarettes?"

The woman bent herself double with laughter over the half-door.

"Did ye hear that, Grania?" she said.

"I did," said Grania, and laughed, too.

She then lost her shyness and became solemn, never taking her big, smoky eyes from me.

"Grania," I said, "you have a name like a queen. What would you do with a shilling?"

She thought a minute, dropped her eyes, and lifted them again, whispering something in Irish:

"She says," said the woman, "that she would buy an apron."

"A blue one like the sky?" I asked.

"Yes," said Grania, in English. (O Grania! and I thought you had no small vanities!)

I held out a shilling in the palm of my hand, and she came slowly like a child and took it with fingers ice-cold with sea-water. . . .

There was an important silence.

"There's no use in telling lies, sir," said the woman earnestly. "It's not an apron she'll buy with a shilling. But," and she paused, looking at me solemnly, "she'd be buying one if it was one and sixpence she had!"

Grania came blushfully and took another sixpence. Then we all burst out laughing.

"I shall come back some day, Grania, and look for you standing by the sea in your red skirt and with our blue apron, looking like a queen in a story. . . ."

"Yes," said the woman, "and if you're a good girl the gentleman will take you away with him, Grania. . . ."

Then we all burst out laughing again and said good-bye. . . .

I turned at the bend of the road and saw Grania standing on a wall with the wind in her matted hair, looking after me and lifting one long arm in farewell.

8

The one-room cabin lies a mile or so from the road over a hill; and inside live a man, a woman, and eight children. The next cabin, which is rare in this district, is three miles away, and the nearest shop, such as it is, ten. They are in the backwoods of Connemara. This family is linked to the world of men only by a belief in God, otherwise they would be as lost as mountain sheep without a shepherd.

As it is, they are a lonely outpost of Christian culture —if that is not too strong a word —rather like a wild flower springing in the footprint of a saint. They live in the Shadow of God. They talk about Him as though He helped them that morning to bake the soda-bread in the peat-embers, and was with them last night to drive the pig in from the perils of the peat-bog.

St. Columba, who left Ireland, 1,365 years ago to convert the north of England, is a greater reality to them than any living man. They talk about him with the circumstantial detail of eye-witnesses, so that at first you think they are describing someone encountered last week in the hills. They tell how he cured his mother's toothache and how he rebuked his son that day when they were driving black cows from the fair at Ballyhean—simple stories made up by them and their fathers on the hill-side or round the fire at night, and repeated so often that they have become true.

They live in a cruel beauty, for the wildness around them was never meant to give food or shelter to man or beast. Their consumptive-looking cow roams the rock sadly in search of herbage, a poor scapegoat creature, lean as a rake, and their three potato-patches, none larger than a small carpet, are dotted about the landscape, ten minutes' walk one from the other, because only in these patches does some geological crack or seam permit the presence of a thin soil.

They are so used to insufficient food that hunger is fortunately something they do not notice. . . .

But if you offered to remove them to better land in another county they would fight you with pitchforks to the death!

The man is a mystery. He is not aware that I know he "did" six months recently, for making poteen. They caught him red-handed one misty day in the hills—fell right on him, in fact—as he was brewing "the stuff" over peat in a cave. Prison has left no mark on him. I suppose he just sat in his cell thinking about St. Columba—or Columcille as he calls him in Irish.

I have never seen a more ragged man. His trousers are unbelievable. He must have owned and inherited perhaps twenty pairs during his life, every one of which is represented in the present astonishing garment. If he fell asleep in the hills, I am sure the leprechauns would come out and play chess on him!

Like all his tribe, he is gentle, well-mannered, with thoughtful, dark eyes, and a thin, high nose. There is a stray touch of decayed aristocracy about him. The first time you see him you think: "Hullo, what an old tramp!" and you address him gruffly, anticipating roughness, but when he replies courteously with a smile and a well-turned sentence you feel abashed and apologetic!

How he keeps his large family I do not know. (Perhaps they keep themselves.) He appears to sit about all day on a big stone, smoking his pipe, looking round the hills, waiting apparently for something that never happens. . . .

I wonder if the peat-bog could tell a different story . . . but, let us change the subject, and meet his wife!

The cabin is dark because the windows, which are set high up, are no larger than sheets of foolscap, and everything in it smells of peat. A peat-fire, that has not gone out probably for centuries, burns with a clear vermilion flame and powders into white ash as fine as talc. Above this fire hangs a big black pot. On the wall are pictures of the Holy Family and the Flight into Egypt.

The woman kneels on the earth floor, rocking a cradle in which peeps the monkey face of a five-months-old infant; round her crawl and climb, bubble and dribble, three babies between the ages of one, two, and four years. Two bigger boys are at school. Two strapping girls, one twelve and the other fourteen, are vaguely useful about the place, slapping an infant out of the fire, stirring the black pot, or taking a turn at the cradle.

The mother of this hearty tribe is about thirty-six, but she looks quite fifty. Beauty seems to fly in a night in Connemara. It is distressing to see lovely young girls aged by hard work in the twenties, and by lack of care and insufficient food. This woman has been romantically beautiful, and even now, with care, kindness, flattery, a visit to a dentist, a hairdresser, a dressmaker, and a bathroom she would still be attractive. She belongs to that thin, whip-cord Latin type, and her big eyes, dark, gentle, and warm, with long centuries in the depth of them, look straight into you.

The most earnest social reformer could not patronize these people. There is no class barrier to negotiate. There is grim poverty, but not the squalid poverty of a slum; it is not pitiful poverty, because these people feel no self-pity.

They would be very puzzling to a parson's wife, or to a busy, bent-on-improvement district visitor!

So we sit and talk intimately about babies, teething, coughs, the difficulty of bringing up babies. In other words, we discuss her life.

She rocks the cradle, a hen walks in, takes a look at the assembled multitude, makes a querulous comment, pecks something from the floor, and wanders out.

"And it's only two I'm after losing," says the mother, with a touch of pride. So there were two more children! I ask her how on earth a doctor manages to get to such cabins in the hills, and she says that she has never seen a doctor all her life.

It's hard work to get enough food, she says, with big girls growing up. They live on potatoes and eggs, when there are eggs, and milk. They never have meat. But, glory be to God! they are all safe and hearty, and Brigid is going to America soon. . . .

The two big daughters nudge one another and giggle at this. They are red-skirted, bare-legged, and ragged as their father, and their faces almost as red as their skirts. How on earth do these wild children settle down in America?

It will be better for everybody when Brigid goes to

America because the first thing she will do will be to send a shilling or two home every week to keep the white cabin in Connemara. This is to me a marvellous thing about these people; there is more than filial piety in it; possibly it is another angle of that passionate attachment to the land which can have no parallel in any other country.

The two boys tramp three miles to school, and the whole tribe tramps three miles to Mass, wet or fine, on Sunday morning.

The woman looks curiously at my cigarette-case! Yes, she would like a cigarette! When I hold the match towards her, she grasps the cigarette and holds the end of it to the match as if it is a firework! She laughs, and confesses that she has never had a cigarette in her hand before. I have to show her how to light and hold it. The girls roar with laughter at their mother and make jokes in Irish.

Outside on a stone the head of the family sits smoking and watching the clouds roll up over the hills. We talk of the difficulty of growing food in such a spot. He says that he is, thanks to God, better off than many a man. Over there, now—he points with his pipe across the hills to the sea— men live on the edge of the rocks and carry the seaweed all day and even the earth in wicker baskets. . . .

"But they love their rocks?"

"They do," he says, "and it's not leaving them they'd be, if you gave them all the Plain o' Meath! But 'tis starvation!"

"Yet they are happy?"

"Aye, it's happy they are, sure enough, but—'tis just starvation!"

That seems to me to sum up Connemara! But, for the life of me, I cannot pity them!

CHAPTER X

I go on into the Joyce country, climb Croagh Patrick, and see
Clare Island, where Grace O'Malley, the sea-pirate, was
buried after a tempestuous life

1

THERE is a verse spoken by peasants in the west as they
rake the embers of their turf fires before going to bed. It
has been Englished as follows:

I save the seed of the fire tonight,
And so may Christ save me;
On the top of the house let Mary,
In the middle let Brighid be.

Let eight of the mightiest angels
Round the throne of the Trinity,
Protect this house and its people
Till the dawn of the day shall be.

One night at the end of a long evening spent in a Connemara cabin I watched the farmer rake his fire. He tidied
the little pile of glowing turf, and then he damped it down
with ashes in order that the fire might live until the morning.

This act, which is performed in thousands of white
cabins when night comes over the hills is symbolic of Ireland. The burning peat, one may fancy, is the Gael; the
ashes are the centuries of suppression under a foreign
power; the darkness needs no comment, and the morning
is the Ireland of the future. When these ashes are raked

244

off in the morning there is a faint pinkish heart of fire in the turf, and the peasants blow upon it until a flame bursts out and new fuel is added on the hearth.

The makers of modern Ireland who believe that the future of the nation is bound up with a revival of all Gaelic things have gone to the Gaelic west for their inspiration. Here, it seems to me, is a strange locked-up force. These strong, proud men, technically illiterate yet with the manners and instincts of scholars and gentle-folk, have a racial strength which must influence the future of Ireland. They are the same breed as the Highland crofters. How many famous generals, surgeons, lawyers, and literary men born in small Highland crofts owe their success in life to the fact that the whole family slaved to send the clever one to college?

The same thirst for scholarships, the same almost fanatical faith in a University education is not yet visible in the west of Ireland. But it may come. It seems to me that when these young Gaelic-Irish dream not of Chicago and New York but of academic honours, and an Ireland that can offer them distinguished careers, something new and powerful will have come into the life of this nation. The Gaelic Revival so far has been due to the work of University men and others who have gone from the cities into the Gaeltacht; the second, and more vital, stage will be when these young Gaels of the west come to the cities determined to use not their hands but their brains.

2

Clifden, the capital of Connemara, lies in the shadow of the Twelve Pins. These mountains are among the most fascinating that I have ever seen. They dominate the landscape in Connemara, now to your left and again to your right as you move through this country; sometimes the clouds swing low and decapitate them; often, especially at evening, they stand up in a sky blue as the Bay of Naples.

Clifden is a small, clean, stone-built town with one wide main street. The hill on which it is built slopes to an estuary that points straight out over the Atlantic to America.

In the post office I waited while a young Connemara girl, fresh as a peach, painfully addressed a letter to New York; and then I drew twenty pounds in much-travelled one pound notes—money that had been wired to me—and not one person in the post office showed any surprise, although this sum must have seemed to them real wealth.

It was strange to make contact with the outside world in the hotel. Here were fishermen with the accents of Dublin and England. The most interesting person, however, was a chauffeur whom I met at the bar: rather, his story was interesting. He asked me if I had noticed an elderly American at luncheon. I had. A thin, sallow man who wore horn spectacles.

"That's himself," said the chauffeur; and there was something sympathetic and kindly in his attitude.

He told me in that dramatic narrative manner which most Irishmen possess that as soon as a certain liner had docked at Cobh this American rushed to the garage where the young chauffeur worked, and chartered a car to take him to a little town in County Mayo. He explained that he wanted to "run up" to see his brother and then rush back and catch the next boat to America.

On the journey north from Cork to Mayo there was plenty of time for my companion's honeyed tongue. And the American, proving not so sallow and uncommunicative as he looked, told the Irishman a lot about himself and his mission. He had emigrated from Mayo thirty years previously. For years his conscience had pricked him because, in spite of success, he had never been home to see his elder brother, whose tragedy it was to stay in Ireland to inherit an uneconomic farm. He had returned at last and was about to pay a surprise visit to his brother.

Unlike every American previously encountered by this chauffeur he was a "terrible teetotaller entirely." He even kept a keen eye on his driver, and when once, at Limerick, the young man had been discovered with his face in a pint of porter the American had lectured him sternly, ordering him to abstain from all liquor while in his service.

They arrived in the town in Mayo and the American was appropriately affected. He made his way to the old home, opened the door, but a strange face greeted him:

"Will it be old Pat Murphy ye want—him that keeps the saloon?"

"The saloon?" cried the American, horrified and indignant.

"Aye; that's himself. . . ."

They went to Pat Murphy's saloon in the little street. There, sure enough, was the favourite brother sitting up behind the counter fast asleep. The American's heart melted at the sight so that he forgot the smell of stale drink that haunts all Irish saloons.

"Pat!" he said, going round and shaking him gently. "Pat, do ye know who's here?"

For answer Pat gave a grunt and slid gently to the floor, dead drunk.

"And he stood there and looked at him a while," said the chauffeur; "then he turned on his heel and he said, 'Take me back to Cork. It's the next boat I'll be catching. . . .'"

The young man drank up and put his cap straight.

"An' niver a word has he given me from that time to this," he said. "And to think a man would come all the way from America for that. He's a hard man entirely, I'm thinking. Still, it's sorry for him I am, taking it to heart the way he does. . . ."

I watched the American get into the motor-car and sit there with the set face of a puritan elder.

3

Behind the Twelve Pins lies the lovely mountain country of the Joyces. This was a family of Welsh descent which settled in this part of the west by permission of the dominant O'Flaherties in the last year of the thirteenth century.

Connemara lives on the sea and the fruits of the sea, but the people of the Joyce Country live upon the mountain. Their active little sheep graze on the splendid uplands, and the wool is taken from them, washed, and spun in the cottages on the hill-sides and made into Irish tweed on hand-looms. It would be easy to confound the Joyce Country with Connemara; they exist side by side on the map, but a difference not only of clan separates them: the vast difference in all the ways of life that separates fishermen from mountaineers.

The journey from Clifden through Letterfrack to Leenane is, I think, one of the most perfect scenes in the west of Ireland. I went along this road on a bright day with the sea intensely blue and huge golden clouds sailing above the crests of the hills. Ahead of me, dominating the scene, was the highest mountain of the north-west—Muilrea—and next to him was Ben Bury and Benlugmore, three monsters that rise up into the sky from an arm of the sea.

Leenane lies among the mountains on the edge of a great fiord called Killary Harbour. Connemara is now a dream. The country has changed. The great hills slope up to barren summits, and the sound is not that of a spade hitting the rock but the bleating of sheep and the clack of a shuttle. Near the post office is a wooden shed where all day long a hand-loom bumps and bangs as the wool from the Joyce Country sheep is turned into home-spun. It is a finer, closer tweed than that of Kerry; in fact, rather like Donegal, but lacking the sudden specks of col-our: excellent hard stuff with the colour of the Joyce Country in it.

As I went on round the eastern limit of Killary Har-bour I saw five young men pulling in a salmon net. They formed a group that might have come from the very dawn of the world. They wore homespun tweed. Their sleeves were rolled above their muscular elbows. Their necks were baked red with wind and sun. As they pulled they shouted to one another in Gaelic; and slowly the great net was hauled in to shore.

It was an exciting moment. I nearly broke my neck scrambling down to the water's edge to be in time to see it. As the net was pulled slowly towards the bank, the water, perhaps fifteen yards out, suddenly boiled with furious life, the sun shone on four feet of living silver as the great fish leapt and lashed in the net. The men sang out in their excitement and pulled, one directing them in Gaelic. The salmon leapt up into the sunlight. I saw the whole of him: a silver monster, an eighteen pounder with great shoulders on him and a tail with the kick of a mule in it.

It was a moment I shall never forget: the sun on the opposite hills; the scent of wild thyme; the splashing at the water's edge; the Gaelic shouts that sounded like war-cries; the bright, leaping body in the net: over it all the simple splendour of a lost world.

4

In Connemara and in the mountains of the Joyce Country women age swiftly, but while the bloom of youth is on them they are like queens.

Padraic Colum has beautifully described the women of Connaught:

"The hard conditions of Connacht life have helped the Connacht woman to development and personality. The size of the holding of land does not permit the man to develop his constructive and organizing faculty. The woman becomes the personality amongst the Connacht peasantry. The civilization is of her creating. It is a civilization of the hearth. One cannot fail to note the number of words for 'child' that is in constant use; there is a word for the child in the cradle, the child creeping on the floor, the child going to school, the child well-grown—naoidheah, lanabh, malrach, piaste—words as soft and intimate as a caress. The tragedies of Connacht life come closest to the woman: as a child she sees the elder sister who has reared her leave home for America; as a wife she lives alone while her husband works abroad, and often her child is born while its father is labouring in the fields of England or Scotland; as a mother she sees her rearing go from her as they grow into boyhood or girlhood. . . ."

I realize in Connaught one feature of the English landscape which is seldom or never seen in Ireland: a courting couple. In England boys and girls, arm in arm, are met with on every country road, or you see groups of country lads and lassies walking out together. In Ireland, as I noted in Kerry, the separateness of the sexes is remarkable. Love is perhaps in Ireland not a sentimental obsession as it is in England. In Connaught, and the west generally, men seldom marry for love: they marry, to some extent, for land.

Match-making, which in England would horrify us by its deliberate, cold-blooded unsentimentalism, goes on in the country districts of the west. Stephen Gwynn gives a remarkable account of this formality in his *Holiday in Connemara*:

"The son of the house gave me the fullest description of an Irish match-making that I have ever heard, and I set it down as an inspiration for some novelist.

"He went with the suitor's party, some eight or ten of them. Their coming was expected, for the match had been fixed, so to say, in principle; and accordingly the house was made ready. They were shown into a room with three long tables, furnished with uncut loaves and butter (I heard of no other food), but there was a glass and tumbler to every place, bottles of whiskey on the board, and a barrel of porter somewhere handy. The bride's friends were there in equal numbers, and the parties ranged themselves on opposite sides of the tables. The host sat at the head of the centre table; on his right was the suitor's spokesman, on his left the bride's spokesman. Any student of Ossianic lays will remember that when Finn came to marry Grania, the Fianna were on one side of the board, and King Cormac's chiefs and princes over against them on the other.

"When, after the Homeric fashion, they had 'put off the desire for eating and drinking,' the host opened the proceedings. 'Creud ta sibh ag iarraidh?' he asked— 'What are you come for?' But the phrase ag iarraidh is ambiguous, and means either 'What are you asking?' or 'What are you seeking?' (an ambiguity that reflects itself in the Anglo-Irish use of 'looking.' 'He'll be looking ten pounds for that heifer'). And, singularly enough, the boy's spokesman did not know his manners. 'Ceud punt' (a hundred pounds), he answered brusquely. This was a shocking solecism, but his neighbour saved the situation. 'And a woman with it,' he put in. 'That is a better story,' said the bride's spokesman. But the proper answer should have been, 'Seeking a wife for this boy we are'—and so on by courteous approaches to the real issue. However, battle was joined. The boy's spokesman, backed by the others began praising the suitor: how he had a well-stocked farm; was sober as well as rich; had no brothers to divide his inheritance. To this the bride's party answered by praising the girl, as industrious and (again Homerically) skilled in the arts of needlework. In the upshot the hundred pounds was agreed to. Then a new discussion arose as to whether it should be in stock or in cash, and the award was made at sixty pounds in cash, and cattle to the value of forty. Then the stock had to be discussed and specified. Lastly, the father dealt with the question of the ceremonial heifer, which is always given with the bride by any father who wishes to hold up his head in the country. He must buy one, he said, having no heifer beast that he would think good enough to send with his daughter.

"Then when the business was settled down to the last detail, the father said: 'We don't know yet if the woman you are looking for is in the house at all?' A message was sent, the girl came in and her health was drunk; and after this ceremony was over, the mother emerged from her retreat in a wall cupboard behind curtains where she had been unofficially present. It is not lucky for a woman to assist at a cleamhnas, or matchmaking. Then the tables were ranged aside to clear the floor for a dance; but one table was set in a corner where the old man drank till morning. Tea was provided for the young people.

" 'Was it a love match?' I asked. The boy's mother arranged it all: the girl was older than he.

"And in truth there is no society where marriage is more a matter of arrangement than among the Irish Catholic tillers of the soil—and none where the marriage-tie is more binding."

5

When Lent came in the year A.D. 449 St. Patrick retired to a great mountain in Connaught to commune with God. He fasted there for forty days and forty nights, weeping, so it is said, until his chasuble was wet with tears.

The mediæval monks possessed detailed accounts of St. Patrick's fast. They said that to the angel, who returned to him every night with promises from God, the saint said:

"Is there aught else that will be granted to me?"

"Is there aught else thou wouldst demand?" asked the angel.

"There is," replied St. Patrick, "that the Saxons shall not abide in Ireland by consent or perforce so long as I abide in heaven."

"Now get thee gone," commanded the angel.

"I will not get me gone," said St. Patrick, "since I have been tormented until I am blessed."

"Is there aught else thou wouldst demand?" asked the angel once more.

St. Patrick requested that on the Day of Judgment he should be judge over the men of Ireland.

"Assuredly," said the angel, "that is not got from the Lord."

"Unless it is got from Him," replied the determined saint, "departure from this Rick shall not be got from me from today until Doom; and, what is more, I shall leave a guardian there."

The angel returned with a message from heaven:

"The Lord said, 'There hath not come, and there will not come from the Apostles, a man more admirable, were it not for thy hardness. What thou hast prayed for thou shalt have . . . and there will be a consecration of the men of the folk of Ireland, both living and dead.' "

St. Patrick said:

"A blessing on the bountiful King who hath given; and the Rick shall now be departed therefrom."

As he arose and prepared to decend from the mountain mighty birds flew about him so that the air was dark and full of the beating of wings. So St. Patrick stood, like Moses on Sinai, and round him all the Saints of Ireland, past, present, and to come.

In this we can see the Irish belief in the inflexible determination of their saint: "a steady and imperturbable man." And it was said that while upon this mountain in Connaught St. Patrick banished all snakes from Ireland.

This mountain, Croagh Patrick—or Patrick's Hill— lifts its magnificent cone 2,510 feet above the blue waters of Clew Bay. It is Ireland's Holy Mountain. Once a year in July a pilgrimage is made to the little chapel on the crest. Atlantic liners drop anchor in Galway Bay, bringing Irish-Americans who wish to ascend the mountain for the good of their souls. As many as 40,000 pilgrims have climbed the mountain in one day; and many of the more devout remove their shoes and socks and take the hard path barefoot.

The morning broke dangerously clear and fine. I took a stout stick and prepared to climb the mighty flank of Ireland's Sinai. As I approached it, admiring the high pattern of wheeling cloud over its head, I could see far off the little Mass chapel like a cairn of stones on the crest.

I plodded on over a rough mountain path worn by the feet of the faithful century after century. A wind blew in from the Atlantic bringing rain with it, and in a few moments the earth was hidden in a thin grey mist. I was disappointed, but went on in the hope that the sky would clear in time and give me what must surely be the grandest view in Ireland.

There are few experiences more uncanny than climbing a mountain in mist and rain. As I went on and up, the mist grew thicker, and the drizzle fell in that peculiar persistent Irish way that wets you to the skin before you are aware of it. Above me was this grey wet pall, below me the same mystery; only the rocks under my feet were real, and there was no sound but the falling of water and the click of a dislodged stone rolling behind me down the path.

There is something terrifying, at least to me, in the mists that cover mountains—mists that hide you know not what; mists that cut a man off from the world and deny him the sight of the sky. To be lost on a mountain in mist is to experience all the horror of panic, for it seems to you that you might lose the path and go wandering vainly in circles answered only by a mocking laugh which seems to hide in all mountain mists. But I consoled myself by the thought that Croagh Patrick is a holy mountain from whose ravines and gullies all demons have been banished. Suddenly, right before me rose a white figure, and I looked up to a statue of St. Patrick.

The saint, I discovered, stands there to hearten pilgrims, for the real climb begins behind him. The path ends. The climber ascends, picking his way over a steep gully, the loose stones sliding beneath his feet; and as I went on the joy of climbing in rain came to me, so that I loved the wetness of my cheeks and hair and the movement of the mist which told me that I was in a great cloud that hid Croagh Patrick from the eyes of men.

I came to a cairn of stones: one of the Stations of the

Cross. And as I stood there asking my Catholic ancestors what to do about it I heard a voice, and out of the mist came an unlikely and preposterous sight. A middle-aged woman was painfully descending the path. She looked exactly as though someone had taken her up in the very moment of buying six yards of *crêpe de Chine* at a Grafton Street draper's and had blown her on top of Croagh Patrick. No sooner had she become startlingly clear in the narrow circle of my vision than another figure materialized from the mist: her husband. He also was incredible. He wore a bowlar hat. It seemed so odd to encounter a bowlar hat on a holy mountain. We said what a bad day it was. They asked if there were any more people coming up behind me. They told me it was their first pilgrimage. The woman was worried. She had lost a rosary among the stones. If I found it would I post it to her in Limerick? I thought how strange it was to English eyes: two solid, middle-aged people of the comfortable kind going off together to pray on the summit of a holy mountain.

"God be with you and bless you," they said gravely; and I went on into the damp cloud.

Onward in the mist I went, hot and weary and happy; once I thought I had found the lost rosary, but it was only a piece of torn shoe-lace that had fallen into a hollow of the rocks. I passed another Station of the Cross and soon found myself on the peak of Croagh Patrick, 2,510 feet above Connaught, with the mountains of Mayo north of me, the blue Atlantic west of me, and south the mountains of the Joyce Country and the Twelve splendid Pins of Connemara. But, alas, not one glimmer of it shone through the wet cloud that hung over the holy mountain. . . .

On the summit of this height is a little Mass chapel. I was told in Connemara how this building was made. Cement in seven-pound bags was carted to the foot of the mountain and every pilgrim regarded it as an act of devotion to carry one of these to the top. Many a man, I was told, made the ascent more than once for the honour of carrying up material for the construction of this tiny oratory.

I went inside and knelt down. The place was very small and ice cold. A young priest knelt in prayer. The wind howled round the little building in soft gusts, and I wondered what it felt like to be there in the great storms that swept in from the Atlantic. Even though the walls of the little chapel cut off the sight of moving mists there was something in the air of the chapel that told of a chilly solitude far from the comfortable earth. I was conscious that, outside, the mountain mists were sweeping past; the cold air told of a remote solitude; the rudeness of the little sanctuary was that of a shrine built on an outpost of the world. The kneeling priest never moved. He might have been carved in stone. He reminded me of some knight keeping vigil before the altar.

I tiptoed out and sitting on a wet stone ate the sandwiches and the cheese that I had brought with me. I sat there wet through, longing and hoping against hope that the clouds would rise and show me the distant earth. The wind that sweeps over the head of Croagh Patrick is the cruel whistle that comes to all great mountains; and in the sound of it, even though you cannot see two yards before you, is a message of height, of dizzy drops, of jagged gullies and awful chasms.

It was on this height, as told by the mediæval monks, that St. Patrick flung his bell from him only to have it returned to his hand; and at each sound of the bell the toads and the adders fled from Ireland. . . .

I went down over the wet stones. I came gratefully to the white statue of the saint. I had left the clouds above me, but the rain was falling, blotting out the sea and the hills.

6

From Clew Bay you can see, lying out perhaps four miles from the nearest land, a small green island called Clare Island.

On the shore facing the mainland is the ruined tower of Grace O'Malley's Castle. Legend says that this remarkable Irishwoman was buried on the island in an abbey which now, like her stronghold, is a ruin.

Grace O'Malley—or Granuaile as she is known in song and legend—was a kind of feminine Rob Roy of Ireland. History says little about her, but what little it says is exciting. She was a unique character. Her life and times seem to me ready and waiting for the Irish Walter Scott.

When Queen Elizabeth was ruling England with the help of her astute councillors, Grace O'Malley was ruling the seaboard of Connaught by sheer force of character. She is without parallel in history: a sea-queen or a she-pirate. Her father was Owen O'Malley, called Dhubdara —"of the Black Oak." His authority extended from the sea-coast to Aran, where he was Lord of the Isles. The clan had from the earliest days been famous for its daring deeds by sea, and the old chief was accompanied on many of his piratical voyages by his daughter. When he died she was a girl of nineteen. She had a younger brother, but, like Hatshepsut of Egypt, she calmly set him aside and declared her intention of becoming the chief of the clan. No one knows the composition of her fleet. She must have possessed certain wooden vessels, but no doubt the bulk of her navy was composed of coracles. Her stronghold, Carrigahowly Castle, was built at the edge of the water on

Clare Island, and legend says that the young she-pirate was in the habit of mooring her navy and tying it together, then passing the main rope through a hole in her castle walls, retiring to rest at night with the rope wound round her arm in order to be up and doing at the first alarm.

She lived in an age of piracy. It was the age of Francis Drake. The Spanish galleons which came up the west coast of Ireland with their wine cargoes for Galway were rich prey for her, but, like a good Gael, her chief attacks were made against the merchant ships of Elizabeth. She became so notorious that the English Government proclaimed her an outlaw and offered what in those days was an enormous sum, £500, for her capture. Troops stationed at Galway were sent to take her castle, but after a fortnight's siege they retired, and Queen Grace was left in peace.

Her first husband was O'Donnell O'Flaherty "of the Wars"—evidently a fit mate for her—head of the "ferocious" O'Flaherties. A record of her about this time is contained in a manuscript preserved in the Dublin archives:

"She was a great pirate and plunderer from her youth. It is Transcended to us by Tradition that the very Day she was brought to bed of her first child, that a Turkish Corsair attacked her ships, and that they were getting the Better of Her Men, she got up, put the quilt about her and a string about her neck, took two Blunder Bushes in her hands, came on deck, began damning and capering about, her monstrous size and odd figure surprised the Turks, their officers gathered together talking of her. This was what she wanted. She stretched both her hands, fired the two Blunder Bushes at them and Destroyed the officers."

That was the sort of woman she was!

When O'Flaherty died she chose as her second husband

a powerful Anglo-Norman named Sir Richard Bourke, known to his Irish sept as MacWilliam Eughter. His personal nickname was "Richard in Iron," an allusion to the plate armour which he wore. Grace, it is said, insisted on observing what the Americans regard as the latest thing in unions, a companionate marriage. If after twelve months the marriage was not satisfactory either party to it should have the power to dissolve it. Some reports say that she employed the companionate year to the garrisoning of her husband's strongholds along the coast, and at the end of it closed the gates of her castle upon him and declared the marriage ended.

We touch surer ground, however, in 1576, when Grace O'Malley went to Galway to ask Sir Henry Sidney to accept her fleet of three galleys and 200 men in the service of England. The upshot of her alliance with England was the most surprising event of all: she was invited by Elizabeth to visit London.

This visit took place in 1593, after the sea-queen had spent years in chasing the enemies of England up and down the Connaught coast. Tradition says that the queen and her retinue sailed to England and anchored in the Thames below old London Bridge. There are many accounts of the interview, which, some say, took place in Hampton Court Palace. The meeting of Elizabeth with the dark-haired she-pirate of Connaught must have been one of the most striking audiences of a picturesque reign. She announced herself as "Grainne O'Malley, daughter of Doodarro O'Malley sometime chief of the country called Upper Owle O'Malley, now called the Barony of Murasky."

A fine-sounding title. The Rev. Cæsar Otway gave an account of the interview. It is probably as authentic as most:

"Grana," he wrote, "having made a bow, and held out her bony hand, horny as it was with many an oar she had handled, and many a helm she had held, to sister Elizabeth (as she called her), sat down with as much self-possession and self-respect as an American Indian chief would now before the President of the United States.

"Elizabeth, observing Grana's fondness for snuff, which, though a practice newly introduced, she had picked up in her smuggling enterprises, and, perceiving her inconvenienced, as snuffers usually are when wanting a pocket handkerchief, presented her with one richly embroidered, which Grana took indifferently, used it loudly, and cast it away carelessly: and when asked by Sir Walter Raleigh why she had treated the gift of her Majesty in such a way, the answer of that wild Irish girl was of that coarseness which ought not to be read by ears polite. Moreover it seems that Elizabeth was not happy in the presents which she proffered to the Vathaness: she ordered a lap-dog, led by a silken band, to be given to her. 'What's this for?' says Grana. 'Oh, it's a sagacious, playful, and faithful little creature, it will lie in your lap.' 'My lap!' says Grana, 'it's little the likes of me would be doing with such a thing—keep it yourself, Queen of the English, it is only fit for such idlers as you; you may, if it likes you, fool away your day with such vermin.' 'Oh, but,' says Elizabeth, 'Grana, you are mistaken. I am not idle. I have the care of this great country on my shoulders.' 'Maybe so,' says Grana, 'but as far as I can see of your ways, there's many a poor creature in Mayo, who has only the care of a barley field, as more industry about them than you seem to have.'

"Of course Elizabeth dismissed her soon—she offered at her last audience to create her a countess. 'I don't want your titles,' says Grana. 'Aren't we both equals? If there be any good in the thing I may as well make you one as you me. Queen of England, I want nothing from you— enough for me is it to be head of my nation, but you may do what you like with my little son Toby of the Ship, who has Saxon blood in his veins, and may not be dishonoured by a Saxon title. I will remain as I am; Grana O'Maille of the Uisles.' "

They say that the child was brought into Court and was there created Viscount Mayo, from whom the present Earls of Mayo are descended.

"When Grainne was returning to Connaught, a storm came on and her fleet was obliged to put into Howth Harbour," wrote E. Owen Blackburne in *Illustrious Irishwomen*. "She landed and advancing to the castle found the doors shut and the inmates at dinner. Being refused the hospitality she demanded for herself and her followers, she retraced her steps towards the shore. On her way she met a beautiful child playing in the grounds, and hearing he was the heir to Howth, Grainne deliberately stole him. She bore off her prize with her to Connaught, nor would she give him up until she stipulated for, and obtained as her ransom, the promise that for ever at mealtimes the doors of the castle be thrown wide open, and hospitality extended to all wayfarers who should demand it. This custom is still observed there."

Unfortunately the end of this tempestuous and heroic figure was tame. She was buried in Clare Abbey, where, I am told, for many years her skull decorated with ribbons was shown to visitors. But the story goes that in the nineteenth century a company was formed in Scotland for the acquisition of bones for manure. A ship was fitted out which raided the west of Ireland, where immense quantities of bones were piled up in churchyards and old abbeys. Grania's bones, so they say, went to manure a Scottish acre.

There is, of course, an artistic Irish ending to this story. They say that one of Grania's grinders, discovered in a turnip, choked a Scotsman!

CHAPTER XI

*Describes a sunset at Mallaranny. I hear a story about enchant-
ment and am invited to go to a wake. I cross the little bridge
to the beautiful island of Achill and, continuing my journey,
see Donegal in rain*

1

THERE is a hill above the sea. The heather is bent back
towards the land and the stems shine whitely like the wood
of olive-trees. The hill smells of wild thyme. Below, the sea
sweeps in over a wide semicircle of yellow sand, and behind
also is water, because the sea flings an arm round this hill.
On a clear evening when the sun is setting below the Atlantic this hill above Mallaranny might be on the map of
heaven. An unearthly beauty pulsates in the air: it is an
opalescence which seems to have a music in it, and even if
the Angelus bell were not ringing below in the white convent you would bare your head.

Lifting themselves out of a blue sea, before you, are
the blue mountains of Achill; to your left, rising up from
the blue waters of Clew Bay, are the blue flanks of Croagh
Patrick: beyond him, far off, are more blue heights—the
Twelve Pins and the wild uplands of the Joyce Country.

Such a heartbreaking symphony in blue is rarely seen
in the world. There is sorrow in it, as there is in all sharp
beauty. Standing there, with the gulls crying and the larks
shivering in the sky and the wind going through the
heather, a man goes cold with the beauty of it and is glad
to be alone.

And just as great music sometimes searches out the

heart until it becomes unbearable, so this sunset over Mallaranny becomes more beautiful minute by minute so that you look away from it, unable to endure it, searching the world for some trivial thing: the white smoke going up from a cabin, the way the green light fills the pools in a peat bog, the slow figure plodding on over the white road, and the sweep of the incoming tide.

The mountains and the hills that lie hushed around you are flung up against a background of pale green, but it is like no green ever seen in the sky except at certain times of the year in the Libyan Desert. This green might be the reflection of green fires lit behind the hills; for it is a light with life in it like the light that comes from fire: a pulsing, nervous, intelligent light that throbs and hurts.

And you feel that if God chose a place to reveal Himself it would be upon these western hills at sunset when the whole hushed world is tense with beauty and earth seems waiting for a revelation.

The sun goes down slowly into the sea. There is a minute when the space of a finger lies between its rim and the water; and the rim sinks until it touches the water and the sun dips down and is gone. Now comes the last movement of the symphony. The clouds change colour. They catch fire in the air. They become pink. Little unnoticed wreaths of cloud change from white to red and live and pulse a moment in the sky. But the green light behind the hills does not die, and the blue of the hills does not die: it grows deeper and more intense.

Then the whole scene fades a tone and the music behind it drops an octave; but all the colour is still there, not departing, it seems, so much as sinking into the earth and withdrawing itself into the sky. You stand watching it with tears in your eyes, the first wind of night touching your hair and cold on your face. . . .

The clouds turn grey, the hills go dark against the green of the sky, the little line of water at the edge of cut peat is a line of quicksilver, the sea is a silver sea, and the mountains of Achill are black.

The evening star burns in the sky; and dusk comes to the West.

2

Where the blue hills of Mallaranny look out to the mauve slopes of Croagh Patrick is a fort, or rath, quite near the sea.

It is amusing to ask a countryman why he does not level a fort, because he will evade the question and will rarely admit to you, straight off, that the fairies are living on his land. Many a child is sent on an errand with a piece of coal in his pocket as a charm against the fairies. In the west men still believe in witches. There is a belief, too, in a "headless coach" which passes like a shadow down a road, foretelling death, but far more common is the belief in the banshee, which is by no means a relic of Irish folk-lore, but a real and vivid belief.

I have met many men and women who swear that they have heard the banshee, many of them educated people, but I have encountered only one man who claims to have seen it. He says it was combing its hair beside a stream and stopping now and then to dip its hands in the water.

I can well understand any man in the west of Ireland believing in the supernatural, and it is unfair to call the countryman an ignorant, superstitious creature until you have experienced the almost indescribable eeriness of the wild west country.

An old man who has lived in Mayo all his life was walking with me over the fort at Mallaranny. After we had

THE ROUND TOWER OF ARDMORE

been talking for some time about the strange things that do undoubtedly happen in life, he said:

" 'Tis true that this was a dreadful place for leprechauns and such before the 'Throuble.' But they've gone on—they've gone on. . . ."

(A man in Kerry said the same thing to me. He would not admit that fairies do not exist today; he said they had "gone on" to some other place!)

"But old people talk of them still," he continued; "and there's many a one in Mallaranny who has seen them, little wee men they are, in the lonely places of the hills. I've not seen them myself—and it's up at all hours of the night and day I am—but then it's not every man who is allowed to see them."

He turned to the fort over which we were strolling and remarked solemnly:

"It's a strange story now they tell about this fort. . . . There was once a young man who cared nothing about the fairies or the ghost, and it's past this very spot he'd come from his fishing in the dead of night without a shiver on him. Well, one night as he was on his way home what does he see coming over this very spot but three tall men in black carrying a coffin. Now he thought it strange that no man was walking where the fourth should have been, so up he goes and puts his shoulder to the place; and never a word said. . . .

"And they walked on.

"Now," continued the old man, "they'd been walking wid the coffin maybe a mile when the three men in black let it down from their shoulders to take a rest, but just as the coffin touched the road they disappeared! The young fellow thought it mighty strange, and so he rus the lid off the coffin. . . ."

"What did he do?"

"He rus the lid gently, and looked inside, and there he saw a fair young girl a-lying with her eyes wide open and a smile on her. 'Come out o' that,' he says, 'if it's not dead ye are!' And the young girl gets up out of the coffin, but never a word can she speak to him. . . . She was dumb, ye see! So he takes her home to his father and mother.

"Well, that night twelve months later the young fellow was coming back from his fishing past this very spot again, and as he passes this fort he hears voices inside. 'This night twelve months ago,' he hears a man's voice say, 'he took the girl from us'; and then he heard a second voice inside the fort say that it's little use she'd be to him because she was dumb and him never thinking of pulling out the little silver pin behind her ear. 'No,' said the first voice, 'and it's plenty of talk she'd be giving him if he did that. . . .'

"So he goes home and looks behind her ear, and there, sure enough, is a little silver pin, which he takes out, and the young girl speaks, telling how she was stolen by the fairies twelve months ago.

" 'Bring me some wool,' she says, 'it's a waistcoat I'll be making for ye!' And she makes him a waistcoat! 'Now,' says she, 'ye'll go to the fair,' says she, 'and ye'll put up at a certain house close to the fair green, and ye'll surely,' says she, 'see an old man comin' in, and when he sees the vest on ye he may get angry and he may not. . . .'

"So early the next morning the young fellow sets off for the fair, and it's not long before up comes a man to him asking how he came by his new vest, for, says he, 'there's only one person in the world could have knitted that vest, and the fairies took her twelve months ago. . . .'

"Now he took this man home, and as soon as the girl sees the man she falls weeping and laughing for joy—

for it was her father! So this young fellow and the girl were married, and the father gave him a great fortune in money—two hundred pounds it was—and they do say that from that day to this his family has never lacked money. . . .

"That's one of the things that they say happened where we're standing now!" he concluded, lighting his pipe, which had gone out during the story.

"How much of it do you believe?"

"Well, there's some that believe every word of it."

"But it never happened!" I laughed, sitting down on the fort.

"Stranger things have happened than that," he said almost sternly. "Will ye come up off that fort while I tell ye about the witch Maumakeogh?"

He did! He also told me the story of the lame boy who prophesied the coming of the railway to Mallaranny.

And I must say that the only time to hear such stories is when the wind is going over the sea-banks and the hushed blue hills are also listening.

3

If one lived in Ireland long enough it would be possible to make a wonderful collection of vivid phrases and startling imagery. These things tumble out of Irish mouths in moments of excitement. It is the Gaelic shining through the English.

I have heard a number of them, but they are not as good as some that have been recorded. I am not thinking of comic remarks known as "bulls," but vivid, colourful phrases which hit off a personality or an incident with exactitude and distinction. A labourer in the west giving evidence before a district council objected to a house because he said it was so windy that "a wild duck would get rheumatism in it." Stephen Gwynn tells the story of an Irish cook who when the well had run dry rushed in to her mistress with the announcement that "there isn't enough water in the house to baptize a fairy, and me with the potatoes to put down for dinner!" He also mentions an old Irish boatman with whom he fished a Westmeath lake. The problem was whether the murrough, or stone-fly, had yet appeared. Suddenly one flew past in the twilight:

"Look at he!" cried the boatman in excitement. "Did you see him going by you *like a hin?*"

Padraic Colum mentions a woman who described a slow, cautious character as "Martin-steal-upon-larks."

The same writer has some interesting things to say about the difference between English and Anglo-Irish. Take the English question: "Are you selling the horse today?"

"The speaker of correct English has to move the emphasis from one word to another of the four last according to the information he seeks. Four successive positions of the chief stress give four different meanings to the question. The Anglo-Irish idiom, which in this matter follows the locution of Gaelic, has no need of accentuating. Its user would say: (*a*) 'Is it you who are selling the horse?' or (*b*) 'Is it the horse you are selling?' or (*c*) 'Is it today you are selling the horse?' 'In other words,' says a well-informed writer, 'where the English purist depends upon stress to bring out his meaning the Irish idiom employs construction for the same purpose, and much more effectively.'

"In reply to the query, 'Does it rain here?' the native says, 'It bees raining' or 'It does be raining.' He is making an attempt to reach an exactitude that is possible in Gaelic; in that language there is a distinct form of the verb 'to be' to indicate the habitual, the frequentative tense. The Irishman who has the tradition of Gaelic, even though he may never have heard it spoken, feels the want of the frequentative tense in English, and he attempts to supply it. And so 'bees' and 'does be' are used as a distinct tense in the Anglo-Irish idiom—'He bees lame in the winter' or 'He does be lame in the winter' implies that the man's lameness is intermittent."

I have just been reading one of Mr. Arnold Bennett's pontifical reviews in an English newspaper. In this he mentions that what puzzled him during a visit to Ireland some time ago was "the earnest effort, then just begun, and still being continued," to re-establish the old Irish language as a living tongue.

"Its futile wrong-headedness," he writes, "its childish flouting of the lesson of history, positively shocked me. How could these intelligent Irish start such a scheme, or allow it to be started? Why had not public opinion killed it by laughter on the day of its inception? Could a country which permitted such a tragi-farce to be enacted have any genuine understanding of what literature is? Could literary genius spring from such a soil?"

I suppose when Mr. Bennett mentions "a country" he means Dublin. But had he really travelled in Ireland he would have known that "the old Irish language" is still a "living tongue." Not so long ago, as I have already mentioned, a Connemara girl was sent back by the emigration authorities because she failed the English test. And literary genius has sprung, and is springing, from "such a soil." If the genius of Synge and Yeats is not founded on the "old Irish language," on what is it founded? The Irish revival, which inspired the nationalist movement and led to the Treaty, was founded on "the old Irish language."

Whether it is a tragi-farce or not only time can show. But even if the Gaelic language fails as a modern commercial tongue the attempt to revive it will shine through Irish literature, and the inspiration of it must give force to the Irish genius.

4

The little man who was whitewashing the ceiling asked his mate if he was going to the O'Brien wake that evening.

No, replied the mate, his feet were sore, and it was too far to walk.

That was a pity, said the whitewasher.

I waited for one of those pauses and descents which punctuate the lives of all painters and decorators before I led the little man, without the least difficulty, to Mr. Casey's beershop. Now I had been trying to attend a wake since I set foot in Ireland. This custom is dying out, because the Church regards it as a relic of paganism. Immediately there is a death the relatives are encouraged to send the body to the chapel, there to await burial. In certain districts, I understand, drinking at wakes is punished by excommunication, but priests tell me that in wild corners of the west, such as this, wakes do go on, and will go on.

When the face of the decorator had been buried in a mug of porter I ventured to ask if I could, without offending the susceptibilities of anyone, go with him to the O'Brien wake that evening. I could, indeed, he replied, and it would be a compliment to the corpse. His breezy handling of so grim a topic gave me some uneasiness. Surely, I asked him, a stranger, and one obviously drawn by vulgar curiosity, would be resented by the family and their friends. Not at all, he cried, what were wakes for at all? When he knew that I had a motor-car he became convinced that the O'Brien wake, which was nine miles away, would be incomplete without me.

He then talked about wakes as men in cities might discuss cinema films. That was a rare good wake of Mr. O'Flaherty's, over the hills beyond Lettcrash, and when old Mrs. Dempsey died, out Strahmore way, that, too, was a grand wake with dancing. They appeared to be his only recreation.

"But do you attend every wake?"

"I do," he cried, burying his face in the mug, then, emerging with a cheery laugh, "a good waker gets a good wake himself. . . . You come to mine, I go to yours!"

(This sounded to me a bit involved; but I was out of my depth anyhow!)

Then—for I have a horror of infection—I asked him: "What did he die of?"

"I think it would be her fourteenth child," he replied. "It's Mrs. O'Brien!"

That night, at about eleven o'clock the little decorator, having removed most of the whitewash from his hair and neck, appeared, wearing a collar and tie. He said that the house to which we were going was a poor little house, and there would be no refreshment. It might be as well, therefore, for us to "have one" in order to brace ourselves for our sad duty. He apologized for that evening's wake, because the poor woman was so young. Had she been old there would have been nothing to mourn, and we should, so he said, have had dancing, and a merry evening. A young corpse makes a sad wake, he added . . .

I suggested that a mother of fourteen children could not be so youthful, but he seemed to think that a person of forty, if still alive, might be middle-aged, while a corpse of forty was youthful. I could not understand his point of view.

We motored for nine miles into the heart of a wild and desolate country. The moon was bright. We swung round the edge of mountains, enormous in the night, we passed little arms of the sea, silver-white and still, arriving at length at a group of small cabins scattered over a hill— pale green they looked in the moonlight—and with a light burning in every window. We abandoned the motor-car in a cart track and struck off down a steep and rocky path towards the sea, my friend explaining, as we met bands of men roving about in the darkness, that when any-one dies the whole village stops work until the funeral, the members of every family taking turns in watching beside the body for two days and nights. . . .

We saw a pin-point of light burning at the edge of the water. That was the O'Brien cottage, said my friend. We went on for a quarter of a mile or so, exchanging greet-ings with the men who seemed to pop up out of the ground before us—"Good-night, Pat!" "Good-night, Mick!"— until we came to a small cabin built on the very edge of the sea.

The door was open; and over the little place was the stillness of death.

We knelt on the floor with bowed heads. I could feel that the room was full of people. I could smell peat. I could hear a cricket chirruping in the hearth. As we rose from our knees an old man, who was sitting beside the fire came forward, shook hands, and, without expressing the least surprise at my presence, handed us clay pipes ready filled with shag tobacco and, motioning us to a wooden bench, resumed his seat, his hands crossed over the handle of his stick and his chin bowed over his hands.

The room was lit by three candles in brass sticks on a

table which contained also a pile of clay pipes and a plate of chopped shag. In the full glow of the candle-light lay the dead woman. She was on a recessed bed, built into the wall near the fire. It was draped with white sheets, decorated with black crosses made of cloth. The corpse was robed in a brown habit like that of a nun, which left exposed only the face and hands. The eyes were half open. One of them was fixed on me with an expression of fearful intelligence.

She was worn out with work, and child-bearing, and poor food. She was not young, as my friend the decorator had said. She was probably in the early forties. She was painfully thin. All her meanness and poverty had fallen from her. She lay, in the majesty of death, like a queen.

In the shadows round the room sat about thirty men and women, the men wearing caps and hats, trying to keep their clay pipes alight, and all sitting in dead silence. Only the cricket chirruped monotonously, filling the universe with shrillness. The men were farm-labourers and fishermen; the women were of the same type. Now and then they sighed and shuffled their feet. In the next room a man was snoring loudly. He was the husband. He had been up all the previous night with the dying woman. The old man beside the fire was her father. . . .

The door framed an oblong of bright moonlight, soft as velvet, and I could hear the waves breaking gently on the rocks outside.

The stillness, the silence, cut across by the high chirrup of the cricket—the "singer in the embers"—got on my nerves. We seemed to be waiting for the Resurrection.

"It's fine weather we've been having," said the old man, turning to spit into the peat fire.

"It is," whispered my friend the decorator.

"It's welcome, God knows," said the old man.

"It is," replied the decorator.

The cricket chirruped madly, and the peat fell apart in little puffs.

Several of the fourteen children gazed into the room where their mother lay, grouped round the doorway of the outer bedroom. Two of the family were in America and did not yet know that she was dead.

New-comers knelt a moment on the floor as they entered, making the Sign of the Cross (I would have given anything to silence the cricket, which seemed to be cracking a whip in my head). Would nothing happen? Would we sit all night with the dead in dreadful silence? Where were the keening women who rock themselves with melancholy cries?

There was a sudden commotion behind a curtain of sacking at the end of the room. A pig grunted! I have been in even poorer-looking cabins in Kerry and Connemara, yet never before had I encountered this often-denied presence. There was something stranger still! A thing like a white coffin lifted and tilted itself above the shoulders of the watchers; and a white cow looked in, wondering what was happening at that time of night, dimly conscious that the placid routine of her life was broken. These creatures occupied a kind of annexe, separated from the living-room only by a length of sacking and a long, wooden bar.

The cow, blowing the breath from her wet nostrils into the room, and turning her mild and uncomprehending eyes this way and that, accentuated the classic simplicity of the picture. I found myself thinking of the Nativity.

There was something terrific about it. Here, in a poverty-stricken cabin on the edge of the Atlantic, simple, gentle folk from the fields and the sea sat in the shadow of that mystery which has saddened mankind since the beginning of history. There was no primitive sorrow. The nerve-racking silence was so much more solemn than violent grief. They had faith. They believed, every one of them, that their friend was even now on the stairs of Paradise. As they looked at that frail, generous body which Life had used and flung aside they saw, I think, in the smooth calmness of a face from which all sorrow and pain had gone, proof that she had only preceded them on a beautiful adventure.

I felt myself wishing that a great painter could have captured that scene. The title of his picture was not "Death," but "Faith."

And the cow stamped in her byre, the cricket chirruped in the hearth, the peat fell into ash, the candles in the wind guttered in oily cowls, and men moved their clumsy feet on the stone flags and sighed, whispering a little, saying that she was a good woman, and remembering little things about her.

In one of those epidemic bursts of whispering, common to people sitting under restraint, I asked the man next to me only to hear my own voice, and stir myself from the spell of the scene of what the woman had died.

"Consumption!" he whispered back.

A cowardly panic to get away obsessed me. I wanted to get out into the clean moonlight, and to walk in the wind by the sea. Of course it was consumption! The white cow, too, looked consumptive and sinister, gazing mildly and foolishly at the dead woman.

We left the wake and walked up the steep path.

"It's a sad wake it was," moaned the little decorator. "Now, if it had only been old Mr. O'Brien, we'd have had a happy wake, with dancing maybe. . . ."

The cricket was still snapping in my head.

"Sure, you behaved as if you'd been going to wakes all your life," he added, smiling up at me in the moonlight.

We passed the little white cabins on the hill—washed in green moonlight—and the lights were still burning in the windows.

5

Seven thousand people, connected to Ireland by a narrow bridge, live on the Isle of Achill, in the shadow of blue mountains and in the gloom of brown peat bogs. They think in Irish, and they speak Irish. When the sun shines they inhabit a paradise of colours. Titian-blue hills, blue skies, seas that rival the blue of Naples; but in bad weather the Atlantic waves scream on every side of them, and the winds from the east go tearing round the mountains like forty thousand devils.

Their little white cabins cluster incredibly on rock ledges; their small potato patches are scratched with heroic industry in the hard rock. They love dancing and music. The sound of their fiddles is like the twittering of sparrows. And they are all in debt to the grocer!

There is no money to be made in Achill, so that twelve months' credit is the easy-going custom. The whole island lives on credit. It is in debt from harvest to harvest. In the spring every able-bodied man, and many a sturdy girl, leaves Achill for England or Scotland, where they sell their strong arms to foreign farmers. They put in five months' hard labour and return with their savings to pay last year's bills.

There is nothing in this country of farewells quite like the regular evacuation of Achill in the spring. Special boats put in from Glasgow and Liverpool. The male population troops down to the sea, waves good-bye to its women-folk, and departs overseas on its gold rush.

"And how much do you make in England?" I asked a young giant.

"Sure I saved ten pounds last year!" he replied proudly.

Ten pounds for five months' hard work in another man's fields!

Just now the whole island is preparing for the annual departure. Every man is cutting turf with a feverish anxiety. Turf is cut in Achill before it is touched in any other part of Ireland, because it must be stacked ready to dry before the emigrants leave.

The men stand dotted over the brown peat bogs, digging into the inexhaustible fuel with queer, wedge-shaped spades, working quickly and methodically. The women load large wicker baskets with the cut peat and bear them slowly over the fields on their shoulders.

You meet barefoot girls leading donkeys along the mountain paths, a loaded creel slung across the beast's back; you meet grandmothers with gnarled faces and wrists, like the knots in a tree, bent double with rheumatism and hard work, plodding along bearing a load which many a city man would be unable to carry for fifty yards.

Women are also at work in the fields turning the hard soil with rakes and sowing seeds. Nothing must stand in a man's way in Achill! He must be left free to cut the turf or the hearth will be dead in winter; and then he must leave home and sell the sweat of his brow for as much as he can get for it. . . .

What a strange, pathetic island! Yet none seems conscious of this. God has planted them on a sea-girt rock, therefore God intended them to remain there! Who would dare to murmur against the divine wisdom? The soil is hard. There is no money. But one can earn money in the foreign countries of England and Scotland, situated, also it seems by divine providence, a few short hours off in a boat.

It is not strange to those who have seen the west of Ireland that contact with the great towns and cities of England and Scotland, generation after generation, should have left no mark on Achill. These people are superb conservatives. They appear to be immune from modern infections.

When the men go to the foreign farms Achill becomes an isle of women. They run the home and they work the fields. They strive and plan for the return of their men in the autumn.

These women and the neurotic women of cities belong to different worlds. It is tragic to see beauty withering visibly and so early, under the trials of a hard life. Here a woman is old at thirty and senile at forty. She knows nothing of comfort and care as women in cities know them, and there seems to be no time in her life when she can fold her hands and gaze about her from the privileged harbour of her old age. You will see women labouring in the fields, and coming like beasts of burden along the road, but so bent and so wrinkled that their age defies supposition.

Yet there is laughter in Achill. The young girls laugh as they drive the geese over the rocks; they laugh as they climb the low stone walls with their baskets; they laugh as they call off the wild dogs that threaten to devour the stranger; they laugh most of all, so I am told, on evenings at dance time when the men are home from overseas and the fiddles twitter over the hills of Achill like birds under an eave.

There is a weird spell over this island. Mr. Paul Henry has caught it in many of his brilliant pictures. It is almost with a shock that one realizes that the mountains are as blue as he paints them, that the sea is as blue, that the clouds are as big, that in the evening there is a space above the hills of bright green, that at certain times the whole island, land, sea, and sky, becomes washed in an unearthly splendour for which there are no words.

There is a sandy beach in one corner of Achill on which the Atlantic beats itself in white waves, sending up a wall of blown spray that, seen against the sun, shimmers with diamond colours. There are dark crags and forbidding headlands, wild tracts of desolate bog land, little mountain communities which seem remote from the rest of the island, where men live in huts formed of stones placed one upon the other.

One of the few primitive beehive huts still in occupation is in this part of Achill. It is the home of an old bachelor called Lavelle, a family, by the way, of French extraction, the descendants of Frenchmen who long ago used to fish off the island of Boffin.

This beehive hut is circular and the smoke of the turf fire drifts from a hole in the roof. It is really a stone tent. Mr. Lavelle politely opened his hut for my inspection. He lives inside with a white pony and a quantity of fodder. The place was insufferably hot and stuffy. I avoided the hind quarters of the pony and, entering the place, wondered how it is possible that during the centuries that it must have been occupied it has escaped destruction by fire. Turf is the safest of all fuel. It does not spit out sparks like wood or break like coal and send out red-hot cinders, otherwise the combined hayrick, stable and home would have disappeared long ago.

There are few dwelling places like this left in the British Isles. I remember one or two "black houses" built into the side of a hill in the Isle of Skye, but I was never inside them. I suppose they were much the same as this beehive hut on Achill. It is remarkable to see a human being living in prehistoric surroundings. Even in remote times men decorated their dwellings with rude coloured pictures of beasts like those of the Middle Stone Age in the Grimaldi cavern in Italy. But this hut was devoid of art, or of any expression of a sense of beauty.

Even the local people look on this hut with a certain curiosity. Compared with its primitive simplicity the meanest cabin with a fireside, a half door and a sleeping room is a mansion. It is Achill's link with an Ireland older than the Irish. Strange that it should be occupied by a man of French descent!

Meanwhile the sun burns over Achill, filling the hills with blue shadow, turning the sea blue; and blue also, blue as the sky, are the wet cart tracks that run over the hills. And the priest, sitting by a turf fire nursing his neuritis, says that the people are good people; and the doctor (who is the only other distinguished resident) administers to the ills of Achill in a little makeshift surgery in the local inn and says that he would not exchange his life for the best practice in Dublin.

As the sunset burns over the hills in almost unbearable beauty, as the sea turns silver, and the first stars hang above the dark slopes of Croaghaun, you sigh . . . then you sigh again.

It is one of those places which a man locks up in his heart, promising himself that some day he will go back there—some day.

6

It was raining with a grim, quiet persistence as I left Sligo and took the road through Bundoran into Donegal.

In the wide square a few drovers stood with long sticks while a few cattle stood about and blundered on the pavement. Now and then carts laden with turf or vegetables set off through the drizzle down the road. Ireland is full of towns whose names have gone round the world with a kind of splendour to them, so that the stranger, expecting towers and turrets and great crowds, comes instead with a kind of wonder to a little town like Donegal where men huddle in the drizzle and a few calves low sadly on the pavement.

This is natural; for the fame of these places has been spread abroad by many exiles. Their greatness is founded on homesickness.

Donegal Bay is one of the most magnificent bays in Ireland. But the beauty of this country is the glory of hill and the splendour of cliffs that fall sharply to the sea.

The rain was a mist that hid the hill-tops and hung out at sea like a white cloth. I went to the edges of cliffs and looked through the mists on waves thundering and breaking furiously against the rocks; and all round me were the formless shadows of hills: hills jutting out into the sea; hills piled back against the land; hills sage-green and smooth in the downpour.

Donegal is surely the most enchanting place in Ireland. Connemara is tribal and epic; Donegal is softer. If anything lies buried beneath the stony acres of Connemara it would be a battle-ax lost in some old fight; but in Donegal you might expect to unearth a crock of gold.

It is worth while to endure an Atlantic storm in these hills for the sake of that moment towards evening when it blows itself out and the rain no longer falls. The clouds thin, the blue "Dutchman's waistcoat" shows in the watery greyness and an unearthly beauty falls over the land. The countryside is suddenly transfigured. There is a stack of turf in a field. A moment ago it was merely a damp pyramid of peat standing on the edge of a seam. Now with this sudden magic light upon it a queer new value comes to it: it stands out importantly and holds the attention. The little trickle of peat water at the edge of the seam gains colour. The sky has flown down into it. And, lo, all round you is the same transfiguration: hills come out of the mist and stand up boldly blue as the sea; a lark takes to the sky, a plover wheels and cries above the green bogland; the little oddly-shaped stone walls shine out on the blue hills; white cabins shine; a girl with a shawl over her head comes along the road driving a donkey; and there is something in all this like a fairy-tale. You look at her, half-expecting that she will come to you and tell you that she is a princess in disguise; half-expecting that the poor moth-eaten little beast will lift an eye to you and indicate in some sure dumb way that he, poor fellow, is searching for the enchanted rose.

This light that turns Donegal into a poem for an hour, or for only a second, is a terrible and disturbing thing. If any man with a sense of beauty were compelled to see it every day it would unfit him for the practical business of life. I think that if ever Ireland produces a Joan of Arc the angel will come to her as she is driving an old grey donkey down the road in Donegal after the lifting of a storm.

7

"The whole countryside has a heterogeneous appearance," writes Padraic Colum of Donegal, "arable and grazing land being in pockets and patches, a patch of brown oats slopes up with a patch of green that is root-crop; the heather mounts above both, and then, on a green pinnacle above the heather, a white cow grazes, the whole running down into a little promontory of cabbages that has the sea water each side of it. They are half-acre and quarter-acre patches; they are crossed and re-crossed by walls that are piles of loose stones . . . the cow or the horse or the ass, impounded by a square of walls, looks like a beast that had been quaintly trapped by those villagers. The houses stand everywhere a few yards of ground can be cultivated; they are very numerous considering the poverty of the land. And they are better and more comfortable houses than the houses that stood hereabouts twenty years ago; this improvement is due to the work of the Congested Districts Board. . . .

"Making a living on a ten-acre farm in this windy and rainy countryside is a harassing business. It might not be so harassing if there was a market near for what the houses can most readily produce—butter and eggs and fowl. But there are no such markets. They can sell their stock at the fair—their cattle and sheep; but their butter and eggs and fowl they sell to the shopkeepers in the village or exchange for commodities. It would be impossible, I suppose, to keep up the struggle here if the houses had not all, or practically all, some outside revenue. . . .

"So on their little holdings and with their outside revenue, the people here make shift to live, and keep sturdy and understanding. But their economic conditions are precarious. These nights they lie awake thinking of their oats and turf in the flooding rains. The loss of either, or considerable damage to either, would be a blow that they would not recover from in a year. It is noted how mortality amongst the old goes up with a poor turf supply. . . . The houses are self-contained as far as milk, butter, meal, and firing are concerned. But they are not self-contained enough. They have to go to the shops for a score of things, and the shopkeeper takes advantage of their harassments, their economic short-sightedness, their extravagance.

"The Irish countryside has a very significant word for the shopkeeper who deals with them cunningly. He is 'gombeen,' a name that expresses a mean graspingness. Not all the shopkeepers are 'gombeen-men,' but there are a few in every parish. The gombeen man has the emporium in the village; he gets the farmers on his books, and then they dare not deal in any store but his; they never know how much they owe him, for he charges them interest on their debts. He takes their butter and eggs, but never gives them the full price for them. The money that comes from earnings abroad, the cheque that comes from America, the money got on the sale of a calf or cow—all goes to the gombeen. The exactions that the gombeen-man makes are harsh enough to recall the landlordism of the old regime."

The only opposition that can be offered to this scourge of the Irish peasantry is, as Padraic Colum points out, the establishment of a co-operative store. There are many in Ireland, some of them successful, many of them failures. The Irish Agricultural Organization Society is working to "co-operatize" every detail of the farmer's business. He is to be his own wholesaler, retailer, manufacturer, and salesman. He is, in short, to do for himself all the things for which in the past he has paid countless middlemen to do for him. In this gospel, it seems to me, is the only sound solution to many problems which keep the Irish country-man in what appears to be hopeless and intolerable debt.

8

On the hills of Donegal is one of those scattered communities which for want of a better word I must call a "village." But there are in Ireland no villages as we know them in England. The English village, with its clustered cottages grouped prettily round the church and the manor-

house, is an Anglo-Saxon institution which had no roots
in Gaeldom. In Ireland, especially in the west, a village
may straggle over several square miles of mountainside.
I was walking through this "village" one evening with an
Irishman to whom I had been given an introduction. He
was a great Gaelic Leaguer years ago, and he believes still
that the future of Ireland hangs on the revival of the
Gaelic and all things Gaelic.

He offered to introduce to me an old farmer who was,
said he, typical of his breed. He paused at the door of a
white cabin, knocked, and sang out a greeting in Gaelic.
An old man, clothed in homespun, patched trousers and
a homespun waistcoat, asked us to enter. When I was introduced the old farmer asked if I had the Gaelic, and
then, with the manner of a grand seigneur, he turned to
me and said in English:

"Welcome to my house."

This has happened to me in crofts in the Scottish Highlands, so that I was spared the surprise and the comparison
which most English people must make on such occasions
with the rather embarrassing ordeal of entering a farm-
labourer's cottage in England.

The old man placed a chair and a stool in front of the
fire and asked us to sit down. In spite of my friend's
protests he took down tea-cups and poured out a libation
from a pot that was standing in the embers of a turf fire.
The tea was thick and strong and full of tannin and, to
my taste, undrinkable. I finished it slowly, wondering how
I might avoid a second cup.

Our host settled himself on a bench beside the wall. He
was perhaps sixty-five, or even older, a fine patriarch with
a white beard and a pair of eyes of a kind rather frequent
in the west, a curious compound of monk and playboy. My

friend, anxious to show off to me his knowledge of the Gaelic, launched out in that language, but the old man, with superb good manners, replied in English and drew me into the conversation.

We discussed many things: the work of the Congested Districts Board, with which, I gathered, the old man quarrelled. He did not approve of some land which had been given to him; and there were other grievances which I did not understand. All the time I silently absorbed the atmosphere of the little room. Unlike many of the cabins in the wilder parts of Connemara, it was clean and uncrowded. It contained only the bare necessities of life, and its frugality spoke not so much of poverty as of a life spent out of doors. There was a chair, a stool, a bench, and a small table. A red light burnt before the Sacred Heart. There were two pictures on the walls: one a grocer's calendar showing Christ carrying a lamb, and the other, most incongruously, a violent lithograph of Queen Victoria. The soul of these cabins is the generous turf fire burning in an open hearth. I know of no heat more sociable, more gentle, more appealing in some way to the affection and the imagination. Burning turf is almost like a living presence in a room. It pervades a house. The scent of it lies around a house and promises warmth and shelter to any traveller outside in the open; the pungency of it lives on in your clothes and reminds you days afterwards of the kindness and hospitality of an Irish home.

There was not a book in this cabin. The only visible reading matter was the much-thumbed picture supplement of a New York Sunday paper. The old man told me that his two daughters and his younger son were doing well in the States. But they had been there long enough. They wanted to come home.

My friend steered the old man towards ancient things.

There can be no other peasantry in the world which has since the Irish Revival been more flattered and cajoled by the *intelligentsia* from cities than the country-folk of the west. It would be amusing to read a history of the movement from their point of view!

The old man, finding that he had a perfect audience, launched out into stories. He spoke of the prophecies of Columcille, in which, although I believe they are now proved to be forgeries, he, like most of the peasants of the west, had implicit faith. Columcille, he said, was driving black kine one day from the fair in the village over the hill; the hill shaped like a woman's breast which, maybe, we noticed as we came along. . . .

The story was not interesting. It told how the saint got the better by magic of a man who was trying to cheat him. But the old man's attitude to Columcille was intensely interesting. This saint died in Iona in the year A.D. 596, but the old man talked of him as though he had been seen that week on the roads of Donegal. Columcille was a much more vivid and comprehensible figure to this man than, say, Mr. Cosgrave. The familiarity with which he spoke of him, the way he described his fair hair and skin, told me that if the door had opened and Columcille had stood there the old man would have got up without any amazement to say, "Welcome to my house."

This attitude towards saints and heroes is common to the west of Ireland. If you miss the beginning of a story you never know whether a countryman is talking about a man in the next village or a saint in the next world.

As the old man's voice went on and on, now and then breaking into the Gaelic with an apology to me because, as he said, the Irish words fitted "the sense of it" better than the English, I watched the turf fire falling apart in white, soft ash, thinking that these fires are the true symbol of the Gael. It is above their white ashes that the voice of the Gael has kept alive through centuries of war and trouble the old legends and stories of the race. Even Elizabeth, even Cromwell, could not put out the turf fires of Ireland, and while the turf burned the Gael kept faith with the past.

"God be with you!" cried the old man as we took the road.

We turned and saw him silhouetted against the light of his cabin. There was not a book in that cabin; but he had a library on the tip of his tongue.

CHAPTER XII

I cross into Northern Ireland, see the only frontier post in the
British Isles, walk the walls of Derry, hear about the siege
and remember Columcille, go on into Antrim, explore Belfast,
see the mountains of Mourne and—say farewell to Ireland
on the Hill of Tara

1

WHEN I said good-bye to Donegal I went south into
Northern Ireland. An English reader who has not studied
the map will wonder how I performed such an unnatural
feat. It is simple.

Donegal, the most northerly county in Ireland and
topographically in Ulster, is not in Northern Ireland! It
is Free State territory. When the Irish Free State was
established six of the nine counties of Ulster expressed
themselves ready to die rather than become part of it.
They decided to form themselves into a political entity with
a parliament of their own. And this is Northern Ireland.

The six counties that compose it are: Fermanagh,
Tyrone, Londonderry, Antrim, Down, and Armagh. The
three Ulster counties under the Free State flag are Donegal, Cavan, and Monaghan. The last two, forming, as
they do, the southern boundary of Ulster, melt naturally
into the Free State, but Donegal in the north is cut off
in the most untidy and inconvenient manner from her
parent. She looks almost like an orphan or a foundling.
There is a little back door to her on the south about five
miles wide (from Bundoran to Belleek) but the rest of
her eastern boundary is on the frontier.

It thus happens that when you are in Donegal you can

look south into Northern Ireland, and when you are in either Londonderry, Tyrone or Fermanagh you can look north into Southern Ireland! This is no doubt an excellent joke except to those who have to live in it! It must be exasperating to find yourself barred by a customs barrier from the county town in which you have always enjoyed free trading.

But as long as it profits the Free State to build up her enterprises behind a tariff wall, or as long as Northern Ireland remains outside the Free State (which, I am told, will be for ever), this inconvenient and costly boundary with its double line of officials will remain, the only frontier in the British Isles.

As I approached Strabane, which is one of Northern Ireland's frontier towns, the Free State customs stopped me, groped about in the car for contraband goods, smiled at me in a friendly way when they discovered that I was not a smuggler, and took me into a tin hut to settle the one serious annoyance which faces the motorist in the Free State. If you take a car into this country you have to deposit a third of its value with the customs, and similarly if you remove it from the country, as you do technically when you take it over the boundary into Northern Ireland. Although motoring and tourist organizations will settle this for you in London, it is a tiresome law which, I suggest, if lifted in favour of those who are travelling for pleasure would react to the advantage of the Free State.

What a queer sight it was, this North-and-South Border line. Five or six cars were halted by the road-side waiting to be searched. An omnibus came along. It pulled up. Its passengers got out. Their brown paper parcels were prodded. I looked at the women and wondered how many wore more than one skirt. Several passengers were wearing new boots. They had left their old boots behind a hedge in Northern Ireland!

There was something rather funny about it. I have crossed frontier lines all over the world, but this was unlike any of them. We were going out of one English-speaking country into a part of the same English-speaking country. It would seem more probable if the Free State would make its customs officials speak Gaelic! As it is, the Irish Boundary has all the elements of a game— "Come on, let's play at being foreigners; you be French and I'll be German."

A few yards farther down the road I encountered the officials of Northern Ireland. They were a good advertisement for the manners and cheerfulnesss of the northern province.

After this ordeal I felt that I deserved a large whisky and soda. I was given one in an hotel full of gloomy Victorian mahogany and equally gloomy commercial travellers. Some sat writing their orders in the little compartments fitted up with sides to prevent cribbing; and others sat about with bags, reading newspapers and waiting for a train.

"How's trade?" I asked the least mournful one.

"Rotten," he said.

"When is this idiotic frontier going to disappear?"

"When the Free State income tax is a bob in the pound," he replied bluntly.

"You don't mean that?"

"Well, what the hell do you think I mean?"

"I thought you were making a joke."

"I don't make jokes."

"I'm sorry for you."

"I didn't ask for your sympathy."

"Will you have a drink?"

"I don't mind if I do."

This man told me quite a lot of things. He was a hard, embittered cynic. Some of his opinions I believed and tucked away for future reference; others I abandoned as the illusions of one condemned for ever to wander the face of the earth with some utterly stupid commodity for which he could feel no respect.

2

As I went on into Northern Ireland a strange thing happened to me.

When I landed months ago in the Free State I adopted the attitude of a foreigner in a foreign land. I had been, I hope, respectful, unargumentative, observant, anxious to understand and to be pleased. Now I realized as I went through towns and villages in Ulster that perhaps the boundary was not so nebulous as I had thought it. For I seemed to be in England again. There were war memorials quite as bad as those at home. I saw a Union Jack flying on a railway station. The pillar-boxes were red. The postmen were like English postmen. All trivial things, but after the Free State, which is trying to make itself as Irish as possible, they printed themselves on the mind with agreeable sharpness. In the south the deeds of the Irish troops in the Great War are never mentioned and no stone infantrymen remind one of the dead, but in Ulster every town and village is proud of the Ulster Division, and their war memorials stand beside the road as in towns and villages all over England, Scotland, and Wales. I had to look at the hills to convince myself that I had not, in some miraculous way, crossed the Irish Sea; but the hills were, beyond question, the hills of Ireland.

I arrived in Londonderry—or Derry as it is called—in the late afternoon. I saw a large city on a slight hill beside a wide river, the Foyle. The slim spire of the cathedral lifted itself above the buildings on the crest of the rise; and at the back, in the distance, was a ridge of low hills.

There are only two other cities in Great Britain as easy to see at a glance: York and Chester. The walls of Derry, like those of York and Chester, are complete. They form a rough parallelogram which encloses Old Derry, but, like all walled cities, modern Derry has broken its ancient confines and now spreads beyond the walls on every side.

What a magnificent walk this is, not as beautiful perhaps as a walk round the walls of York, but finer, in my opinion, than the walls of Chester. These walls are wider than those of York or Chester. They are about twenty-five feet high and in a magnificent state of preservation.

The story of Derry, as of Ulster, is one of the most heroic pages in the book of Ireland. The hatred of Celt and Saxon was complicated and deepened during Elizabethan times by the reformation: religious hatred was now added to racial hatred. The consistent rebellion against English government went on, and as each one was crushed by the armies of Elizabeth the lands of the rebels were confiscated and handed over to English "undertakers," or settlers who undertook to live in Ireland and anglicize it. Walter Raleigh was an undertaker; so was Edmund Spenser. Raleigh received 42,000 confiscated Irish acres, and Spenser received Kilcolman Castle, County Cork, where during the years 1586 to 1590 he wrote the *Faery Queen*.

The last great armed struggle of the Irish Nation until modern times began in Ulster in 1598. It was inspired by one of the most gallant warriors who ever opposed the might of England—Hugh O'Neill, Earl of Tyrone. He was educated in England under the eye of Elizabeth; and this handsome Irishman seems to have pleased the queen, who was never too busy to notice a fine young man. Hugh O'Neill returned to Ireland, apparently the friend of England but in reality to plot against her. He set himself to that most difficult of all tasks, the healing of clan quarrels. He ended for ever the bitter feud that had existed between his own clan, the O'Neills, and the O'Donnells by marrying the sister of Red Hugh O'Donnell. Gradually and cunningly he brought the tribes together and trained them in up-to-date warfare. When his wife died he eloped with an English lady, Mabel Bagenal, sister of Sir Henry Bagenal, Chief Marshal of Ireland. From that time onward Bagenal was Hugh O'Neill's implacable foe.

The rebel clans now made war and fought a number of minor engagements, sometimes winning and sometimes losing. Spain sent three ships with arms and troops. The English generals decided to march on Ulster by three different routes and crush the clans. They were beaten back and the war dragged on for two years.

In August 1598, by one of those melodramatic chances so frequent in Irish history, O'Neill found himself at a place called the Mouth of the Yellow Ford, about two miles from Armagh, facing an English army commanded by his still implacable brother-in-law, Sir Henry Bagenal, Chief Marshal.

Sharpshooters picked off the English infantry as they advanced. Bagenal flung his heavy cavalry into the battle, but O'Neill, remembering Bannockburn, perhaps, had dug pits covered with grass into which the heavily armed horsemen fell in a ghastly tangle of lamed animals and dying men. The Irish light horse charged the English cavalry as they struggled in the pits. Bagenal then called up his cannon and drove back the Irish slightly, whereupon O'Neill ordered a general advance, and the Irish army—horse, foot and guns—came on in a mad rush

that must have been rather like the last charge of the
Scottish clans at Culloden. The battle was now a hand-
to-hand struggle. The English ranks were broken and were
giving way. Just at the critical moment as English and
Irish were locked together in the fight, a careless English
gunner exploded a quantity of gunpowder which created
terrible confusion. Sir Henry Bagenal, in an attempt to
rally his army, raised the visor of his helmet and an Irish
musket-ball shot him through the head. When the English
saw the Chief Marshal fall from his horse the army
wavered, gave way and fled, pursued by the clansmen.

The English general, twenty-three of his high com-
manders, and 2,500 rank and file lay dead on the field.
The Irish army captured thirty-four banners, the artillery, money and baggage trains of the enemy. Their own
losses were only 200 killed and 600 wounded.

This battle of the Yellow Ford was the greatest over-
throw of the English since they had set foot in Ireland.
O'Neill was hailed as the deliverer of his country. All over
Ireland the clans rose to drive the English into the sea.
O'Neill had set the heather alight.

Elizabeth, learning of the defeat of her army in Ireland
sent over the greatest expeditionary force that had ever
landed in that country under the command of her favourite, the Earl of Essex. He had with him 20,000 foot and
2,000 horse. He behaved with unusual stupidity, patched
up a peace with O'Neill and returned to England, where,
soon after, he suffered disgrace and death.

His successor was a vastly different man, the crafty
Charles Blount, Lord Mountjoy. He sent forged letters
among the Irish chiefs and sowed discord and mutual dis-
trust among the clans, thus splitting up his enemies. The
decisive battle was fought at Kinsale in September 1601.

A force of 3,000 Spaniards occupied Kinsale. An English army of 17,000 besieged them. The Irish clans under O'Neill and Red Hugh O'Donnell made two magnificent forced marches to come to the rescue of the Spaniards. One of Ireland's most notorious traitors, a person called Brian MacMahon, sold the plan of campaign to the English for a bottle of whisky! On a dark night the English armies surprised the Irish and utterly routed them.

But Hugh O'Neill fought a losing fight for another two years. It was no good. His cause was lost. At Mellifont in Meath the great chieftain fell upon his knees and implored the mercy of the English queen. He was permitted to retain his title and part of his lands.

This is how Professor G. M. Trevelyan in his brilliant *History of England* sums up the Elizabethan Age in Ireland:

"The policy of colonization was favoured by government as the only means of permanently holding down the natives, who were growing more hostile every year. This opened the door to a legion of 'gentlemen-adventurers' and 'younger sons' from the towns and manor houses of England. It has been said that the Elizabethan eagles flew to the Spanish Main while the vultures swooped down on Ireland; but they were in many cases one and the same bird. Among the conquerors and exploiters of Ireland were Humphrey Gilbert, Walter Raleigh, Grenville of the *Revenge*, and the high-souled author of the *Faery Queen*. They saw in America and Ireland two new fields of equal importance and attraction, where private fortunes could be made, public service rendered to their royal mistress, and the cause of true religion upheld against Pope and Spaniard. When Raleigh and Spenser were stone-blind to the realities of the Irish racial and religious problem under their eyes, it was not likely that the ordinary Englishman at home would comprehend it for centuries to come.

"And so in the last years of Elizabeth's reign, Irish his-

tory, till then fluid, ran into the mould where it hardened
for three hundred years. The native population conceived
a novel enthusiasm for the Roman religion, which they
identified with a passionate hatred of the English. On the
other hand the new colonists, as distinguished from the old
Anglo-Irish nobility, identified Protestantism with their
own racial ascendancy, to retain which they regarded as a
solemn duty to England and to God. Ireland has ever since
remained the most religious part of the British Islands.

"In such circumstances the Irish tribes finally became
welded into the submerged Irish nation. The union of
hatred against England, and the union of religious observance and enthusiasm became strong enough to break
down at last the clan divisions of dateless antiquity, which
the English were also busily destroying from outside. The
abolition of the native upper class to make room for Irish
landlords, began under the Tudors and completed under
Cromwell, left this peasant nation with no leaders but the
priests and no sympathizers but the enemies of England."

And now the walls of Derry rise out of history. When
the O'Neill begged mercy from Elizabeth she had been
dead (although they did not know in Ireland) for six days.
Already Sir Robert Carey had ridden through the wild
March weather from London to Edinburgh to offer the
Crown to the King of Scotland, James VI (and I of Eng-
land), the mean-spirited son of Mary, Queen of Scots, and
Darnley.

James decided to "plant" the north of Ireland with
English and Scottish farmers. The first thing to do was to
get rid of the Ulster chieftains, the O'Neill, Earl of Tyrone, and Red Hugh's brother, Rory O'Donnell, Earl of
Tyrconnell. A trumped-up charge of conspiracy was
brought against them and they, seeing that a defence
would be useless, decided to fly from Ireland.

On a September day in 1607 a ship put out from Rathmullan on Lough Swilly and set its course for France. The two earls saw the green hills of Donegal go down into the sea; and so, like countless sons of their country, known and unknown, they went away in order to live.

The "Flight of the Earls" decided the fate of Northern Ireland. The moment they had turned their backs on their country Protestant Ulster was born. O'Donnell died the following year, and the O'Neill in nine years' time, in a city that has soothed many a broken heart—Rome.

So ended an old song.

3

Now, said James and his ministers, was the time to try the experiment of a "plantation" on a grand scale. Over three and three-quarter million acres in Ulster were declared forfeit to the Crown, or practically the whole of the six counties of Donegal, Derry, Tyrone, Fermanagh, Cavan and Armagh.

Every inch of ground owned by the earls was promptly confiscated. In Irish eyes this land was not the property of the earls: it belonged to their clansmen. That did not matter to James or his ministers. They pressed forward their scheme for a solid Protestant colony in the north. The Corporation of London was approached by the Lords of the Privy Council with the suggestion that the rich City Companies might care to acquire land in Ulster. This is how the conquered territory was described to the merchants of London:

"The country is well watered, generally, by abundance of springs, brooks, and rivers; and plenty of fuel, either by means of wood, or where that is wanting of good and wholesome turf. It yieldeth store of all necessary for man's sustenance, in such measure as may not only maintain itself, but also furnish the City of London, yearly, with manifold provisions, especially for their fleets; namely with beef, pork, fish, rye, bere, peas, and beans, which will also in some years help the dearth of the city and country about, and the storehouses appointed for the relief of the poor. As it is fit for all sorts of husbandry, so for breeding of mares and increase of cattle it doth excel, whence may be expected plenty of butter, cheese, hides and tallow.

"English sheep will breed abundantly in Ireland, the sea-coast, and the nature of the soil, being very wholesome for them; and, if need be, wool might be had cheaply and plentifully out of the west parts of Scotland. It is held to be good in many places for madder, hops and woad. It affordeth fells of all sorts, in great quantity, red-deer, foxes, sheep, lamb, rabbits, martins, squirrels, etc. Hemp and flax do more naturally grow there than elsewhere; which being well regarded, might give great provision for canvas, cable, cording, and such like requisites for shipping, besides thread, linen cloth, and all stuffs made of linen yarn, which is more plentiful there than in all the rest of the kingdom.

"Materials for building—timber, stone of all sorts, limestone, slate, and shingle—are afforded in most parts of the country; and the soil is good for brick and tile. The harbour of the river of Derry is exceedingly good; and the road of Portrush and Lough Swilly, not far distant from the Derry, tolerable. The sea fishing of that coast very plentiful of all manner of usual sea fish, especially herrings and eels; there being yearly, after Michaelmas, for taking of herrings, above seven or eight score sail of his Majesty's subjects and strangers for lading, besides an infinite number of boats for fishing and killing. . . .

"The coasts be ready for traffic with England and Scotland and for supply of provisions from or to them; and do lie open and convenient for Spain and the Straits, and the fittest and nearest for Newfoundland."

The City of London, approached by this auctioneers' circular, wisely sent four "grave and discreet" citizens to spy out the land. Their report was favourable. On March 29, 1613, the Irish Society was formed under the title "The Society of the Governor and Assistants of London of the new Plantation in Ulster within the Realm of Ireland." The land was divided into twelve parts which the companies drew by lot.

It is not unnatural that in the events which followed the prefix London should have been tacked on to the ancient name of Derry. Only the map-makers and the tourists, however, call it Londonderry. The older name persists.

It is, to a Londoner, strange to walk round the splendid walls of Derry and be told by any lounger how the Skinners or the Merchant Taylors did this or that and how the Grocers gave this gun and the Haberdashers that one; for old cannon still point their black noses above the Derry walls. You look from the ramparts down the chimneys of the city, you can pry into a thousand back yards, you gaze down into streets and squares, you pass over massive gateways which must be rather like the vanished gates of London Wall; and you come at length to a veteran of the Siege called Roaring Meg, an old cannon which made a great noise at that time. It was provided by the Fishmongers of London!

So London merchants built an Anglo-Scottish bulwark in the north. The "plantation" went on. The country of the clans was split up and redistributed. Many of the dispossessed Irish were allowed to enlist in foreign armies—a trial flight of the Wild Geese.

From this time dates the title of Baronet. James, who was full of schemes for raising money, had the happy idea of creating a new order of chivalry and conferring the dignity on certain men who paid for it by maintaining thirty

armed men in Ulster at eightpence a day for three years. I
have been told that the Act authorizing the creation of
baronets has never been repealed, so that anyone who can
prove that he is a gentleman by birth, not in trade, and
possessing property valued at £1,000 a year can theo-
retically become a baronet if he can find men-at-arms willing to serve in Ulster for eightpence a day!

By a grim touch of irony baronets use the Red Hand of
O'Neill as the mark of their rank.

4

I imagine that no other city, except perhaps Limerick,
has such a single-minded memory of its history as Londonderry. You cannot live even for a few hours in this city without hearing the story of the Closing of the Gates of Derry.

It is, thanks to Macaulay, the only incident in Irish
history which is thoroughly well known in England. Here
they tell it all over again with just pride: how the thirteen
'prentice boys shut the gates of Derry in the face of a
Catholic army sent to win the town for James II; how
Derry declared for William of Orange; how the town endured the worst horrors of starvation and disease for one
hundred and five days; how the Jacobite army placed a
great boom of fir logs bound with cable across the River
Foyle to prevent the relief of the city from the sea, and
how, on a Sunday night in August 1689, the starving gar
rison saw two ships loaded with food break through the
barrier and sail right up to the walls of Derry.

It was one of the most gallant defences in the history of
siege warfare. It links Derry with Limerick. But Derry
was holding greater stakes. The siege of Limerick was
fought on the old racial quarrel between Irish and English; the siege of Derry lifted the curtain on greater issues;

the survival or defeat of Protestantism in Western Europe. Ireland for the first time in her history had become a European battle-field, and the thirteen 'prentice boys of Derry shut the gate on someone more dangerous to England than James: they shut it on Louis XIV.

Few Catholics seem aware, by the way, that the Pope knew or, and approved, William's Protestant Armada. Innocent XI had himself urged all Catholics to resist the French Jesuits and the Gallican Church, so that when William of Orange set sail from Hellevoetsluis on a November day in 1688 he took with him, paradoxically, the blessing of the Holy See and the united hopes of Protestant Europe! In a similar way Gustavus Adolphus, struggling against Spain and Austria, had been helped by Catholic France and by the Pope.

The gallant defenders of Derry must have known the utmost horrors possible to a beleaguered town. Three days before the boom was broken and the food-ships came up a member of the garrison compiled a list of food and prices. A rat cost a shilling. A cat cost four and sixpence. No money would buy a small fish from the river. It would be exchanged only for a quantity of meal. A quart of horse blood cost a shilling. There is one savage entry in the list:

"A quarter of a dog, five and sixpence (fattened by eating the bodies of the slain Irish.)"

The men of Derry take you to the lofty Doric column erected to the memory of the hero of the defence, the Rev. George Walker, who later died at the Battle of the Boyne. They take you to the cathedral and show you the graves of the defenders, a bomb which was hurled over the walls with a proposal of surrender, two white flags and a red flag.

And in the evening, even when the streets of Derry are full of young small girls, plump and thin ones, who make

shirts and control the purse-strings in these bad times
when so many men are out of work, it is never possible to
feel that Derry is an ordinary city. Look where you will
and you see the wall and a peeping cannon. The memory of
1688–9 is as vivid as though the smoke of Roaring Meg
was still blowing from the Walls.

5

One evening I mounted the Walls of Derry and looked
down over the city with its clustered chimneys. I stood
there a long time, dreaming of that far-off time in the history of Ireland when the twin lamps of faith and learning
went out one by one all over Europe until only in Ireland
was there the Light.

> *For the end of the world was long ago*
>   *When the ends of the world waxed free,*
> *When Rome was sunk in a waste of slaves*
>   *And the sun drowned in the sea.*
>
> *When Cæsar's sun fell out of the sky*
>   *And whoso hearkened right*
> *Could only hear the plunging*
>   *Of the nations in the night.*
>
> *When the ends of the earth came marching in*
>   *To torch and cresset gleam,*
> *And the roads of the world that lead to Rome*
> *Were filled with faces that moved like foam,*
>   *Like faces in a dream. . . .*
>
> *Misshapen ships stood on the deep*
>   *Full of strange gold and fire,*
> *And hairy men as huge as sin,*
> *With horned heads, came wading in*
>   *Through the long, low sea mire.*

Our towns were shaken of tall kings
With scarlet beards like blood;
The world turned empty where they trod,
They took the kindly cross of God
And cut it up for wood.[1]

In this time, when the barbarian armies marched and counter-marched across Europe, gathering like vultures round the corpse of Rome, this little island in the West knew its Golden Age. The weeds pushed apart the Roman pavements all over England. The nettles and the bramble grew on London Wall. The wild Saxon war bands halted outside London and blew their horns, but there was no answer. Roman London was dead.

In France, in Spain, in Germany the barbaric cavalry of Vandal and Hun swept to the four corners of the world; and there was no sound in Europe but the whistle of swords and the death-cry of civilization.

Then the great army of Irish saints set out to rekindle the Faith of Europe. Century after century saw them sailing off into sunrise or sunset to clothe the land with Christ. St. Fridolin, "the traveller," crossed the Rhine and set up the Cross at Seckingen; St. Kilian converted Gozbert, duke of Wurzburg; St. Columbanus of Bobbio went through Burgundy with twelve other Irish monks and founded the monasteries of Luxeuil and Fontaines; St. Gall, one of his monks, pushed on over the Alps into Switzerland and founded the monastery known by his name; St. Molaissi of Leighlin, in Carlow, journeyed to Rome where he studied for fourteen years; St. Fursa, son of a South Munster prince, passed through France and founded a monastery of Lagy, near Paris; St. Buite of Monasterboice travelled to Italy, where he studied for years; Vir-

[1] *The Ballad of the White Horse* by G. K. Chesterton (Dodd, Mead & Co.)

gilius, Abbot of Aghaboe, explored France and became bishop of Salzburg.

There was St. Cataldus, educated at Lismore, who became bishop of Tarentum. There was John Scotus Erigena, the great Greek scholar, who taught philosophy in Paris at the Court of Charles the Bold. There was St. Fiacre who died at Breuil in France and gave his name to the vehicle—*fiacre*—which was used to convey pilgrims to his tomb.

And on the Walls of Derry a man remembers the best-loved of them all, Columcille, "Dove of the Church," who founded the monastery of Derry in the year 546. There could have been nothing on the hill above the Foyle but perhaps a grove of oak trees. The word Derry, or Daire, means oak or oak wood. We can imagine the young saint, for he was then only twenty-five years of age, building a little oratory of wattles and oak boughs and listening at the end of his day's labours to the wind going through the leaves. When he was far away in after years he used to think of Derry. He once wrote that the angels of God sang in the glades of Derry and that every leaf held its angel.

Even St. Patrick is not more dearly beloved by the common people of Ireland than Columcille. He is as real and vivid in the country places today as he was during his lifetime thirteen hundred years ago. Every age has told stories about him. Century after century has lovingly embroidered his memory so that he lives so vividly in Ireland that I believe there are many country people who would not be surprised to meet him on the road some morning.

He was born at Gartan in Donegal in 521. The royal blood of Ireland ran in his veins. He belonged to the northern Hy Neill, the descendants of Niall of the Nine Hostages. Over the green mountains of Donegal, beside a little lake, tradition has preserved a stone on which he lay. It is said that if anyone sleeps on this stone he will be saved the agonies of home-sickness. Many a pitiful journey has been made to the stone of Ráith Cnó by men and women on the eve of their exile.

His first name was Crimthann, but the children with whom he played, watching him come from the church near the house of his fosterage, called him "Colum from the Cill"—Columcille.

The education of a child like Columcille in the Ireland of the sixth century illustrates more clearly than anything, I think, the culture of a State that had survived the wreck of Western civilization.

First the child was sent to the school of St. Finnen at Moville on Lough Foyle. This saint was of royal blood and had, as I have already mentioned, spent seven years as a student in Rome. He then went to the Leinster School of Bards which was ruled by an ancient poet, Gemman, who must have taught the boy the ancient druidic lore of Ireland. His next school was that of Aranmore, founded by St. Enna. He passed on into the great college of Clonard on the Boyne, where St. Finnen taught three thousand pupils from every part of Europe. His last school was that of Mobhi at Fin-glas—the "fair stream"—at Glasnevin, near Dublin. This school was broken up by the plague that swept Ireland in the year 544.

When we realize the powerful and ordered State behind such a remarkable system of education and such wealth of knowledge, and when we realize that at this time England was still in the nebulous, legendary period of King Arthur, does it not seem one of history's puzzles that the Irish did not invade and dominate England after the departure of the Romans?

Columcille, in order to avoid the plague, went into Ulster, where his cousin, Prince of Aileach, gave him the oak grove of Derry as his first monastery. During the next fifteen years of his life he founded monasteries at Kells, Swords, Tory Island, Lambay, near Dublin, and Durrow.

His new monastery of Durrow was the cause of his exile and the cause of the coming of Christianity to Scotland and the north of England. It happened in this way. His old master, St. Finnen of Moville, had returned from a second journey to Rome with a rare manuscript, probably the first translation of the Vulgate of St. Jerome to reach Ireland. Finnen, like a true bookman, valued his manuscript so highly that he did not wish anyone to copy it. He desired to be the sole owner of it. Had Columcille waited a while no doubt the bibliophile's enthusiasm would have been tempered by generosity. But Columcille could not wait. He wanted a copy of St. Jerome for his new foundation. So he borrowed the book and secretly copied it, sitting up by night and working by the light of a lamp. When Finnen knew of this he was furious. He appealed to the High King at Tara and brought forward the first action for violation of copyright. The king decided in favour of Finnen on the theory that as every cow owns her calf so every book owns its child, or copy. This greatly angered Columcille, who, like St. Patrick, had a temper.

Another event complicated matters and hastened Columcille's departure from Ireland. During the Festival at Tara the son of the King of Connaught lost his temper and killed another youth, thus violating the annual truce proclaimed at this time. The murderer fled to Ulster and was placed under Columcille's protection. The High King had the boy seized and, in spite of Columcille's protests, put to death. His anger again burst out. The saint raised his clan against the High King. A furious battle was fought in which 3,000 lives were lost.

The legend is that in order to make penance for the

battle Columcille decided to leave Ireland and seek some desolate place from which he could no longer see his native land. But it is more reasonable, perhaps, to believe that he was animated merely by the missionary zeal of his age and nation. However, two years after the battle of Cuil Dremne, the saint set out in a boat with a few companions to take the Word of God into heathen places. His sorrow in leaving Ireland expresses the centuries of exile which this country has known. As he listened to the sounds of the gulls on Lough Foyle, he turned to his monks and said:

"The sound of it will not go from my ears till death."

They landed on the little, unearthly island of Iona that lies in bright blue water facing the red granite cliffs of Mull.

"It is well that our roots should pass into the earth here," said Columcille.

Nobly and eternally did they root themselves into the earth. It was from Iona that Christ went through Scotland, and from Iona that He went to Lindisfarne, off the Northumbrian coast. So Christianity came to England from Ireland.

Columcille died before the high altar of his church at the age of 75 and in the year 596. In the following year there landed on the south coast of England a band of forty monks, led by St. Augustine. They had been sent by Pope Gregory the Great to convert Britain. But for more than thirty years the Light from Ireland had been burning in the north.

So one turns from the Walls of Derry as dusk falls. There is nothing now to remind one of the oak grove on the hill. But as the wind passes over Derry from Lough Foyle, as the gulls cry over the water one thinks of a boat

Photo. F. Frith & Co., Ltd., Reigate

SUNSET AT PORTRUSH HARBOR

turning from Ireland and a saint who expressed so simply the ache of exile:

"The sound of it will not go from my ears till death."

6

The afternoon was sunlit and warm. A fresh wind blew inland from Lough Foyle. I left Derry with regret because seldom, except in Scotland, have I met a place so full of kindly people. I went through country as beautiful as anything in Ireland: a well-ordered landscape on which man has left his mark. The crops were high in the fields. The neat farms lay back from the road. Over Ulster was that peace which makes a landscape happy, the mark of good and faithful husbandry.

What a varied beauty is that of the road from Derry to Magilligan. There are cliffs that go down to salt water. There are lanes as heavenly as any in Devon or Somerset. There are cornfields as good as any in Norfolk, and meadows as green as any in Yorkshire. Over the wide, still waters of Lough Foyle rise the mountains of Donegal, blue in the sunlight, the clouds passing over their heads. What a country to paint and what a country to love!

The bright, firm sands of Magilligan are magnificent. I adore sands. I think the act of running with bare feet on firm sand or of riding a horse on sands at the very edge of the sea are two most wonderful physical experiences. I looked at the Magilligan sands. I looked out to the point where the Derry bank thrust its sharp nose almost into Donegal. I looked at the Donegal hills opposite. I looked out over the lovely waters of Lough Foyle, and I promised myself that I would come back one day with nothing to do but lie about in old clothes and with an old Irish hat on my head. . . .

I crossed the River Bann and came to a town called Portrush. It is built on a promontory that thrusts itself for three-quarters of a mile into the Atlantic and thus was designed by nature as a perfect holiday resort. Here people go to play golf, bathe, swim, dance and to endure all the other hardships of a summer holiday. Portrush will remain for ever in my memory as the place where I saw one of the most perfect sunsets it has been my luck to see in any part of the world.

I was on Ramore Head. The sun was setting in the west. A few clouds were lying in the sky. They caught fire and burned for a little while in bright red, that faded to pink and grew dim and dun-coloured. I could see far to the west the faint blue hills of Donegal. When I looked north I could see the Western Isles of Scotland—Islay and Jura —and to the south of them the dim line of the Mull of Kintyre. It was a magnificent sight. The sea swept in over the sands in long, lazy half-moons; and as the light grew less, the sea was the colour of silver; the sands were grey and the afterglow throbbed and trembled in the sky. Mists hid Donegal. Mists hid Scotland, and the first star lit the sky.

7

Dunluce is an extraordinary castle mounted high on a rock above the sea. It has the misfortune to be next door to the Giant's Causeway so that its features are often appreciated from a distance by people who would explore them if it were not so near a more famous place.

I must confess that I was so anxious to see the Giant's Causeway that I gave Dunluce a miss after very carefully raking it with field-glasses. This suggested to me that the ruin is almost as decayed as Tintagel and looks important

only because its builders spread it over a singularly unfriendly headland. It has a good banshee and a tower in
which it used to cry. It has not been heard, I believe, in
our time.

The Giant's Causeway, like an over-photographed ac-
tress, is a rather surprising sight to encounter in real life.
It exists in memory from my earliest days. As children we
see it framed in railway carriages when we go on our holi-
days. Most of us have received a post card of it. In later
life when condemned to live in one or other of those hotels
run by railway companies we meet it once more, greatly
enlarged, in billiard and smoke-rooms all over the country.
It shares with the Blarney Stone in the south the distinction
of being the only natural feature of Ireland which is well
known by the ignorant world.

Well; I looked at the Giant's Causeway, unable, of
course, to feel any surprise, but aware of a certain relief.
It was all quite true. I felt like the ardent maiden who
rushes home with the news of "I've seen Gladys Cooper
and—she's exactly like her post cards!"

Some writers confess themselves disappointed with the
Causeway because it is not as big as photographs have led
them to believe. I cannot agree with them. Although I have
been familiar with this sight since I was born, it impressed
me more than I would have believed possible.

There is something inexpressibly weird about those millions of mathematically formed pillars which thrust themselves upward at the edge of the sea. And the whole scene
is a shade of metallic grey. I have never seen stones that
so closely resemble iron or steel. The Causeway has a
queerly modern look! It is Cubist. It suggests that the
architects who are designing the new shop-fronts in Paris
have been trying out their octagons!

There are, of course, guides but very different from the

guides of Killarney. The Ulster guide is a more solemn and factful person. The Killarney guides are poets; the Causeway guides are amateur geologists.

"I've had the British Association here and not one of them could agree with the other about it," said my guide. "Aye, even the Americans who have something bigger and better in their ain country are beaten at the Giant's Causeway. . . . It's one of the seven wonders of the world; and I think so still though I've been here since I was a barefoot lad. . . ."

Then he took me over the three divisions of the geological freak: the Little Causeway, the Middle and the Grand Causeway, and described with zeal how the basaltic lava cooled and contracted and became columnar. He was a grand lecturer. He told me, if I wanted a simple illustration of the formation, to make some starch in a basin and watch it cool!

The enthusiasm which these local men have spent on the Causeway would in a different channel of inquiry have given them a University degree. Imagination has, of course, been as busy with the Causeway as with the Lakes of Killarney. There are the usual legends and the usual supposed likenesses to men and beasts.

It is the extraordinary mathematical exactitude of the Causeway that impresses one. The vertical columns are all separate but set so closely together that a knife cannot be thrust between them. Most of them are six-sided, some have five or seven sides. There are said to be only three nine-sided columns in the estimated 40,000 which compose the Causeway. There is only one three-sided column. On the Little Causeway my guide pointed out an octagon, a pentagon, a hexagon, and a heptagon all together. He made me sit in the "Wishing Chair" which is formed of columns which rise to a height of ten feet or so to a little platform on which is a comfortable natural seat with a back and two arms.

On the Grand Causeway is a marvellous arrangement of five perfect pentagons sunk round a heptagon known as the "Lady's Fan." Here also is the Keystone—a sunken octagon.

Although the Giant's Causeway is the subject of a photograph as hackneyed as any in the British Isles it is a sight which must not be neglected by anyone who visits Ireland. I was agreeably surprised to find myself gazing at it with the same expression of wonder which I probably assumed when, at the age of six, I saw the Causeway framed in a railway carriage.

One other memory I took from this place. The second bay beyond it is called Port-na-Spania because in the great storm that drove the Spanish Armada before it round the northern coasts one galleon was driven ashore there and all lives lost. What a fearful scene for a shipwreck. One can imagine the great ship driven mercilessly upon the jagged rocks, the waves piling up against it, and ahead nothing but the steel grey Causeway with its weird pinnacles piled up in the storm.

In this horrible place Admiral Alonzo de Leya and his crew met death.

8

What a magnificent road is the coast road from the Causeway to Belfast. On a day of brilliant sunlight it is finer, to my mind, than the Corniche Road in the South of France.

The hills lie backward to your right all the way; to

your left is a blue sea and on a clear day you can see Scotland over the water, at some points only about twelve miles distant. You can see Islay and the unmistakable Paps of Jura rising above and beyond it; you can see over the low Mull of Kintyre the head of Goatfell and the mountains of Arran.

I do not know eighty miles of road anywhere in the British Isles which can show more varied or entrancing beauty. There are hills that rise to the height of mountains, low lands and high lands, glens and waterfalls, with slow rivers slipping through them, fairy-like woodlands, broad pasture lands, sudden stretches of brown Irish bog and, always, either in sight or within hearing, the sea thundering on rocks or sweeping in long waves over yellow sands.

Not far from the Causeway, near Ballintoy, a path leads down to a sharp chasm in the cliffs over which is one of the nastiest bridges you will see anywhere. It is made of two long parallel ropes, with cross ropes on which planks are laid. There is a rope handrail that swings about in the wind. In fact, the whole bridge sways in a sickening manner. Below is a drop of about a hundred feet to sharp rocks.

This bridge is used by the fishermen who work the salmon fishery at the foot of the cliffs. I saw one of them run lightly over this horrible bridge with a box of fish on his shoulders! Opposite, and a few miles out at sea, is a fascinating little island called Rathlin. This is where Robert Bruce when hidden in the cave had his historic interview with the spider.

I went onward through Ballycastle to Cushendun, a heavenly place beside the sea, and then due south to Cushendall and the glory of Glenariff. Here all the beauty that Nature can crowd into two miles has been spread out in an Antrim glen. Two streams come singing down over the

Photo. F. Frith & Co., Ltd., Reigate

THE GIANT'S CAUSEWAY

rocks. The trees form a green shade. There are wild flowers, a whisper of leaves, a roar of white water falling, green and brown mountains enclosing this beauty, and eastward the sea. It is one of those happy places which a man can never forget.

And as I sat listening to the sound of the Vale I took out a book that every man who goes through Antrim should have in his pocket: *Songs of the Glens of Antrim*, by that sweet singer, Moira O'Neill. Many of them are well known to Ulstermen all over the world but they can never be too frequently quoted:

> *Slemish an' Trostan, dark wi' heather,*
> *High are the Rockies, airy-blue;*
> *Sure ye have snows in the winter weather,*
> *Here they're lyin' the long year through.*
> *Snows are fair in the summer weather,*
> *Och, an' the shadows between are blue!*

> *Lone Glen Dun an' the wild glen flowers,*
> *Little ye know if the prairie is sweet.*
> *Roses for miles, an' redder than ours*
> *Spring here undher the horses' feet,*
> *Ay, an' the black-eyed gold sunflowers—*
> *Not as the glen flowers small an' sweet!*

> *Wathers o' Moyle, I hear ye callin',*
> *Clearer for half o' the world between,*
> *Antrim hills an' the wet rain fallin',*
> *Whiles ye are nearer than snow-tops keen;*
> *Dreams o' the night an' a night-wind callin'—*
> *What is the half o' the world between?*

Best of all, and possibly best known of all, is Corrymeela, the name, I believe, of a little place between Cushendun and Tor Point. I can imagine how an Ulsterman feels as he reads Moira O'Neill in some distant and unfriendly part of the world. I like this poem because it voices the truth that home-sickness can be just as acute in England "helping with the hay," as in Canada helping with the cattle or the corn. Here it is:

Over here in England I'm helpin' wi' the hay,
An' I wisht I was in Ireland the livelong day;
Weary on the English hay, an' sorra' take the wheat.
    Och! Corrymeela, an' the blue sky over it.

There's a deep dumb river flowin' by beyont the heavy
        trees,
This livin' air is moithered wi' the bummin' o' the bees;
I wisht I'd hear the Claddagh burn go runnin' through the
        heat,
    Past Corrymeela, wi' the blue sky over it.

The people that's in England is richer nor the Jews,
There's not the smallest young gossoon but thravels in his
        shoes!
I'd give the pipe between me teeth to see a barefut child.
    Och! Corrymeela, an' the low south wind.

Here's hands so full o' money, and hearts so full o' care,
By the luck o' love! I'd still go light for all I did go bare.
"God save ye, colleen dhas," I said; the girl she thought
        me wild.
    Far Corrymeela, an' the low south wind.

D'ye mind me now, the song at night is mortal hard to
        raise,
The girls are heavy goin' here, the boys are ill to plase;
When one'st I'm out this workin' hive, 'tis I'll be back
        again—
    Ay, Corrymeela, in the same soft rain.

The puff o' smoke from one ould roof before an English
town!
For a shaugh *wid Andy Feelan here I'd give a silver crown.*
For a curl o' hair like Mollie's ye'll ask the like in vain;
  Sweet Corrymeela, an' the same soft rain.

And the road ran on through Antrim from beauty to
new beauty, mile after mile of it with the blue mountains
of Scotland shining over the sea. Then it swung south
towards Belfast Lough. There were tram-cars, factories,
people on bicycles, ships. I had come to the capital of
Northern Ireland.

9

Belfast is a great modern city with a population of
384,000. It is, even more so than Glasgow, a swift creation
of the Industrial Revolution and the great expansion of
Empire and trade that followed the eighteenth century. It
is, like all modern cities, an eloquent tribute to the long
start Great Britain once had over the rest of the world in
the race for industrial supremacy. That time is now over
and the rest of the world has caught up with us, hence
many of the troubles of the Clyde and of the Belfast docks.

There is no grace about Belfast as there is about Dublin.
Belfast plays the Glasgow to Dublin's Edinburgh. Instead
of grace and tradition Belfast has vigour and ambition.
Dublin is feminine; Belfast is masculine. Could they
marry, the child of their union would be a great and balanced nation. But the male is rather shy; he is afraid of
losing his independence. He fears the woman. He thinks
she might run up big bills and drag him into all kinds of
unnecessary extravagance. She might also develop religious mania. He has therefore set up for himself a very

expensive bachelor establishment; but—you never can tell!

At first sight Belfast is more like Glasgow than any other city, an impression due, perhaps, to a Scottish burr in the air and to a great herd of tram-cars painted like Neapolitan ices, after the Glasgow manner. The chief building of distinction is a big Renaissance palace, the City Hall, which also is strongly reminiscent of Glasgow's municipal building, except that instead of a campanile it has a dome that owes something to St. Paul's.

The city is an expression of the vitality which has made Ulster the progressive province of Ireland. There is no Celtic twilight about Belfast. There is a hard Scotch mist. The enterprise which has made Belfast links it mentally and physically with Glasgow, Manchester, and Liverpool. It is one of the great industrial capitals of our time.

Here again the unconquerable enterprise of Belfast men links their city with Glasgow. Glasgow made the Clyde. The river is a narrow stream, so narrow that some of the greatest vessels have been launched sideways into it. It has been embanked and deepened. Every day it is dredged. Similarly Belfast has made for itself a firm footing on marshland. Mr. St. John Ervine wrote of his native city:

"The visitor, when passing judgment on Belfast, will do well to remember that it grew quickly and that it grew recently. In eighty years, its population increased seven-fold. About half of it was built within the past thirty-five years, and it was built by men in whom the pioneering instinct was stronger than any other. The city's centre was made out of a marsh. A river runs below one of its chief streets, High Street, and the ground below Donegall Place is so waterlogged that it had to be piled before shops could be raised on it. So soft and sodden is the ground about the

City Hall that a single blow from the hammer on the pile
has driven a heavy log out of sight into the soil. Out of
this stretch of mud and water the grandfathers of our generation made Belfast. They came from cottages and farms,
men of high stature and resolution and hard muscles and
faith, and they wrought on this unpromising marsh until
too swiftly for planning, they made a town. Ulster is a
small place in a small island, but it has taken an extraordinary part of the establishment of the British Empire
and of the United States. The pioneering and unquenchable spirit which seized on the mudflats of the Lagan and
turned them into a thriving city went everywhere."

Everything in Belfast is on the big size. All the clichés
are applicable to it, It is a "hive of industry." Its chimneys
"tower." Its mills are "mammoth." Its workers "pour out"
of factories. Its docks could, and let us hope soon will,
"hum" with activity. It is, therefore, thoroughly comprehensible to most people. There is no mystery about it. It is as
serious as a child playing a game.

Dublin, on the other hand, has the gaiety of a middle-
aged woman. She has no reserves. (Mr. Belfast, by the
way, is full of them!) Mrs. Dublin, if she likes you, will
ask you out to dinner with a shrill little laugh and a tap
on the cheek. And you will dine in her home and possibly
spend the night there, quite morally, of course. Mr. Belfast,
if he asks you out, not to dinner but to lunch, will take you
to a rather grim club. Here he will solemnly introduce you
to his friends, all of whom will talk about trade. This is
the only subject never discussed in Dublin.

But the Belfast man has—and it is the men you meet
in Belfast and not the women, as in Dublin—all the qualities of his defects. He is, first of all, a perfectly comprehensible person, a staunch good fellow. He would never
stab you in the back or forget you the instant you left the

room. He prefers to praise rather than to blame. There is no malice in him. If he likes you he is your friend. If he dislikes you he says so, and there's an end of it. He is blunt, outspoken, and at times, even a bit crude. Loyalty to the Crown, and to the half-crown, is also a strong factor in his make-up. He enjoys power. He loves to make things. He has a great and unphilosophic pride in material achievement. He is not a Scotsman, as so many people consider him: he is a Calvinistic Irishman. The greatest of his qualities is perhaps honesty and reliability. He would never let you down. . . .

Mrs. Dublin, dear, now that your *decree nisi* is pronounced—what a perfect husband!

10

I have heard people say that Belfast has no history.

In the eighteenth century the town—it had then a population of about 15,000—became the centre of nationalist aspirations and won for Ireland a political independence similar to that of the Free State today.

It was the time when the American War of Independence let loose on the British coasts a number of privateers, chief among whom was the Scottish gardener's son, the famous Paul Jones. There was also the fear of a French invasion. Ulster's sympathies were wholeheartedly with the American colonists. Were they not suffering similar injustices?

On April 20, 1778, a ship disguised as a merchantman appeared off Carrickfergus. She was the notorious *Ranger*, commanded by Paul Jones. The crew of a fishing smack boarded her, and Jones, on learning that they were pilots, detained them. They told him that the ship which he could see lying in Belfast Lough was the *Drake*, a

British sloop-of-war of twenty guns. Paul Jones then planned an attack that was to reverberate all over Britain, and, incidentally, lead to the temporary independence of Ireland.

Jones, who loved to write long-winded narratives, has left a detailed description of the fight. His idea was to lumber up to the warship looking like a harmless merchant-man, overlie her cable and fall upon her bow, this exposing all her decks to his fire. But things went wrong. A storm blew up, and Jones made off to carry out his daring and historic raid on Whitehaven. He burnt the shipping in this port, and a few hours after landed on St. Mary's Isle, Kircudbright, with the strange idea of capturing the harm-less Earl of Selkirk. On the morning of the 24th he was again off Carrickfergus, where he saw the *Drake* moving out of Belfast Lough. News of his wild escapade at White-haven had, as he guessed, reached Belfast, and the *Drake* was under orders to find him.

The *Drake's* boat was sent to reconnoitre the *Ranger*. When the officer boarded the privateer he was at once made prisoner. The British ship was accompanied by five small vessels full of Belfast folk who wanted to see a naval fight. As the *Drake* approached and the *Ranger* manoeuvred for position alarm smokes appeared on both sides of the chan-nel, and, as Paul Jones says, the sightseers "wisely put back."

The *Drake* came within hail and hoisted the Union Jack. The *Ranger* ran up the American stars. (Surely this was the first occasion on which the American flag was hoisted in British waters!) In a few moments the first broadside broke from the side of the *Ranger* and swept the *Drake*. The two ships then engaged hotly and ob-stinately for over an hour. The *Drake* then called for quarter. Her fore and main-top-yards were cut away. Her top-gallant yard and mizzen gaff were both hanging up and down along the mast. Her ensign was riddled with shot and hanging in the water. Her hull was galled with shot.

Such was America's first naval victory won in open fight and in view of thousands of Belfast people. No matter what may be said of the morals and manner of Paul Jones none can deny that his seamanship was magnificent.

The alarm created throughout Great Britain by this incident, and the raids on Scotland, was something like that caused thirty years later by the fear of a Napoleonic invasion. The alarm was based, of course, on the French treaty with America, so that Paul Jones must have seemed like the advance-guard of war. Militia camps sprang up all over England. "Camps everywhere," wrote Horace Walpole, "and the ladies in the uniforms of their husbands. All the world are politicians or soldiers or both, servants are learning to fire all day long."

The Irish, Protestants and Catholics, demanded that as England could not defend them in the event of war they should be allowed to organize a volunteer force similar to the militia that was training all over England. It was the old story of England's difficulty and Ireland's opportunity. Belfast led the way. She enlisted 40,000 men within a year, put them in uniform and armed them. This force was officered by the public men of the time. Henry Grattan and Henry Flood were colonels. Grattan, who had represented Charlemont in the British Parliament at the age of twenty-nine, was the leader of the Patriot Party. The volunteer movement spread all over Ireland. Grattan, with the immense influence of an armed country behind him, pressed for the lifting of the restrictions on Irish trade and the repeal of the harsh laws against Catholics. (Grattan was, of course, a Protestant.) He won freedom for

Irish exports and in 1782 certain of the penal laws were lifted. Grattan then fought for Parliamentary independence under the British Crown. On May 16, 1782, Ireland went wild with happiness. She had received legislative independence. She had achieved Home Rule. An Irish Parliament sat in Dublin.

In the years that followed another great Irishman trod the streets of Belfast. He was Wolfe Tone, the founder of the United Irishmen. This society sought only the welfare of Ireland. It was joined by Catholics and Protestants. Then, denied a constitutional outlet, it became a great secret society and a means for hatching rebellion.

In a few years Ireland was once more at war with England. The terrible years dragged on in bloodshed. Gallant men, mistaken men and evil men added their story to that of Ireland's sorrows. In 1800 the Irish Parliament listened to the impassioned voice of Grattan, then an invalid of fifty, as he sat in his seat too weak to stand, wearing the faded blue and red coat of the old Volunteers. He pleaded with his fellow-Irishmen not to fling away their political independence by supporting the Act of Union. The inspired voice fell on deaf ears. The Act of Union became law. Over a century was to pass before England's extremity was again Ireland's opportunity. History has never repeated itself with more unfailing and consistent regularity than in Ireland. The Act of Union went down and the Free State Flag went up.

But Belfast was no longer the Belfast that Grattan knew.

11

The Ulsterman is, I believe, less understood in England even than the southern Irishman. You frequently hear him called an "Ulster Scot." Were I an Ulsterman this would make me see red. It is so ambiguous and untrue. An Englishman who has settled in Canada for a generation or so becomes a Canadian, or if in Australia an Australian, or if in New Zealand a New Zealander. Why should the Ulsterman be the only man to whom it is necessary to attach an explanatory label? If upwards of three centuries of Irish life do not make a people Irish what, I would like to know, does?

During the war 75,000 Ulstermen fought, not for England or for Scotland, but to defend their own part of Ireland.

The dialect of the Northern Irish is a wonderful and a fascinating thing. Many of the words are pure broad Scots, and many are obviously Irish. I believe Burns would find it easier to understand the speech of an Ulster countryman than that of a modern Dumfriesian. There are also, in the north as in the south, many pronunciations regarded by novelists and others as ignorant vulgarisms, but they are really interesting survivals of Elizabethan pronunciations. In the south of Ireland the sounds of "ie" and "ea" have not changed as they have changed in English. A word such as "defeat" pronounced today so as to rhyme with "feet" was originally rhymed with "fate." When an Irishman talks about "defating" anyone he is merely using the word as it was spoken by Shakespeare:

> *And for a woman wert thou first created,*
> *Till nature as she wrought thee, fell a-doting*
> *And by addition me of thee defeated.*

Ulster can boast many Elizabethan words and phrases. They say: "It's a brave night." This is pure Shakespeare. The word "brave" in modern English is never employed except to denote courage. They say: "I'll learn ye" instead of "I'll teach you." In *As You Like It* Shakespeare says: "You must not learn me how to remember."

Mr. James Logan in his popular book, *Ulster in the X-rays*, has a fascinating chapter on Ulster words. "Skunner" is a good word. It means disgust. "Bad eggs gie onybody the skunner." "Pushin' hame" is going home. "The win's in a guid airt" is pure Scots; so is "Houl' yer wheesht!"

I like some of Ulster's onomatopœic words: "scrunchin' " the gravel, a dog "youghin'," a tired person "spraghling" out to post a letter, a pig "nyirping," a child "yammering." On a cold day an Ulsterman will say "It's gye and coul." They have a fine collection of derogatory terms: "coof," "gommeril," "tappy," "haveral," "gazook." Like the Scots, the Ulster folk frequently use the word "ye." "Man, John, how are ye?" They will also use the word "man" to a woman: "Man a dear, 'Liza, wasn't that a great fechtin' match?"

But, as Mr. Logan points out, many an Ulster word is Gaelic, such as "caelie" (pronounced Kail-ye), meaning a gathering or meeting, which comes from the Irish "ceilide."

Ulster is a perfect treasure-house for any student of philology. The Elizabethan settlers, unexposed to the current changes in English speech, have preserved a great glossary of words used probably nowhere else in their original purity and pronounced as Shakespeare spoke them. I wish Mr. Logan would write a book about them.

12

Two things must strike the visitor to Belfast as remarkable. Here is one of the greatest ports in the British Isles, serving a country with an area less than Yorkshire. And on a slight hill a few miles east of Belfast on the road to Dundonald is rising a huge white palace of Portland stone, the new Parliament of Northern Ireland. In a princely moment Westminster agreed to give Ulster this immense building to house fifty-two M.P.s and twenty-six senators. It will cost £850,000.

It is not yet finished. It rises on a terrace and wears an expression very similar to an over-grown Buckingham Palace. Not far away is Stormont Castle, a Scottish baronial building, the official residence of the Prime Minister.

"And what are you going to do with the place when Ireland becomes one country?" I asked the Belfast man who had taken me out to see this building.

"We'll never join in with the south," he said indignantly. "We'd die first."

"Yes, but would you? Suppose the Free State became a prosperous agricultural State with no national debt and an income tax of one shilling in the pound. Could you afford to stay outside?"

"Our future doesn't lie with the south. All we want from the south is bacon from Limerick and stout from Dublin. . . ."

"But the Free State may need Ulster as she develops. Is it right that an industrial north should be a separate entity in any country?"

"How could we be ruled by a lot of Catholics," he blazed up.

I had scratched a business man and found John Knox. I cannot help feeling that if the right moment came the Churches could bring north and south together in six months. The religious animosity is not half so bitter as it appears to a newspaper reader.

13

I visited a linen mill in Belfast. The manager sat at a desk marked by bullet holes, a souvenir of Ulster's "crossness."

"I'm always glad to show anyone over the place," he said. "I regard them as attending the obsequies of a dead industry."

It was one of the most depressing openings I remember to any conversation. He told me that the Belfast linen trade had been badly hit by the world depression following the War and also by the surplus linen which Belgian factories are dumping in Great Britain. We went through a magnificently equipped factory. There were sheds in which some of the most up-to-date looms in the world were silent under white sheets. In other sheds girls sat tending that most complicated-looking of all inventions— the most noisy, the most rapid, and the most fascinating to watch—the power loom. In other sheds the perforated mats danced the Jacquard jig above looms weaving damask. They were making something very expensive for America.

We talked about the busy days of the War. In 1914 there were in Belfast 90,000 workers and 37,000 looms. Earl Haig paid Belfast a pretty tribute when he said that "victory in the air was won by Belfast linen wings."

The post-War hardship has to be faced today as the linen trade faced it in 1816 after the Napoleonic Wars. At that time linen found itelf elbowed from the market in favour of cheaper substitutes. But at that time the linen trade was not directed from mills and factories. The cottagers used to spin the thread by hand and weave it on hand looms. The lack of markets caused terrible hardship.

Then came steam power. In 1828 a Belfast mill decided to re-open after a fire with an up-to-date steam plant for spinning thread. The linen industry had entered on a new and triumphant life.

I spent a happy afternoon in the new Belfast Museum which has been sensibly planted on the edge of the Botanic Gardens. It is a small young collection, beautifully arranged and perfectly displayed. One is not dismayed and confused by the cluttered mass of objects which older museums have not the heart to consign to the cellar.

The Magowan collection of old Belfast scenes by Mr. Frank McKelvey is a possession which a changing city will find of priceless value in another fifty years. Sir John Lavery, a Belfast man, has given a whole room-full of pictures which show his work in all its variety.

There are some fascinating Celtic relics recently excavated from the religious ruins on Magee Island as well as perfect copies of the Bell Shrine of St. Patrick, the Monasterboice Cross, the Cross of Cong, the Tara Brooch, and the Ardagh Chalice.

The mysteries of the museum are the queer little Chinese apes found in County Down. How old are they? How did they get there? Many have been discovered in places which suggest that in remote ages there must have been traffic between Ireland and China. There is no satisfactory explanation, so far as I know, of these puzzling figures.

14

Near Belfast is the ancient capital of Ulster, Carrickfergus, which remembers the time when her great neighbour was a humble fishing village. There is a magnificent castle on a rock—a square Norman keep and a great wall

—and the guns of this castle could, if they were not muzzle-loaders, command Belfast Lough.

The castle has just been created an "ancient monument." The admirable Government department which controls abbeys, castles, and other historic relics has begun the necessary task of restoration. Experts are stripping the walls of ancient plaster, pulling down partitions and generally restoring Carrick Castle to its original condition. When they have done their work they will have given Northern Ireland one of the finest Norman strongholds in the country.

I would like to suggest that when the keep has been restored, the great hall in which, so it is said, King John slept should be furnished with wall hangings and furniture of the period. One of the tragedies of reconstruction is that no matter how well the archæologists do their work there is always something lacking if children cannot become excited about it. Students know perfectly well what a castle like Carrick was in the days of its power. It would not really matter very much to them if it fell into decay. It has no sentimental value and little historical value. What does matter tremendously, and what seems to me to justify the expenditure of a few thousand pounds, is the effect which this castle will have on the minds of young children and adult persons who are unaware that there was any other age than this. The Office of Works, the only Government department to which an intelligent man can extend unqualified approval, should open a furniture department. Wherever a castle is sufficiently complete to justify furnishing, the experts should have the power of fitting it out in the period. I could name countless ancient monuments in England, Ireland and Scotland which would become instantly alive and unforgettable if a little imagination was spent on them. The great hall of

Carrick Castle would be a magnificent thing to bring back to life. The long Norman windows look out over Belfast Lough, the great arches tower up into the gloom of the stone roof, the spiral stairways are complete, so is the floor.

The ex-soldier who takes you round has a neat sense of humour. He mounts before you into the gatehouse where he explains the working of the portcullis which is still in position. He shows you the holes from which boiling lead was poured on the heads of attacking troops. He lifts the lid of a black well in the keep and tells you that it is haunted. He takes you into a dungeon as foul as anything in the tower of London, a black hole into which thirty Scottish soldiers were treacherously flung by an English garrison in the time of Bruce and, so legend says, devoured by the starving garrison.

Carrick Castle takes us into the wildest days of Ireland's history when the Anglo-Welsh adventurers were riding over the country staking out their claims. It is said to have been built by one of the most tempestuous of these, a knight called John de Courcy. He was, like so many of the men let loose on Ireland in the reign of Henry II, a penniless adventurer. De Courcy was a discontented giant who had heard a legend—one of the spurious prophecies of Columcille—that Ulster would be conquered by a pauper knight from a foreign country, a white knight on a white horse bearing birds upon his shield. So great would be the slaughter that men would wade up to their knees in blood. This prophecy suited De Courcy down to the ground. It obsessed him. He even kept a little book of Columcille's with him although he could not understand one word of the Gaelic.

He made himself as much as possible like the knight of

legend. He was a fair-haired man. He rode a white horse and he bore heraldic birds upon his shield. With a small, well-armed band of 320 knights and Welsh archers he set out to conquer Ulster; and the terror of the prophecy preceded him. He advanced on Downpatrick so swiftly that the town was surprised by the sound of bugles and the clatter of his cavalry. The half-starved troops sacked the town. They ate and drank everything. They slaughtered. They pillaged.

The Pope's legate, Cardinal Vivian, who happened to be in Downpatrick, witnessed the scene and attempted to persuade De Courcy to go back to Dublin. When he refused the indignant cardinal exhorted the Irish to defend themselves and drive back the invaders. They fought a tremendous battle, but they broke themselves against the steel mail of the trained soldiery. What hopes had the Irish with their Danish axes and their javelins against the finest cavalry at that time in Europe and the best archers in the world? In this battle part of Columcille's prophecy was said to have been fulfilled, for De Courcy's men when chasing the Irish along the shore sank to their knees in the blood-stained sand.

De Courcy fought for years to conquer Ulster, consolidating any victory with a castle like Carrick, a policy in Ireland, as in England, which was the basis of Norman rule. The end of this adventurer was ruin and disgrace. His enemies, the De Lacys, intrigued against him with the King and procured his arrest as a traitor. His own servants betrayed him at Downpatrick. They came upon him on a Good Friday when, unarmed and in sackcloth, he was kneeling in penance for his many sins in the cathedral. When he saw De Lacy's men advancing to slay him he sprang up, in rags and barefoot, rushed into the churchyard and grasping the nearest weapon, a huge wooden cross on a grave, dashed out the brains of thirteen men before he was overpowered.

But for some strange reason he was not killed. His end is a mystery. There are entries in the Irish Annals which suggest that he, like many another ruffian, went on a Crusade in the Holy Land. Then this wild character is lost to history.

In the harbour at Carrickfergus is a stone low down in the wall on which King William landed. Probably few people could tell you much about De Courcy but there is not a man, woman or child in Carrickfergus who could not describe to you how on June 14, 1690, King William III stepped ashore on this stone on his way to fight the Battle of the Boyne.

This and the Treaty Stone at Limerick are, for opposite reasons, Ireland's most venerated boulders.

15

No matter which road you take from Belfast, north, south, east or west, you arrive in some beautiful place. I know few capitals which are camped in such varied splendour. To the north are the exquisite Antrim glens, to the west is the great inland sea, Lough Neagh, the largest lake in the British Isles, to the south are the Mourne Mountains, and to the east is the ravishing beauty of Strangford Lough with its salt water and its white gulls.

I left Belfast by the eastern road through Dundonald, where I branched off and came to Comber. I went south into County Down along the west bank of Strangford Lough. County Down is a place of little friendly green hills. It is rather like parts of Somerset where the small green domes rise up, looking rather as if many buried St. Paul's had been sown with corn, oats and mustard. I took the west bank of Strangford Lough, a name given to it by the Vikings—Strang Fiord, the "violent inlet"—a tribute to the force of the tides that force themselves through a narrow opening about a mile in width.

I shall never forget the sight of this lough from a high hill near Killinchy. The salt water was stirred by a sea wind. The edges of the lough were fringed with that glorious golden weed called by Western Islesmen in Scotland *femin feàrnaich* (I cannot guarantee the spelling), a weed full of iodine, from which, I imagine, the ancient Irish obtained the saffron dye for the kilt. The near bank of the loch was dotted with small green islands which looked as though the children of the hills of Down were playing in the water. These miniature hills lifted their green domes out of the green sea water and some of them were sown in vertical strips with different root crops, strips of bright mustard-yellow would alternate with squares of golden wheat or the dark green of beet. The gulls circled over the water and stood in white companies in the yellow weed on the shores of these fairy islands. Strangford Lough is Ulster's Killarney.

In nine miles or so I came to the town of Downpatrick, and I went straight up to the top of the hill where, it is said, the bones of St. Patrick lie in the shadow of the cathedral. There was no need to ask anybody the way to his tomb. A much-trodden path led through a graveyard overgrown with trees. There is a big slab of rough granite with a Celtic cross on it and the word "Patric."

Several places have claimed to be the burial place of St. Patrick, among them Armagh. There is a legend in Downpatrick that St. Brigid and the great Columcille lie also buried with St. Patrick in this little graveyard. The truth of this will perhaps never be known.

St. Patrick died about the year 465, probably in the little village of Saul in County Down. The whole of Ireland went into mourning. From every monastery monks with heads shaven from ear to ear set out to attend his obsequies. Great saints and scholars of the Celtic Church converged on Saul from every part of Ireland. For twelve days and nights the sound of chanting rose round the body of St. Patrick. The night was as bright as day with the fire of torches. The Chiefs of Oriel demanded that the saint should be buried in Armagh; those of Ulidia demanded that he should lie in their capital of Dun-da-leth-glas, which became Downpatrick. The tradition up to Norman times was that:

> *In burgo Duno tumulo; tumulanter in uno*
> *Brigida, Patricius, atque Columba Pius.*

> *In Down three saints one grave do fill,*
> *Brigid, Patrick and Columcille.*

Strangely enough this couplet is attributed to that bad man, John De Courcy, who, it is said, took the remains of St. Brigid, who died at Kildare in 523, and Columcille, who died in Iona in 597, and placed the three great saints of Ireland in one grave.

It is certain that Columcille was buried first in Iona and that when centuries later the Danes ravaged the Western Isles his followers took up his relics and translated them to another place, just as the followers of St. Cuthbert fled with their saint's bones from Lindisfarne and wandered all over the north of England with them until they built over them the church that became Durham.

Whether or not Columcille or St. Brigid lie in Down-patrick, it is certain that St. Patrick was believed to lie there in the time of De Courcy. There are letters in existence from the abbot of a Norman monastery founded in Downpatrick offering the bones of St. Patrick in exchange for a summer, or holiday, establishment in England.

16

If you would see something equal to the beauty of the Antrim coast road go to Ulster in summer and, choosing a day of bright sunlight, go south from Downpatrick to Newcastle and then right on the edge of the coast to Kilkeel and Warrenpoint.

Here, lying back only a little way from the sea, are some of the most beautiful mountains in all Ireland—the Mountains of Mourne. They are different from the blue hills of Donegal, different from the weird peaks of Kerry or the wild highlands of the West; yet they are linked to all these by that unearthly quality of the Irish landscape which I can describe only as something which seems half in this world and half in the next. There is a curious dream-like quality about all Irish mountains. While they lacerate the feet and send the blood into the ears and tear the muscles there is something about them that uplifts the spirit—something that is not in the higher mountains of Europe. I have climbed mountains in Switzerland and in Africa, on the edge of the Sahara and the Libyan deserts, but I have never encountered this mystical beauty which exists in the high places of Ireland. I have often wondered during my travels in Ireland whether this country would have produced so many saints had she been a flat, practical land like Holland.

The Mourne Mountains contain eleven peaks over two thousand feet in height and one of them, Slieve Donard, is nearly three thousand feet. There are ten peaks, just under two thousand feet in height. And all these mountains are grouped together in exquisite beauty in an area only about fourteen miles long by seven miles broad.

The mountains lie against one another in soft and gentle lines. They thrust their feet into pine woods and the clouds swing above their heads. Slieve Donard lies against the sky escorted by peaks that look almost as great but are in reality a thousand feet below him. The green waters of the Irish Sea break almost among the woodlands at the feet of these mountains.

What a climb on a hot day is the ascent of Slieve Donard! You attack him from Newcastle. You climb for nearly a thousand feet until you come to stone quarries. You keep a little stream to the left of you and go on with beating heart and aching limbs until you leave this stream and, looking down, see it rising from a mountain bog whose many pools shine like silver coins in the brownness of peat and heather. After you have been climbing for an hour, or an hour and a half if you are a sensible, slow climber, you see above you the magnificent broad, granite cone of Slieve Donard. Your climb is over! He does not torture you on the last mile as Goatfell does in the Isle of Arran or as Ben Nevis does after you leave the half-way hut; he is a decent-minded, kindly mountain with no evil in him but sufficient hardness to make you respect him, and yourself, when at last you fling down by the cairn on top. The last slope is fairly tough and steep, but the foothold is good and—what an incredible view!

Look north and all County Down lies beneath you. You can see Downpatrick lying on its wooded hill, and beyond is the glorious fretted outline of Strangford Lough dotted with its green islands. Look north-west and you will see the broad silver sea that is Lough Neagh, and east of this are the Belfast Hills. Westward are miles of brown mountains lifting their lonely ridges to the sky, and in the south you can see the cone-shaped hills that lie south of Dublin in County Wicklow, eighty miles away.

Look eastward over the Irish Sea. At your feet is Dundrum Bay with the waves sweeping in, blue as Capri, and far off, opposite you, is the Isle of Man lying half-way between Ireland and England like a blue ship at sea.

You can explore the mountain at the back where there is a lake as blue as a spoonful of the Mediterranean. Here is a quarry and—so strangely do the sublime and the ridiculous rub shoulders in this world—from this mountain of Mourne came the stone for the Albert Memorial!

There are in every country beauties which have rooted themselves in the hearts of men. How can we achieve a cold internationalism when to each one of us there is a little piece of the world so dear that we would not exchange the wide earth for it? This sea-ward side of County Down is plainly, even to a stranger, a corner of the world to love and remember. Wherever men from County Down are to be found throughout the world, the words "Mountains of Mourne" must bring back to them the line of hill against hill, the shine of white heather stems, the sound of bees, the bog myrtle, the brown peat water, the shadows of clouds sweeping over the fields and the sound of waves rhythmically falling against rocks.

And with this memory must come something which no outsider can know: that sense of kinship with the hills, that knowledge of belonging to something infinitely good and enduring, a feeling of possession and of being possessed; in other words that irrational emotion which has spilt so much of the earth's best blood—love of home.

17

I went on all that afternoon through gentle country where the broad fields rose and fell on either side of me. Fields were full of millions of the minute blue flowers of the flax plant. In mid-August these crops are taken up and placed in bog-holes and ponds to rot. They are then spread lightly over the fields to dry. This simple process removes the woody portions of the plant and makes it a stem of dry, hair-thin fibres. Before it can be called "flax," as it is known to the spinning mills, it goes through a further refining process in a "scutch" mill.

But no lovelier sight is to be seen in an Ulster field than flax in bloom. They call it "lint" and have a charming phrase to describe it in mid-summer—"when lint is in the bell."

As it was growing dusk I entered Armagh, a city of red marble. Romance will always linger in the quiet streets of Ireland's Canterbury, for although there is little about it today to remind one of ancient times its fame is not written in stone but in the history of faith and learning. The two cathedrals, the Catholic and the Protestant, rise on their hills. The Protestant cathedral is a small, modest building of red sandstone; the Catholic Cathedral is an imposing but unattractive and un-Irish building that lifts twin towers on the highest hill. But the story of this cathedral is remarkable. It was erected "to the Glory of God and the Honour of Ireland" by Catholics in every part of the world. One looks at its stones knowing that they have been bought by a nation at home and at the ends of the earth. "I wonder how many thousands of day labourers gave their mite to its building in the thirty years since the work began," wrote Stephen Gwynn.

The peace that enfolds all cathedral cities lies over

Armagh. It has known peace and storm and peace again. St. Patrick founded his church there in A. D. 432, and a beautiful legend says that when the saint was solemnly consecrating the site with bell, book and holy water a timid doe followed by her fawn broke from a thicket, startled by the crowds that had gathered to witness the strange rites. Some bystanders would have slain her, but the saint, rebuking them and offering them a first object lesson in Christian tenderness, picked up the poor, trembling fawn and carried it down the hill where he set it at liberty, the doe following. Then he returned to the place where the doe had lain and said that on the spot should God's altar stand.

The Book of Armagh was written in the monastery in A. D. 807. It is a copy of the New Testament in Latin, and bound up with it is the *Confessio* of St. Patrick. At the end of the Confession the scribe Ferdomnach wrote: "Thus far the volume which Patrick wrote with his own hand." This was written three centuries after the saint's death and suggests that Ferdomnach was copying a manuscript—now, alas, lost—in St. Patrick's writing. Those who look at the book, now in Trinity College, Dublin, will see with interest a much-thumbed page at the end with an entry dated A. D. 1004, stating that the great King Brian Boru on his triumphal journey through Ireland visited Armagh, made an offering of gold on the altar of St. Patrick and confirmed the city in its ancient religious supremacy.

For centuries the Book of Armagh was the most venerated of all Irish manuscripts.

The school of Armagh that grew up beside the monastery was one of the most celebrated in the Ireland of the sixth century. It opened its doors to scholars from every part of Europe. One part of the city was called Trian-

Saxon, the Saxon's Third, from the numbers of Saxon students who lived there. When the Norman invaders wrecked the ancient Gaelic civilization there were 3,000 scholars in residence at. Armagh receiving knowledge which Ireland alone among nations had saved from the wreck of the Western world.

18

I went from Armagh to Newry, which is the frontier post. I was again in the Free State. I came by mid-day into a magnificent example of a prosperous Irish market town—Dundalk.

Everything that can happen in an Irish market town was happening in Dundalk. The wide central place before the town hall was packed with people; and I have never seen so many women taking part in an Irish market day. Carts were piled up in the main street. Calves mooed under string nets. Pigs squealed and grunted. Geese hissed and gobbled. On trestles before the town hall were set out all sorts of things from silk stockings to tin buckets. Strange and alien in this typical Irish crowd was one of those Orientals who hopelessly peddle rugs and bits of bright cloth round the world. He was a young fellow and he spoke rather bad English. He told me that he was born near Calcutta:

"How do you get on in Ireland? How do they treat you? Where do you live?"

"The Irish—good peoples," he said. "Kind peoples. They let me sleep in stables and they give food. I know Scotland too. Good people there far north in the mountains but in the south not so good. They think you come to steal. But the Irish kind, good peoples, share food with you. Oh, very nice and very kind. . . ."

I thought that this was rather a fine tribute from a helpless and pointless visitor to these shores.

A surprising sight in Dundalk is the Chapel of King's College, Cambridge! It is called the Pro-Cathedral of St. Patrick, and it is an excellent and beautiful smaller version of King's College.

I had lunch in a room full of the biggest and the loudest Irish farmers I have ever encountered. We had tepid soup and the carelessly cooked meat served in so many Irish hotels. There is absolutely no imagination in Irish cooking. The quality of the food is perfect. Where else do you get such butter, such fresh eggs, such bacon and such meat, and such vegetables straight from a garden? One of the mysteries of Ireland is the way these things become either definitely unpleasant and even uneatable after they have passed through a kitchen! Even potatoes, which are supposed to be an Irish speciality, are often either pounded into a watery mess or are just frankly objectionable. I do not know whether there is an Irish school of cookery. I feel that Irishwomen do not enjoy cooking as Scotswomen do. Nothing pleases a Scotswoman more than if you praise her scones or her soup or her oat cakes—specially her soup, and nearly every Scotswoman can make soup that casts the best and most intricate concoctions of a French chef for ever into the outer darkness.

But in Ireland you often forget the food because of the bright and cheerful maids who set it down before you. It was so in this place. We drank beer and passed the bread to one another and talked about the price of calves, pigs, ducks, geese and acres. It was like an Irish Salisbury. There was a robustness and a frank heartiness about this gathering of men from Louth and Meath and Cavan quite unlike the silent, furtive gatherings in the south. All the time a buxom wench with soft blue eyes passed round, giving us food and addressing the farmers by name.

Then we all trooped into another room and ponderously chaffed a barmaid who stood behind a counter catching the chaff in mid-air and tossing it back with interest in the neatest and swiftest manner of Wimbledon. As we sat, booming away, we could hear through the open windows the mooing and cackling and barking and gabbling of Dundalk.

Then we tramped heavily out into the main street to conclude our business. I like Dundalk. I don't care how soon I go back to another of its market days.

19

Drogheda. . . .

This ancient town stands full of heavy memories on the estuary of the River Boyne. A great Elizabethan gate spans its streets and there are ruins like old teeth, brown and jagged, many of which go back to the bad times of Cromwell. It was here that Cromwell made clear his intention to subdue the Irish nation and stamp out its consistent demand for independence. He turned his cannon on Drogheda, battered down its walls, slew every tenth man in the garrison and sent the rest as slaves to the Barbados.

Not far from Drogheda are the famous ruins of Monasterboice. More interesting than the ruins or the round tower are the Celtic Crosses. The Great Cross is nearly 1,000 years old and it stands twenty-seven feet in height, covered with sculptured figures depicting Biblical scenes. One shows, or is thought to show, Christ between a band of armed men in Gethsemane. Our Lord wears the cloak of an Irish chieftain of the period, while his enemies have the long beards of Vikings. There are two other magnificent crosses, Muiredach's Cross and the Cross of Columcille. Many people have said that the faces on these crosses are exactly like those of modern Irishmen. Padraic Colum says that he can recognize likenesses of two particular friends of his!

A mile above Drogheda you come to the site of the Battle of the Boyne. When James II could not take the town of Derry he decided to risk his fortune on a pitched battle. William III had landed at Carrickfergus with a varied army of raw English recruits and hardened foreign mercenaries: French, Fins, Swedes, Danes, Dutch, and Brandenburgers. Anyone who saw this army on the march must have felt that it adequately represented the international interests at stake: Protestant Europe versus the French Catholic stalking horse, the luckless James. I have already said that the Pope was unofficially on the Protestant side, which makes it difficult to see why Catholics and Protestants can still feel sore about the Boyne!

James, with his army of 25,000 men, occupied the height of Donore Hill on the south bank; William, with a much better army of 36,000, encamped on Tullyesker Hill on the north bank. This was on the last day of June 1690. In the early morning William rode out to reconnoitre the ground and was struck on the shoulder by a cannon ball. He was not hurt, although the rumour spread that he was dead. On the next morning the battle began. William's army was split up into three divisions and advanced to ford the Boyne. The first division, the right wing, attempted the crossing at Slane; the famous Blue Guards of the Dutch army, ten abreast, entered the water opposite Oldbridge to attack the centre of the Jacobite army; William himself led his cavalry.

The Irish Dragoons put up a magnificent defence. They held the river for an hour in the face of a raking fire. They drove the infantry back into the water and met sabre charges of greatly superior strength. In this assault the great Schomberg was killed. The Williamite army eventually reached the opposite bank. They outflanked the French troops. James's French general, Lazlum, flung his infantry, his artillery and the cavalry under Patrick Sarsfield to drive back the enemy, thus leaving the centre without cannon. But there was no hope. The Irish horse made charge after charge, but bit by bit the Jacobite forces were pressed back in retreat to fall at bay late at night at Duleek. But the battle was won. James fled, taking Ireland's best soldier, Sarsfield, with him in command of the bodyguard. The losses on both sides were about a thousand killed and wounded.

"Change kings," Sarsfield is reported to have cried before he left the battle-field, "and we will fight you again."

"The outcome of that day," writes Professor G. M. Trevelyan in his *History of England*, "subjected the native Irish to persecution and tyranny for several generations to come, but it saved Protestantism in Europe and enabled the British Empire to launch forth strongly on its career of prosperity, freedom and expansion overseas. . . . The restored English rule in Ireland reflected very little of the wise and tolerant spirit of William. In this Catholic island he was powerless to do anything to protect the Catholics, whose lot he mitigated in England. The new regime in Ireland reflected the rash ignorance and prejudice of the Whigs and Tories of the Westminster Parliament, who were the real overlords of the reconquered dependency."

And the calm, weedy river runs on to the sea beneath a summer sky, gentle, remote from all passion, unconscious of the things that men have done upon the banks.

* * * * * * * *

I came to the Hill of Tara as a man should at sunset, and alone, to say good-bye to Ireland. The sun was low in the west and soon the night mists would fall over the grasslands of Meath. Five broad ways once led to the Hill through all the provinces; but now there is nothing but the wind in the grass and the sound of sheep. Ireland is full of old unhappy things that strangely shake the heart; and this mound of earth is one of them, lonely, remote and withdrawn like "something left on earth after a judgment day." The figure of St. Patrick, mitred and crozier in hand, stood against the sunset. He made the sign of the Cross over Ireland. Near him an old stone leaned upward from the grass, the Lia Fail.

And as I stood there in this queerly alive place memories of Ireland came to me, little happy pictures sharp as in sunlight: the homes of Ireland, the kindness, the laughter, the music, cabins of the West white on the hill, the smell of turf fires, the light throbbing in the sky, lapwings tumbling over wild marsh-land, the stone walls, the green light shining on the edge of peat scums, the wild wind of the moor and all the little winding roads among the hills.

When my feet first trod Irish soil I felt that I had come to a magic country and now, as I said good-bye, I knew it truly as an enchanted island. That minor note which is like a vibration in the air, something that lives in the light and in the water and in the soil, runs through every

Irish thing, but, like the cry of a bat, it is too high to be heard. But a man is conscious of it everywhere.

Some day, I thought, a great Irishman will stand upon this hill and make faith with Ireland. He will take the story of his country in strong hands and give it to the world. He will love the past of Ireland as much as he believes in her future. In him the unhappy Irish trick of looking backward instead of forward will spend itself, and Ireland, sure of her future, will forget old wounds. And this man will do for her what Walter Scott did for Scotland: he will fuse two races and unite his country and make it whole. He will bring to Ireland the love and affection of the world. I like to think of him as a blend of north and south, a mingling of Catholic and Protestant. The southerner in him will watch the past and the northerner will reach forward into the future.

Ireland of the Sorrows is no more. The Ireland of romantic nationalism, the beautiful tragedy queen among nations, has gone, let us hope for ever. Ireland has emerged from the Celtic twilight into a blaze of day. In spite of her ventures, and she has lost no time in proving to the world that she can govern and embark on great enterprises, it may be that she is feeling, perhaps, that disillusion which a sleeper experiences when he awakens from an heroic dream into cold reality. But that will pass. The future is with Ireland. She is the only European country, with the exception perhaps of Spain, which is not dehumanized by industrialism. The typical Irishman is the only eternal figure the world has known: the man who guides a plough. . . .

The sun sets, and the Hill grows dark. I know that in the West at this moment men are raking the ashes of the turf fires. In thousands of little white cabins they are kneeling before the wide hearth, piling up the ashes round the red glow, and in the morning there will be new light.

The shadows have fallen over the fields of Meath. The air is grey with night. St. Patrick rises up over the mounds of Tara, his hand uplifted. And in the silence and darkness I listen again for that hidden music. It is not for my ears. I hear nothing but the night wind in the grass; and I say good-bye to Ireland.

APPENDIX

HERE are some Irish facts and figures which I think may be of interest:

GOVERNMENT

The Legislature of the Free State (Oireachtas) consists of the King and the Senate (Seanead Eireann) composed of 60 senators, and the Chamber of Deputies (Dáil Eireann) composed of 153 Deputies.

The Parliament of Northern Ireland at Belfast consists of 26 Senators and 52 elected members. Northern Ireland continues to return 13 members to the Imperial Parliament.

POPULATION. 1926 CENSUS

The Free State	2,971,992
Northern Ireland	1,256,561
Total	4,228,553

In 1911 the percentage of Roman Catholics throughout Ireland was 73.9 per cent of the population. In the same year Protestants in Ulster numbered 886,333 and Catholics 690,134.

FREE STATE CUSTOMS

Travellers' baggage is subjected to a Customs examination at all ports of entry into the Free State and on the frontier of Northern Ireland. This is done quickly and politely. (A passport is not necessary for travellers from Great Britain.) There is a customs duty on tobacco, cigarettes, cigars, matches and all new wearing apparel and new boots and shoes. Among the principal prohibited, or restricted, articles are foreign reprints of registered copyright work, including music, dogs from all places other than Northern Ireland, the Channel Islands, and the Isle of Man.

IMPORTATION OF MOTOR-CARS INTO THE FREE STATE

Motor-cars and motor-cycles imported into the Irish Free State are subject to 33⅓ per cent Import Duty. Where *temporary importation* only is desired the importer, if a member of a recognized Automobile Club or Association, can avoid payment of duty by obtaining from his Club a Pass Sheet (Triptyque), the production of which to the Customs and Excise authorities will enable him to introduce his car for a temporary stay in the Irish Free State.

If the importer does not desire or is unable to avail himself of this arrangement he may, at the time of importation, deposit with the Customs Officer at the Port or Customs Station of importation a sum sufficient to cover the duty, which is repayable provided—

(1) That the Officer is satisfied as to the identity of the motor-car or cycle and

(2) That exportation takes place within twelve months from the date of importation or within such extended period as the Revenue Commissioners may allow.

Motorists resident in Great Britain or abroad, and who intend visiting the Irish Free State, must, *if not in possession of an International Travelling Pass*, secure an Official Licence or Permit, and also a Driving Licence valid in the Irish Free State.

Residents of Northern Ireland need obtain only an

Irish Free State Driving Licence if their visit is for touring only and not connected with trade or business.

POSTAGE STAMPS AND COINAGE

The Irish Free State issues its own stamps. British postage stamps cannot be used except in Northern Ireland. British money is, of course, current.

ROUTES TO IRELAND FROM GREAT BRITAIN

From (British Ports)	To (Irish Ports)	Services	Distance Miles	Time
Holyhead	Dublin (Dun Laoghaire)	Morning and .... Evening (Night Service only on Sundays)	64	2¾ h.
Liverpool	Dublin	Every week day .	136	—
Glasgow	Do.	Every week day .	192	—
Heysham	Do.	Every week day .	125	9 h.
London, Southampton & Plymouth ...	Do.	Saturdays (dep. . London)	667	4 dys.
Douglas (I.O.M.) ...	Do.	Seasonal	—	—
Silloth-Douglas	Do.	Tues., Sat.	136	—
Fishguard	Rosslare	Every week day .	54	2¾ h.
do	Waterford ..	Mon., Wed., Fri. .	92	8 h.
London, Southampton	Do. ..... {	Wed. (d. London)	590	4 dys.
Plymouth	Do. ..... {	Fri. (d. Plymouth)	250	3 dys.
Glasgow	Do.	Bi-weekly Sail'gs .	—	2 dys.
Fishguard	Cork	Tues., Thurs., Sat.	—	10 h.
Liverpool	Do.	Wed., Sat.	239	—
Glasgow	Do.	Every Tuesday ..	396	—
Liverpool	Drogheda ...	Tues., Fri.	135	9 h.
Glasgow	Belfast	Every week day .	112	—
Heysham	Do.	Every week day .	140	—
Liverpool	Do.	Every week day .	356	—
London	Do.	Tues., Fri.	—	3 dys.
Douglas (I.O.M.)	Do.	Seasonal	—	—
Stranraer	Larne	Every week day .	25	70 m.
Heysham	Derry	Wed., Sat.	—	14 h.
Glasgow	Do.	Regular Sailings .	141	—

INDEX